SMALL NATIONS, HIGH AMBITIONS

Economic Nationalism and Venture Capital in Quebec and Scotland

Studies in Comparative Political Economy and Public Policy

Editors: MICHAEL HOWLETT, DAVID LAYCOCK (Simon Fraser University), and STEPHEN MCBRIDE (McMaster University)

Studies in Comparative Political Economy and Public Policy is designed to showcase innovative approaches to political economy and public policy from a comparative perspective. While originating in Canada, the series will provide attractive offerings to a wide international audience, featuring studies with local, subnational, cross-national, and international empirical bases and theoretical frameworks.

Editorial Advisory Board

For a list of books published in the series, see page 279.

Small Nations, High Ambitions

Economic Nationalism and Venture Capital in Quebec and Scotland

X. HUBERT RIOUX

UNIVERSITY OF TORONTO PRESS
Toronto Buffalo London

ISBN 978-1-4875-0582-0 (cloth)
ISBN 978-1-4875-3276-5 (PDF)
ISBN 978-1-4875-3277-2 (EPUB)

Library and Archives Canada Cataloguing in Publication

Title: Small nations, high ambitions : economic nationalism and venture
    capital in Quebec and Scotland / X. Hubert Rioux.
Names: Rioux, X. Hubert, 1988– author.
Series: Studies in comparative political economy and public policy ; 57.
Description: Series statement: Studies in comparative political economy
    and public policy ; 57 | Includes bibliographical references and index.
Identifiers: Canadiana (print) 20190203307 | Canadiana (ebook)
    20190203412 | ISBN 9781487505820 (hardcover) |
    ISBN 9781487532765 (PDF) | ISBN 9781487532772 (EPUB)
Subjects: LCSH: Venture capital – Government policy – Québec (Province) |
    LCSH: Venture capital – Government policy – Scotland. | LCSH: Public
    investments – Government policy – Québec (Province) | LCSH: Public
    investments – Government policy – Scotland. | LCSH: Nationalism –
    Economic aspects – Québec (Province) | LCSH: Nationalism – Economic
    aspects – Scotland. | LCSH: Québec (Province) – Economic policy. |
    LCSH: Scotland – Economic policy.
Classification: LCC HC117.Q4 R56 2020 | DDC 330.9714—dc23

This book has been published with the help of a grant from the Federation
for the Humanities and Social Sciences, through the Awards to Scholarly
Publications Program, using funds provided by the Social Sciences and
Humanities Research Council of Canada.

University of Toronto Press acknowledges the financial assistance to its
publishing program of the Canada Council for the Arts and the Ontario
Arts Council, an agency of the Government of Ontario.

Canada Council   Conseil des Arts
for the Arts   du Canada

ONTARIO ARTS COUNCIL
CONSEIL DES ARTS DE L'ONTARIO
an Ontario government agency
un organisme du gouvernement de l'Ontario

Funded by the   Financé par le
Government   gouvernement
of Canada   du Canada

Contents

Illustrations

Graphs

Tables

Figures

Acknowledgments

The completion of this book would not have been possible without the financial support of the Social Sciences and Humanities Research Council (SSHRC). For their generous participation and very useful conversations, I am grateful to all interviewees from Quebec and Scotland. For their comments on previous versions of this book, I am thankful to my editor, Daniel Quinlan, and to the three anonymous reviewers who took the time to read it. For all their help and support, I finally thank Dr. Peter Graefe, Dr. Stephen McBride, Dr. Robert O'Brien, and Dr. Stéphane Paquin, as well as my family, friends, and (past and present) colleagues. Anyone who thinks he or she contributed to making this book a reality is probably right.

Acronyms and Abbreviations

ACLDQ	Association des centres locaux de développement du Québec
AQC	Anges Québec Capital
AQVIR	Agence québécoise de valorisation industrielle de la recherche
BBB	British Business Bank
BBRS	Business Birth Rate Strategy
BDC	Business Development Bank of Canada
BDÉQ	Banque de développement économique du Québec
BES	Business Expansion Scheme
BG	Business Gateway
BGF	Business Growth Fund
CAQ	Coalition Avenir Québec
CBI Scotland	Confederation of British Industry – Scotland
CCPME	Capital-Croissance PME
CDPQ	Caisse de dépôt et placement du Québec
CLD	Centres locaux de développement
CMEs	Coordinated Market Economies
CRCD	Capital régional et coopératif Desjardins
CSN	Centrale des syndicats nationaux
CUFTA	Canada-US Free Trade Agreement
DARPA	Defense Advanced Research Projects Agency
ELLD	Enterprise and Lifelong Learning Department
ERDF	European Regional Development Fund
FA	La Financière agricole
FACSN	FondAction CSN
FAIRE	Fonds pour l'accroissement de l'investissement privé et la relance de l'emploi
FDÉ	Fonds du développement économique
FDI	Foreign Direct Investment
FDQ	La Financière du Québec

FDT	Fonds de développement technologique
FIER	Fonds d'intervention économique régionale
FIRA	Fonds d'investissement pour la relève agricole
FLI	Fonds locaux d'investissement
FMQ	Fonds manufacturier québécois
FQDI	Fonds québécois de développement industriel
FRQ	Fonds Relève Québec
FRS	Fonds régionaux de solidarité
FSTQ	Fonds de solidarité FTQ
FTQ	Fédération des travailleurs du Québec
GDP	Gross Domestic Product
GEM	Global Entrepreneurship Monitor
GVA	Gross Value Added
HIDB	Highlands and Islands Development Board
HIE	Highlands and Islands Enterprise
ICF	Institut Català de Finances
ICT	Information & Communication Technologies
INNQ	Innovation Québec
IPOs	Initial Public Offerings
IQ	Investissement Québec
ITIs	Intermediary Technology Institutes
LECs	Local Enterprise Companies
LGS	Loan Guarantee Scheme
LINC	Local Investment Networking Company
LMEs	Liberal Market Economies
LSIFs	Labour-Sponsored Investment Funds
MDEIE	Ministère du développement économique, de l'innovation et des exportations
MEI	Ministère de l'économie et de l'innovation
MIC	Ministère de l'industrie et du commerce
MICST	Ministère de l'industrie, du commerce, de la science et de la technologie
MICT	Ministère de l'industrie, du commerce et de la technologie
MNA	Member of the National Assembly
MP	Member of Parliament
MRC	Municipalité régionale de comté
MRST	Ministère de la recherche, de la science et de la technologie
NAFTA	North American Free Trade Agreement
NDP	New Democratic Party
NEB	National Enterprise Board

NRIF	National Renewables Infrastructure Fund
OECD	Organisation for Economic Co-operation and Development
OVCF	Ontario Venture Capital Fund
PASI	Programme d'appui stratégique à l'investissement
PLQ	Parti Libéral du Québec
PQ	Parti Québécois
R&D	Research & Development
RÉAQ	Régime d'épargne-actions du Québec
REIF	Renewable Energy Investment Fund
RoC	Rest of Canada
RoUK	Rest of United Kingdom
SBA	Small Business Administration
SBDB	Scottish Business Development Bank
SBIC	Small Business Investment Company
SBIR	Small Business Innovation Research
SCC	Scottish Constitutional Convention
SCDI	Scottish Council for Development and Industry
SCIF	Scottish Co-Investment Fund
SDA	Scottish Development Agency
SDF	Scottish Development Finance
SDI	Société de développement industriel
SE	Scottish Enterprise
SEP	Scottish Equity Partnership
SFE	Scottish Financial Enterprise
SGF	Société générale de financement
SGS	Scottish Growth Scheme
SIB	Scottish Investment Bank
SID	Société d'investissement Desjardins
SIF	Scottish Investment Fund
SIGM	Société Innovatech du Grand Montréal
SIQCA	Société Innovatech Québec & Chaudière-Appalaches
SIRR	Société Innovatech Régions-Ressources
SISQ	Société Innovatech du Sud du Québec
SLD	Scottish Liberal Democrats
SLF	Scottish Loan Fund
SLP	Scottish Labour Party
SLSF	Scottish Life Sciences Fund
SMBs	Small and Medium Businesses
SMEs	State-Influenced Market Economies
SNIB	Scottish National Investment Bank
SNP	Scottish National Party

SO	Scottish Office
SODEQ	Sociétés d'investissement dans l'entreprise québécoise
SOLIDE	Sociétés locales d'investissement dans le développement de l'emploi
SOSS	Secretary of State for Scotland
SRI	Sociétés régionales d'investissement
SSF	Scottish Seed Fund
STF	Scottish Technology Fund
SVF	Scottish Venture Fund
TCFI	Teralys Capital Fonds d'innovation
UK	United Kingdom
US	United States
VC	Venture Capital
VCs	Private Venture Capital firms
VoC	Varieties of Capitalism
VRQ	Valorisation-Recherche Québec

SMALL NATIONS, HIGH AMBITIONS

Economic Nationalism and Venture Capital in Quebec and Scotland

Nationalist Underpinnings of State-Backed Entrepreneurial Finance

"Economists and economic historians discuss endlessly the reasons for the relative prosperity of nations, for their success or failure in the industrial race, but they do not ask why such a race exists at all and why nations should want to enter it. This they regard as self-evident. But there is nothing self-evident about it."

Liah Greenfeld, *The Spirit of Capitalism:*
Nationalism and Economic Growth, 5

As early as 2009, Harvard Business School professor of investment banking and venture capital (VC) specialist Josh Lerner remarked that "the financial crisis of 2008 opened the door to massive public interventions in the Western economies. In many nations, governments responded to the threats of illiquidity and insolvency by making huge investments in troubled firms, frequently taking large ownership stakes" (Lerner 2009, 1). As Lerner went on to explain, however, most of these interventions in the wake of the crisis indeed consisted in the bailout and/or acquisition of ailing financial institutions and businesses, and were therefore primarily reactive in nature and focus. In other parts of the world, by contrast, and notably in East Asia since the 1997 Asian financial crisis, state intervention in the economy and public support to growing businesses and "national champions" through government-owned or government-backed investment funds had persisted and even accelerated (Carney 2018; D'Costa 2012). The case of China is of course particularly striking in that regard, as the influence and activities of its gigantic publicly owned investment funds never ceased to grow, both internally and now even in foreign – and increasingly, Western – markets (Carney 2018; Chen 2011; Liu and Parenti 2019; Zheng and Pan 2012).

Over the last ten years or so, however, such public sector activism and interventionism, through the use of state-owned corporations and government-backed investment vehicles, has been spreading to Western economies as well. Liberalizing tendencies that had dominated previous decades have progressively been receding, as policies deemed "protectionist," "illiberal," and/or "nationalist" have been rapidly multiplying and even surpassing the volume of liberalizing measures implemented (Altenberg 2016; Evenett and Fritz 2015; OECD 2018a). Among such policies, moreover, the measures having experienced the most rapid growth are not tariff or non-tariff barriers to trade and investment but rather various types of industrial and export subsidies, notably allocated by a soaring number of state-owned agencies and public investment banks (Bernier and Reeves 2018; OECD 2018b; Schmit et al. 2011; Thomsen and Mistura 2017). Already by the early 2010s, even excluding Chinese institutions, state-owned enterprises represented over 10% of the world's gross domestic product (GDP), and this proportion has kept increasing since (Bernier and Reeves 2018; OECD 2016, 2017). Similarly, assets held by sovereign wealth funds more than doubled between 2007 (US$3.3 trillion) and 2015 (US$7.2 trillion), and national governments all over the world have been acquiring rapidly increasing amounts of assets through stock purchases (Carney 2018, 3).

Thus not only has recourse to state-owned corporations been progressing, at the level of OECD member countries and worldwide, since the financial crisis of 2008, but the financial sector is clearly the one in which the highest proportion (over 25%) of such state-owned enterprises are now concentrated (Bernier and Reeves 2018; OECD 2017). Public investment banks and government agencies devoted to entrepreneurial financing, export credit, or economic development more generally have indeed been multiplying. In Europe, for instance, some estimates indicate that several hundreds of such fully or partially government-owned financial institutions were in operation by 2010, controlling over 20% of the total assets managed by the financial sector as a whole (Schmit et al. 2011). Among those, moreover, an increasing number have been actively intervening in private equity and VC markets (OECD 2018b), which is consistent with the fact that today's most dynamic and/or rapidly emerging VC hubs – such as Silicon Valley, Tel Aviv, or Singapore – have all benefited from and continue to enjoy significant public sector support in many forms, from direct investments and subsidies to the setting up of hybrid (public-private) co-investment funds (Lerner 2009, 5).

There are many economic rationales explaining this increasing involvement of states in entrepreneurial finance and VC, ranging from the need to fill in market gaps left open by the private sector all the way to the strategic will to *create* new markets for promising but still unprofitable innovations (Lerner 2009; Mazzucato 2014). This book, however, covers the other side of the equation: the *ideological* and *political* rationales for intervention, as well as their impacts on the specific scales, forms, and objectives of state involvement. Although some level of public support and intervention in these sectors is now likely to be found pretty much everywhere, because of the sheer importance of entrepreneurship and technological innovation for economic development and growth (OECD 2018b), the fact remains that various policy models subsist, producing different levels and means of public intervention. In some cases state involvement is long-standing and extensive, while in others it can be relatively recent and limited, if not marginal. Trying to understand why that is, where this policy diversity comes from, and which economic and political variables affect such policy trajectories is an interesting and, in the present context, particularly relevant challenge for economists and social scientists.

This book's contribution to this challenge rests on an investigation of two specific and particularly interesting cases, which because of their small size and provincial/regional status have escaped the attention of VC and entrepreneurial finance scholars. There are many reasons why the cases of Quebec and Scotland are of particular interest, three of which can be mentioned from the onset. First, researchers have to account for the fact that, in an increasing number of countries, government involvement in corporate financing (including in VC) operates more and more often at the *subnational* level, which "allows for more tailor-made policy reforms and enables a better uptake of policy" (OECD 2018b, 79). Accordingly, second, even though central state intervention in entrepreneurial finance and VC is certainly present in both Canada and the United Kingdom (UK) – one can think of the activities of the state-owned Business Development Bank of Canada and British Business Bank, most notably – the Quebec and Scottish VC ecosystems, as described in detail in this book, have long diverged from the Canadian and British models by the magnitude and design of public sector involvement.

Third, and perhaps most importantly, Quebec and Scotland constitute especially interesting test cases for an investigation of the ideological and political determinants of entrepreneurial finance and VC policy. The influence of a strong nationalist current in both regions, favouring their political, economic, and policy autonomy from Canada and the UK (Henderson 2007; Bélanger et al. 2018), allows for a study of the policy impacts of a specific set of political and ideological preferences, constituting what I henceforth refer to as "economic nationalism." In a context where political events such as the recent referendums on secession in Scotland (2014) and Catalonia (2017), or the UK's withdrawal from the European Union and the election of President Donald Trump in the United States, have highlighted the resurgence of both minority nationalism and economic nationalism around the world (Bélanger et al. 2018; Boylan 2015; Chandan and Christiansen 2019; Clift and Woll 2015; D'Costa 2012; De La Calle and Fazi 2010; Eatwell and Goodwin 2018; Gray 2015; Hepburn 2008), attempting to circumscribe some of the policy impacts of *minority economic nationalism* in regional contexts seems relevant and promising. Besides, many indicators suggest that the sectors of entrepreneurial finance and VC may be particularly permeable to nationalist policy considerations, as the example of the powerful American VC ecosystem helps illustrate.

Indeed, strategic state intervention in entrepreneurial finance and VC has a long history even in the United States (US). In her book *The Entrepreneurial State*, for instance, economist Mariana Mazzucato (2014) – a member of the Scottish Government's Council of Economic Advisers – studied Apple's enormous commercial successes since the early 2000s and highlighted the following:

> Apple was able to ride the wave of massive State investments in "revolutionary" technologies that underpinned the iPhone and iPad: the Internet, GPS, touch-screen displays and communication technologies ... While the products owe their beautiful design and slick integration to the genius of [Steve] Jobs and his large team, nearly every state-of-the-art technology found in the iPod, iPhone and iPad is an often overlooked and ignored achievement of the research efforts and funding support of the government and military. (2014, 88)

In fact, if the central importance of federal state funding for the emergence and success of Apple is not often recognized, the same can be said of the American VC ecosystem and of the Silicon Valley high-tech cluster more generally (Lerner 2009). As economic sociologist Fred Block (2008) remarked, there remains a deep gulf between mainstream public discourses about American entrepreneurialism on the one hand, centred on the "free market" and private-sector leadership, and the historical roles government initiatives played in the emergence of research and development (R&D) and VC industries in the US on the other. Thus, a "hidden developmental state" has emerged in the US since the 1960s, with the multiplication of government and military programs for R&D commercialization and entrepreneurial support (Block 2008).

The Small Business Investment Company (SBIC) program, for instance, launched by the US federal government in 1958 to leverage the growth of the country's VC industry, backed most American VC investments during the 1960s (Florida and Kenney 1988; Lerner 2009, 37–9; Mazzucato 2014, 94). Administered by the US Small Business Administration (SBA), SBICs are private VC funds that benefit from government-guaranteed loans for up to two-thirds of their investment budget in return for a commitment to finance eligible small businesses. By 2018, the SBA had licensed 2,100 such funds, for a total exceeding 166,000 investments worth over US $67 billion.[1] Also launched in 1958 was the Pentagon's Advanced Research Projects Agency, now known as DARPA, which was instrumental in the development of both personal computing and the Internet (Block 2008, 175). The idea behind DARPA was to fund the commercialization of R&D to provide the US military with cutting-edge technology (Mazzucato 2014, 74–5) and to foster con-certation between the public, corporate, military, scientific, and invest-ment communities.

Such concertation gave way to yet another public sector program for R&D and entrepreneurial support in 1982, as the SBA formed a con-sortium with large government agencies and departments such as the Department of Defense, the National Aeronautics and Space Adminis-tration (NASA), and the Department of Energy to create the Small Busi-ness Innovation Research (SBIR) program (Block 2008, 180). Each agency and department participating in the SBIR must now dedicate 3.2% of its R&D budget to fund the projects of small private-sector firms. As with DARPA, the impacts of the SBIR extend far beyond financing, how-ever, and include managerial support for start-ups, the linking of entre-preneurs with venture capitalists, and the opening of fast-track access routes to public procurement contracts (Keller and Block 2013; Lerner 1999). Besides, many support programs for technology-intensive entre-preneurship as well as several public VC funds have been created, often in close coordination with the SBIR and DARPA, by individual states since the 1980s (Block 2008, 191).

Yet the prime driving forces behind the establishment of such pro-grams in the US have not been technological innovation or the lever-aging of private VC for their own sake, but national security concerns and import substitution objectives. The effects of economic nationalism – traditionally defined as "a body of economic policies aimed at the loos-ening of the organic links between economic processes taking place within the boundaries of a country and those taking place beyond these boundaries" (Heilperin 1960, 27) – therefore constitute the forgotten links explaining the advent of a "hidden developmental state" in an otherwise liberal, free market-oriented economy such as the US (Block 2008, 174; Lerner 2009, 32–5). The SBIC and DARPA were indeed direct policy responses to the successful launch of the Sputnik I satellite in 1957, perceived both as a threat to national security and as a sign of the Soviet Union's technological superiority (Mazzucato 2014, 75–6). DARPA was thus always "aggressively mission oriented" (Mazzucato 2014, 104), and similarly the SBIR emanated from projects conducted under the Richard Nixon, Jimmy Carter, and Ronald Reagan administrations in response to the US's "declining competitiveness" against Japan in high technology sectors (Keller and Block 2013, 639–40).

The fact that such a "hidden developmental state" could emerge even in the US is thus not all that surprising when taking economic nationalism into account. Even as the process of globalization deepened, nationalism remained a powerful motivation and justification for state intervention in industrial development (Abdelal 2001; Carney 2018; Chandan and Christiansen 2019; Clift and Woll 2015; Helleiner and Pickel 2005; D'Costa 2012; Weiss 1998, 2003). This is perhaps particularly evident in the case of entrepreneurial finance and VC, given that these are policy sectors specifically dedicated to the creation, development, and growth of *domestic* businesses in what are often high-value-added, technology-intensive sectors. Besides, entrepreneurship and technological innovation represent basic pillars of capitalism, itself rooted (as it arguably always was) in competitive growth imperatives fueled in part by nationalism and the nation-state system (Greenfeld 2001, 2006).

Not only was this true of the second half of the 20th century, with national security issues and economic nationalism having strongly motivated state-sponsored entrepreneurial support in the US and, to a much larger degree, in East Asian "developmental states" such as South Korea, Taiwan, Japan, Singapore, Malaysia, Hong Kong, and China (Galenson 1985; Noland 1990), but it largely remains so today (Carney 2018; D'Costa 2012; Woo-Cumings 2005). This is especially evident in the case of Chinese "state capitalism" and "techno-nationalism" (Chen 2011; Zheng and Pan 2012), with the aggressive "promotion of indigenously developed technologies as industry standards" being a central part of its National Medium-and-Long-Term Plan for the Development of Science and Technology (2006–2020). In some cases, however, economic nationalism affects policy in opposite directions, such as in Japan, where some level of liberalization and state retrenchment in industry and trade were perceived as national imperatives from the mid-1990s onward, but where state involvement grew in other high value-added strategic sectors such as finance and banking, high-tech R&D, green technologies, and aerospace (Hall 2005; Suzuki 2012; Ozaki 2012).

The argument that public support for high-tech sectors, businesses, and entrepreneurs is in part fueled by economic nationalism and the "race" for industrial and technological competitiveness is far from novel. The case has even been made that nationalism, scientific advancement, and technological innovation have been consubstantial throughout the emergence of the capitalist system itself. Building on Max Weber's insights regarding the development of the "capitalist ethic," for instance, American sociologist Liah Greenfeld (2001) argued that the rise of nationalism as a cultural phenomenon, ideology, and (geo)political system was and remained the prime driving force behind the perpetual growth imperatives constitutive of capitalism. Nationalism (i.e., the definition of the community and body politic as a "nation") allowed for the development of a "flexible system of stratification" in which citizens could henceforth aspire to social and economic mobility through individual effort (Greenfeld 2006, 69). Scientific inquiry and technological innovation, in turn, were and remained at the core of this conjunction between nationalism and capitalism, most notably because of the industrial and military advantages they could procure for nation-states over their rivals (Greenfeld 2001, 2006).

This co-extensivity between nationalism, capitalism, and technological innovation gave way to a wide variety of policy models – and, in fact, to "varieties of capitalism" (Hall and Soskice 2001; Hancké 2009) – up to this day, some more interventionist, some less. One of the most important contributions of the recent literature on economic nationalism, accordingly, has been to demonstrate that it should not necessarily be conflated with protectionism or collectivism, but instead should be studied from the perspective of policy *intent* and *content*. In other words, economic nationalism should not be approached as a pre-defined set of policies incompatible with liberalism; instead, "the study of economic nationalism involves examining how national identities and nationalism shape economic policies and processes" (Helleiner 2005, 221). The development of innovation policy in the US, for instance, unfolded under the influence of national security and import substitution imperatives but also under those of the rootedness of American identity in free market, liberal principles that simultaneously *discouraged* state intervention and contributed to containing it to decentralized forms and relatively low levels (Block 2008).

Nationalism can thus have concrete impacts on economic policy, notably by motivating government involvement for innovation and entrepreneurial support even in countries known for their liberal approach to development. In federal states or decentralized countries, however, VC ecosystems are often best studied at the subnational level, both to reflect the VC industry's tendency for geographical concentration and to get a better grasp of the various policy models that can distinguish such

Graph 0.1. Annual venture capital investments' value as % of GDP, 2006–2016 average

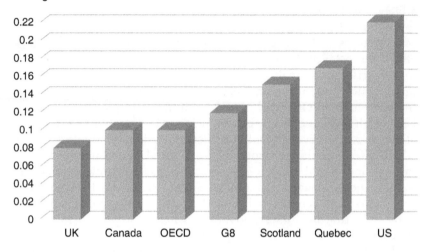

Sources: Institut de la statistique du Québec (2017); Young Company Finance (2017).

ecosystems *within* individual countries. From this perspective, a study of states, provinces, or regions where minority nationalism is a salient political force indeed becomes particularly interesting. In the wake of the most recent secession referendums in Quebec, Scotland, and Catalonia, revived interest has been given to such regions' economies and development models, thereby inviting more detailed investigations of their policy trajectories in various sectors. The ways and extent to which their economic policy models differ from their respective country's, as well as the institutional and political implications of such differences, have been increasingly common objects of study (Boylan 2015; Haddow 2015; Gibb et al. 2017).

Even among social scientists interested in both minority nationalism and political economy, however, the specific sector of VC has been largely ignored in spite of its growing importance for development policy. Yet a quick glance at our two cases, with both regions also evolving as part of "liberal market economies" – Canada and the UK – raises interesting questions. The VC industries of Quebec and Scotland are indeed particularly dynamic (graph 0.1): as measured on the basis of annual VC investments' value as a proportion of GDP, the relative size of the VC sector in Scotland (0.15%) was for the 2006–16 period almost double that of the UK (0.08%), while Quebec's VC industry (0.17%) was

70% superior to Canada's, approaching the scope of the mighty US eco-system (0.22%). These proportions tend to vary from year to year, but the fact remains that both Quebec and Scotland have long been recipients of a greater proportion of total Canadian and British VC investments than their economic or demographic weight would justify. As mentioned, moreover, the Quebec and Scottish VC ecosystems differ from the Canadian and British models not only in size but also, and in many ways, in form.

Given the current contexts of rapid technological transformations, increasing state intervention, and resurging economic *and* minority nationalisms around the world, this book thus offers a timely contribution, answering the following questions: Why is it that entrepreneurial finance and VC ecosystems in regions such as Quebec and Scotland diverge from their respective country's, notably with respect to their size and the roles of the public sector, and what kind of influences has minority nationalism exerted on regional VC policies there? From a policy standpoint, what I found is that in both Quebec and Scotland nationalism indeed played crucial roles in justifying higher levels of state involvement in VC, notably in the name of the preservation of *local ownership* over innovative firms. The economic implications of such policy choices are debatable, but as with the story of the US's success in information and communication technologies (ICT), it can reasonably be argued that they are not foreign to Quebec and Scottish major accomplishments in artificial intelligence or renewable energy, among recent examples (Frangoul 2017; Holder 2018; Lalonde 2018; Rioux and Paquin 2017). If only for this reason, the development of their VC ecosystems over the last decades is, like that of Apple or Silicon Valley, a story well worth telling.

At the foundation of this book thus lies a crucial assumption: ideologies and identities affect many aspects and sectors of policymaking in various and important respects, even though the precise ways their effects unfold are difficult to establish empirically. The main objective of this book is to overcome this difficulty, and to investigate the tangible effects that a specific set of ideas – economic nationalism – has had on a particular policy sector within the larger fields of economic development and entrepreneurial finance: that of venture capital. By focusing on this sector and by pursuing "deep knowledge" of the cases of Scotland and Quebec, I am determined to go "from whether to how" (Mehta 2011) with regards to the policy effects of nationalism. My main challenge is to demonstrate how it is linked not only to the elaboration and implementation of policy decisions but also to the structures and functioning of evolving entrepreneurial finance ecosystems in these regions.

In so doing, I deal with different organizations and actors upstream and downstream of industrial policies and strategies, from economic ministries and government officials to venture capitalists and private investment funds. My contention is that economic and political actors' ideas and ideological preferences can have decisive effects on economic policymaking, and that such effects often provide crucial explanations for the elaboration of specific policies. My goal is to establish if, and how, minority nationalism had such effects in Quebec and Scotland over the last three decades. Unlike the US case, of course, I did not expect national security issues to have played a key role in the development of entrepreneurial finance and VC ecosystems in these regions. However, I did expect to find – and I did find – that Québécois and Scottish nationalisms fueled state intervention and the crafting of policies geared toward the development and preservation of *local* production and ownership in key industries, notably in technology-intensive, high-value-added sectors. After all, small nations can also have high ambitions.

Chapter One

Minority Nationalism and Economic Policymaking

The vitality of nationalist movements in regions such as Quebec and Scotland has indeed sustained constant interest in "minority nationalism" as well as the development trajectories of "national minorities," "small nations," and "small states" over the recent past (Boucher and Thériault 2005; Cardinal and Papillon 2011; Keating and Baldersheim 2016). These movements and trajectories, highlighting issues relating to the political and economic *autonomy* of such nations, have been objects of puzzlement not least because their vigour seems to have been co-extensive with a "changing international order" characterized by increasing *interdependence* (Keating and McGarry 2001). Studying secessionism in Quebec and Scotland, Holitsher and Suter (1999) famously referred to this as "the paradox of economic globalization and political fragmentation."

Remarkably, a widely shared explanation for this paradox has attained paradigmatic status since the mid-1990s. Notably drawing from economic geography, economic sociology, and political economy,[1] the argument basically runs as follows: international trade liberalization, both by weakening nation-states' capacities for (macro)economic intervention and by providing wider market opportunities to regional or local economies, conferred new (micro)economic responsibilities and tools on subnational governments, thereby necessitating decentralization and lessening the economic uncertainties associated with enhanced autonomy or secession as promoted by nationalist movements (Boylan 2015; Drover and Leung 2001; Guibernau 1999; Hamilton 2004; Hechter 2000; Kacowicz 1999; Keating and Loughlin 1997; Meadwell and Martin 1996, Paquin 2001). Contemporary minority nationalism has thus been widely perceived as deriving from *changing scales of economic development*, most importantly below nation-states' control, a phenomenon conceptualized as a "rescaling" of political economy along regional lines (Keating 1997a, 1998, 2001, 2013).

Minority Nationalism and Policy Asymmetry

This explanation has often been applied to Quebec and Scotland. It has been opposed to arguments depicting Scottish nationalism since the late 1970s as a mere defensive reaction against Thatcherism, as the reforms imposed in the UK by the Thatcher and Major administrations, combined with further economic integration in Europe, offered Scotland new and politically significant opportunities for autonomous economic development (Paquin 2002; Rioux 2012b). Gagnon and Montcalm (1992) also developed an early version of this argument to explain the rapid rise of economic nationalism and state intervention in Quebec between the 1960s and 1980s, demonstrating that it responded to structural westward shifts in the North American economy and thus to a corresponding need for Quebec (and especially for the emerging Francophone business class) to break its dependence upon Anglo-Canadian and American capital markets.

Although such economic explanations gained saliency, minority nationalism is rarely used, in turn, to explain economic policy choices and trajectories among subnational jurisdictions. Two trends can be distinguished in the literature on minority nationalism: most authors have sought to explain the phenomenon and thus to approach it as a dependent variable, while a minority has, more recently, tried to use it instead as an independent variable, as an *explanans*. Yet, despite growing interest for ideational approaches in policy analysis and comparative political economy (Béland and Cox 2011a; Blyth 1997, 2002; Campbell, 1998; Schmidt 2008, 2010), and notwithstanding existing literature on "economic nationalism in a globalizing world" (Helleiner and Pickel 2005), even fewer scholars have tried to link minority nationalism and *economic* policymaking in particular.

One important reason why this is so is that "economic nationalism" has almost always been conflated with protectionism (Boulanger 2006). Therefore, because governments of subnational jurisdictions rarely control traditional protectionist tools (most tariff and non-tariff barriers, for instance), and because nationalist parties such as the Parti Québécois (PQ) or Scottish National Party (SNP) mostly embraced trade liberalization since the late 1980s, it has been assumed that minority nationalism and economic policymaking now relate very indirectly, if at all. Yet this gap in the literature on minority nationalism's policy effects contrasts with both the economic rhetoric of parties such as the PQ or SNP and the programs, strategies, and specific policy choices of governments in regions such as Scotland and Quebec.

Accordingly, I intend to put the aforementioned paradigm on its head: if the resurgence of minority nationalism has been caused in good part by the changing scales of economic development, then it is reasonable to think it also had some causal effects on economic policymaking at the regional level. The main contribution of this book, thus, is to identify the precise impacts minority nationalism has had, since 1990, on economic development strategies and policies in Scotland and Quebec. This effort is not completely innovative, however: although economic policymaking in particular has been overlooked by recent literature on minority nationalism, previous work exists on its impacts in other policy fields.

Without revisiting the numerous definitions and theories of nationalism (Breuilly 1994; Smith 1995; Calhoun 1998; Beiner 1999; Roger 2001; Dieckhoff and Jaffrelot 2006), suffice it to say that although there are probably as many definitions of nationalism as there are "types" of nationalism, all variants revolve around the same ideological principle, famously summarized by Ernest Gellner (1983): that *political* and *national* "units" should be as congruent as possible. The different meanings attached to the "national unit" – i.e., the diverse definitions of the "nation" – as well as the various forms political power, unity, and autonomy can take explain, in turn, the polymorphism that distinguishes nationalism. What I henceforth refer to as "minority nationalism" thus comes down to collective commitments *to* and demands *for* significant policy self-determination, carried by national communities forming demographic minorities within sovereign nation-states.

Minority nationalism is sometimes labeled as "substate" nationalism, because "in articulating and accentuating the distinctiveness of nations within the state, and in making claims on behalf of national minorities, substate nationalism implicitly competes with the dominant nation-building project of the center. In so doing, it challenges the state's claim to represent a united people, going to the heart of its claims to legitimacy" (McEwen 2006, 47). I prefer the concept of *minority nationalism* because Scotland and Quebec already enjoy degrees of governmental autonomy that could be said to amount to a status of "statehood." Yet Quebec and Scottish nationalisms do challenge, in many ways, the Canadian and British states' claims to represent a united people, and do articulate competing nation-and-state-building projects, notably through policy asymmetry.

In "multinational democracies" (Gagnon and Tully 2001) such as Canada and the UK, such policy asymmetry can take different forms. First, it can refer to *policy divergence*, where one part of the country – Quebec in Canada, or Scotland in the UK – pursues policy objectives and thus implements policies that are relatively distinct from those prevalent in most other regions of the country. It can also point to *policy autonomy,* where policy objectives and policies remain relatively similar countrywide but where those objectives and policies are pursued through autonomous institutions and/or to a greater extent by one region of the country while other regions collaborate closely or remain, on their own, less active.

These two forms of asymmetry are not mutually exclusive. Scottish and Québécois nationalisms can help explain the advent and persistence of both policy divergence and autonomy in economic development, which is a shared responsibility between the federal and provincial governments in Canada, and between the central and devolved administrations in the UK. Besides, many authors have already established that minority nationalism can lead to asymmetry – through divergence and/or autonomy – in other policy areas. Best known among these are Béland and Lecours (2004, 2005a, 2005b, 2006a, 2006b, 2007, 2008), who developed an extensive literature on the different impacts minority nationalism has on social policy "decentralization" in regions such as Quebec, Scotland, Flanders, and Wallonia.

In their book on the subject, Béland and Lecours developed arguments about what they call the "nationalism-social policy nexus," among which is the assertion that "it is intrinsic to the nature of contemporary (sub-state) nationalism that it puts forward claims about the existence of a national unit of solidarity where co-nationals have a special obligation to each other's welfare, ... viewed as being best fulfilled by having control over social policy" (2008, 26). Their main contribution, in this regard, was to show how different regimes' institutional arrangements provide nationalists with distinct opportunities to push for social policy asymmetry at various points in time. This is perhaps best demonstrated by their comparison of welfare policy decentralization in Quebec and Flanders (Béland and Lecours 2005b, 2006b, 2007).

Case studies have also been conducted regarding minority nationalism's impact in various policy sectors. McEwen (2002, 2006) showed that Scottish nationalism fed the rejection of welfare retrenchment in the UK during the 1980s and 1990s, leading to policy divergence after devolution on matters such as long-term home care for the elderly. Law and Mooney (2012) also argued that growing economic and social policy asymmetry between Scotland and the rest of the UK (RoUK) since the late 1990s resulted in good part from the influence of the SNP's nationalist framing of Scottish policymaking. Arnott and Ozga (2010, 96), relatedly, argued that this nationalist framing resulted in "a move away from referencing England as a comparator nation" on education policy, leading to divergence on the issue of university tuition fees.

A relatively abundant literature likewise exists on the relationships between minority nationalism and the conduct of international relations (Aldecoa and Keating 2013; Lachapelle and Paquin 2005; Rioux 2015). As early as 1977, Paul Painchaud described the rapid intensification of Quebec's "paradiplomacy" as the natural extension of an internal "modernization" and "state-building" process fueled by nationalism. Three decades later, Paquin (2004a, 2004b) popularized the concept of *"paradiplomatie identitaire"* to describe the dynamic international activities of Quebec, Catalonia, and Flanders. Paquin argued such activities mainly stem from a desire for the external recognition and legitimation of these regions' nation-and-state-building initiatives.

A number of authors have also investigated the impacts of Québécois nationalism on attitudes toward free trade since the late 1980s. Rocher (1994, 2003) argued that government support – of both Liberal (PLQ, Parti Libéral du Québec) and PQ administrations – for free trade was informed by "neo-nationalist" ideas and strategies rather than "neo-liberal" ones (1994, 479). Such a support aimed to reduce the Francophone business class' reliance on interprovincial trade and would entail, as a counterpart, the intensification of government involvement in the development of sectoral "competitive advantages." Martin (1997) followed a similar logic when he argued that, unlike for Ontario, structural or class-based variables could not explain this support, which, as an instance of "free-trade nationalism," was underpinned by the pursuit of provincial autonomy through economic internationalization.

Scottish nationalism too had important effects on attitudes toward trade and continental integration since the 1980s, impacting British institutional arrangements regarding Scotland's international prerogatives (Balke 2005; Dmitrieva 2008; Henderson 2001; Mitchell 1997; Robbins 1998; Trench 2004). Interestingly, the SNP only abandoned "Euroscepticism" in the late 1980s, when trade liberalization and European integration opened new opportunities to push for autonomy within the UK, or even for secession followed by EU membership (Tarditi 2010). Smith (2010) showed how the SNP then began to pressure for enhanced Scottish influence in EU affairs as soon as it formed a minority government in 2007 (Scotland 2008a, 2008b). In fact, however, the promotion of Scotland's interests in Europe and elsewhere had already been a central aspect of the Scottish Labour Party-Scottish Liberal Democrats (SLP-SLD) coalition's economic strategies since 1999 (Imrie 2006).

This book, in sum, builds on a rich literature on minority nationalism and policy, although one in which important blind spots persist when it comes to the specific field of economic development. My intention is thus to bridge the gaps that exist in the literature between minority nationalism, political economy, and policy analysis. By trying to understand how nationalism impacts economic development policy, I draw lessons as to what those impacts mean in terms of government involvement in the organization of entrepreneurial funding chains and investment ecosystems in Quebec and Scotland. So far, however, much of the literature in comparative political economy has had a tendency either to focus solely on nation-states, to overlook the organizational influence of governments, or both.[2] I offer an alternative approach.

Comparative Political Economy

By the end of the century, nationalists in Quebec, Scotland, and other regions had become well aware that trade liberalization would provide not only access to wider markets but also new state-building opportunities, relating to the responsibilities it would impart to regional governments in terms of industrial reconversion and support for businesses in emerging sectors. These new responsibilities would indeed call for new forms of supply-side state intervention and policy asymmetry – through divergence or at least through autonomy – in economic development (Keating and Loughlin 1997; Paquin 2001).

Yet since the mid-1990s many authors have also demonstrated that trade and financial liberalization have been compatible with the persistence of economic policy diversity at the nation-state level (Berger and Dore 1996; Boyer and Drache 1996; Chang 2003; Crouch and Streeck 1997; Hall and Gingerich 2009; Hall and Soskice 2001; Hancké 2009; Helleiner 1994; Leibfried et al. 2015; Schmidt 2007; Weiss 1998, 2003). Nation-states adapted to the "changing international order" in different ways, based on distinct institutional and regulatory legacies, the structure of their economies, the prevailing ideologies of their elites, the dynamics of partisan politics (Garrett 1998a), or even simply citizens' "everyday agency" (Hobson and Seabrooke 2007).

A specific literature on the "competition state," for instance, emerged since the late 1980s. This literature illustrated how advanced industrial nations, in the face of trade liberalization, turned away from macroeconomic policies aimed at shielding strategic sectors or businesses from international competitors and instead adopted various microeconomic, supply-side policies aimed at providing such clusters and businesses with "competitive advantages" over foreign rivals (Cerny 1997, 2010; Fougner 2006b; Genschel and Seelkopf 2015; Jessop 2002; Vukov 2016). In many countries – and in many regions such as Quebec and Scotland[3] – policymakers notably turned to the development of competitive advantages through territorialized "industrial clusters" (Porter 1994, 1998).

This widespread shift toward the "competitive" paradigm among developed market economies was also deeply influenced by export-led growth theories (Palley 2011), which replaced domestic demand-led growth and protectionist import-substitution principles from the late 1970s onward. The central tenets of the competition state's internationalization strategies can be said to rest on two main objectives: (a) attracting and retaining foreign direct investments (FDI) in order to foster growth and provide new jobs with imported capital; and (b) facilitating the internationalization of domestic firms through exports, outward FDI, and overseas expansion, in order to free corporate value chains and revenues from the limited domestic market.

As it became clear that the most "innovative" firms – often young and growing small-and-medium businesses (SMBs) – would be important engines of economic growth (Birch 1979), states also started to pursue "industrial reconversion" toward high-value-added, high-tech sectors, notably through increased R&D and strategic VC spending. Such "innovation-led growth" and industrial reconversion, indeed, warranted government intervention: "studying firm behavior and competition has led to a 'systems of innovation' view of policy where what matters is understanding the way in which firms of different types are embedded in a system at sectoral, regional and national levels. In this system view, it is not the quantity of R&D that matters, but how it is distributed throughout an economy, often reflective of the crucial role of the State" (Mazzucato 2014, 35).

Industrial policymaking at the "subnational" or "regional" level thus attracted renewed attention given the territorialized nature of competitive advantages, systems of innovation, and clustering. There is a substantial literature, for example, on the way Scottish economic development strategies and policies diverged from English ones since devolution and even before (Brown and Mason 2012; Coyle, Alexander, and Ashcroft 2005; Devine, Lee, and Peden 2005; Hood et al. 2002). After her mandate (2000–2) as Minister for Enterprise in the Scottish Executive, for instance, Wendy Alexander wrote a lengthy account of how her government drew lessons from Ireland's "low-road to competitiveness" – based on corporate tax cuts – and tried to devise a "high-road" based on investment, clustering, professional training, and the "building of a new national consensus" (2003, 53).

Despite such convergence toward clustering, innovation-led growth, and export-led growth, diversity in "competition state" models persists when it comes to industrial strategies and the roles of government. The 1990s' "first-wave" literature on "globalization and the state" – very much focused on the "varieties of state capacity" (Weiss 1998, 194) – therefore gave way, in the early 2000s, to a blossoming "second-wave" literature on the "varieties of capitalism" (VoC). Among its common research objects were corporate governance and financing, firm-firm relationships, industrial relations, wage bargaining dynamics, professional training programs, and the "institutional complementarities" allowing for coherent and "competitive" systems (Hall and Soskice 2001; Hall and Gingerich 2009; Hancké 2009).

This "firm-centered" typology (Hall and Soskice 2001), distinguishing "liberal" and "coordinated" market economies (LMEs/CMEs), became the foundation on which many scholars have built to offer new comparisons and additional typologies. First, some claimed the VoC perspective could benefit from renewed attention to *government involvement and policymaking* as crucial driving forces behind economic organization. Vivien Schmidt (2002, 2007, 2008, 2009) even suggested a third ideal type, the "state-influenced market economy" (SME), to cover regimes that fit neither the LME nor CME categories and in which state involvement can be protean, strategic, and/or sector-specific.

Schmidt (2009) illustrated her argument by classifying LMEs, CMEs, and SMEs along axes measuring the extent to which governments substitute themselves to "market actors" such as businesses, labour unions, or financial institutions (figure 1.1). Despite overlap between the three ideal types, states in CMEs are thus mainly "enabling," as they coordinate very closely with market actors on numerous policy matters (hence *"faire avec,"* i.e., "do with market actors"). This is typical of corporatist and social-democratic systems such as Germany or the Scandinavian countries. In LMEs such as Canada or the UK, the state generally prefers establishing conditions conducive to market *competition* rather than coordination (hence *"laissez-faire,"* i.e., "let market actors do"). In SMEs, finally, the state is "influencing" in that it often intervenes directly in the market through state corporations or public agencies (hence *"faire,"* i.e., "do in place of market actors"), in addition to pushing market actors in strategic directions through various fiscal, financial, or policy incentives (hence *"faire faire,"* i.e., "have market actors do"). According to Schmidt, this is typical of a country like France.

The VoC perspective was enriched by exploring variety below the nation-state level but also across industrial and/or policy sectors; in other words, by accounting for "regional" and "sectoral" varieties of capitalism. This approach was notably applied to the comparison of specific regions, clusters, and even localities within nation-states.[4] Crouch,

Figure 1.1. VoC and state activism

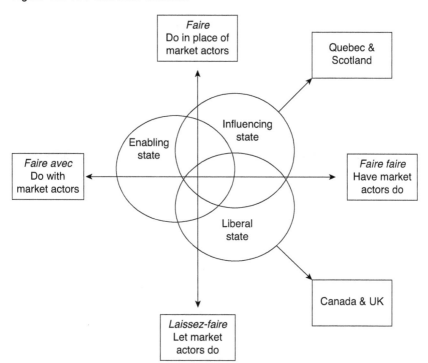

Source: Taken from Schmidt (2009, 526). Quebec/Scotland and Canada/UK labels are my additions.

Schröder, and Voelzkow (2009) for instance, compared the dynamics of economic organization in German, Swedish, Hungarian, and English regions, but also across production sectors such as furniture manufacturing, the auto industry, biopharmaceuticals, and the film industry. Case studies were also conducted this way, such as Rafiqui's (2010) on Sweden's local furniture industry clusters.

To draw a clear picture of government involvement in any polity's economic development and to get a better grasp of the main influences affecting policy choices, such a focus on specific sectors is particularly useful. This is especially true when studying regions such as Quebec or Scotland, given their limited degrees of policy autonomy. This explains this book's focus on a very specific policy sector within the larger field of economic development. The inspiration for the choice of this sector came in part from the work of Linda Weiss (2005), who established a shortlist of those sectors where, even in a liberalized international trade environment, state involvement can remain highly strategic ("strategic activism") and policy diversity significant.

Reminiscent of the literature on "competition states," Weiss mainly identified sectors conducive to export-and-innovation-led growth, among which was that of "innovation & investment support" (2005, 728). This is the policy sector this book covers, with a specific focus on the subsector of *venture capital* – high-risk equity investments in unlisted start-ups and SMBs (Cumming 2012). This sector and subsector, indeed, provide opportunities for regions such as Quebec and Scotland to promote the birth and expansion of indigenous businesses in strategic industries. I contend that over the last thirty years, through policy asymmetry and government activism in entrepreneurial finance and VC, Quebec and Scotland have been moving toward the SME model while remaining part of Canadian and British LMEs.

With a mix of *faire, faire faire*, and *faire avec*, Quebec and Scotland have been pushing market actors in strategic directions, strengthening funding chains and high-tech clusters via the multiplication of public funds, tax-advantaged funds, hybrid co-investment funds, and limited partnerships. An introductory glance at the two regions' ecosystems as of 2019[5] indeed portends similarities, but most importantly the uncharacteristic extent of public intervention (figures 1.2 & 1.3). Within the two regions' "entrepreneurial finance" ecosystems – including VC, private equity, mezzanine finance, equity loans, loans, loan guarantees, and grants – government involvement is key, as it both complements funding chains in strategic sectors and incentivizes market actors to invest in such sectors.

Still, Quebec and Scotland diverge in two important respects. Since the 1980s, first, Quebec supported the development of labour-sponsored investment funds (LSIFs) – the Fonds de solidarité des travailleurs du Québec (FSTQ) and FondAction CSN (FACSN) – and of the tax-advantaged Capital régional et coopératif Desjardins (CRCD) fund, investing in regional businesses and co-ops. This model distinguishes Quebec from the rest of Canada (RoC), a clear case of policy divergence, but is almost completely absent in Scotland. Second, the central role of business angel syndicates in Scotland's VC market differentiates it from Quebec's, where organized angel syndicates are almost absent – although business angels collaborate through the centralized Anges Québec network – and represent a relatively small share of the VC industry.

These differences are however much less significant than the two models' convergence in the widespread use of public funds, hybrid funds,[6] and limited partnerships (capitalization of private funds by public and/or tax-advantaged partners) designed to leverage and steer private investment in strategic sectors. Aside from public funds and agencies, both regions have indeed increasingly resorted to hybrid funds and limited partnerships since the late 1990s. Given that the UK and Canada, although to a much lesser extent relative to their means, also adopted this approach – notably through the British Business Bank and the Business Development Bank of Canada – what is of interest in this case is most importantly (1) the comparatively early development of such funds in Quebec and Scotland, and (2) policy *autonomy*, that is to say the peculiar extent to which, compared to other subnational jurisdictions in Canada or the UK, these regions act on their own.

The scope of state intervention in their entrepreneurial finance and VC ecosystems, I argue, shows that Quebec and Scotland have been moving toward the SME model. One major argument of this book, accordingly, is that in the area of entrepreneurial finance both Quebec and Scotland can be described as autonomous "sponsor states" given the significant influence of their public sector. Through policy asymmetry, the strategic role of Quebec and Scottish governments has consisted in "sponsoring" domestic SMBs in order to develop and sustain internationally competitive clusters. Such public sponsorship mainly consists in:

(a) allocating significant quantities of public resources to the development of start-ups, early-stage businesses, and high-growth companies or "gazelles," either through direct investments or via co-investment funds and limited partnerships with institutional and private funds;
(b) assisting businesses in locating the appropriate funding chains and securing the appropriate funding opportunities throughout their growth stages;
(c) supporting the establishment of and collaborating with private/non-for-profit organizations promoting sectoral coordination in entrepreneurial finance and the attraction of foreign investors.

Other jurisdictions in Canada and the UK – as well as central governments – also engage in such activities, but the magnitude of public involvement in Quebec and Scotland remains proportionately much greater. A number of general arguments can thus be articulated. Firstly, in various institutional contexts and policy fields, minority nationalism generally fosters policy asymmetry. Secondly, its effects on economic development policy remain understudied. Thirdly, such effects and

Figure 1.2. Quebec's entrepreneurial finance ecosystem, 2019

Government

- Ministère de l'Économie et de l'Innovation

- Ministère des Finances

Public funds & investors

- Investissement Québec
    - Ressources Québec
- Fonds du développement économique
- Fonds pour la croissance des entreprises québécoises
- Caisse de dépôt et placement du Québec
    - Fonds Espace CDPQ
    - Fonds Croissance CDPQ
    - Fonds Relève CDPQ
- Fonds locaux d'investissement
- Société de développement des entreprises culturelles
- La Financière agricole
- Fonds d'initiatives autochtones
- Fonds d'action québécois pour le développement durable

Tax-advantaged funds

- Capital régional et coopératif Desjardins

- Fonds de solidarité FTQ

- Fond*Action* CSN

Main private funds

- Anges Québec (angel network)
- Novacap (ICT)
- Real Ventures (ICT)
- AmorChem (life sciences)
- Panache Ventures (ICT/cleantech)
- Cycle Capital Management (cleantech)
- iNovia Capital (diversified)
- Lumira Capital (life sciences)
- XPND Capital (tech/cleantech)
- White Star Capital (ICT, fintech)
- Luge Capital (artificial intelligence, fintech)

Hybrids

- Teralys Capital
- Teralys Capital Fonds d'innovation
- Anges Québec Capital
- Fonds Capital Croissance PME
- FIER-Partenaires
- Desjardins-Innovatech
- Fonds de transfert d'entreprise du Québec
- Fonds Manufacturier Québécois
- Fonds Innovexport
- SIDEX
- Fonds Femmessor Québec
- Fonds Biomasse Énergie
- Fonds d'investissement pour la relève agricole
- Capital Financière agricole
- Fonds Tourisme PME
- Fonds Capital Culture Québec
- Fonds Capital Mines Hydrocarbures

Source: Author.

Figure 1.3. Scotland's entrepreneurial finance ecosystem, 2019

Government

- Cabinet Secretary for Finance, Economy, and Fair Work
- Minister for Business, Fair Work, and Skills
- Minister for Trade, Investment, and Innovation
- Economic Development Directorate
- Scottish National Investment Bank Directorate

Non-for-profit organizations

- LINC Scotland
- Prince's Trust Enterprise
- Royal Society of Edinburgh
- Social Investment Scotland
- DSL Business Finance

Public funds & investors

- Scottish Enterprise
- Highlands & Islands Enterprise
- South of Scotland Enterprise
- Scottish Investment Bank
-SME Holding Fund
- Scottish Growth Scheme
- Co-operative Development Scotland
- Regional Selective Assistance
- Business Gateway
- Local Authority Councils
- Ayrshire Loan Fund
- Marine Renewables Commercialisation Fund
- Creative Scotland
- Scottish Funding Council

Main private funds & angel syndicates

- Highland Venture Capital (diverse)
- Par Equity (diverse)
- Archangels (ICT/cleantech)
- Strathtay Ventures (diverse)
- Gabriel Investment Syndicate (ICT/diverse)
- Amadeus Capital Partners (diverse)
- TriCapital (diverse)
- Equity Gap (diverse)
- Maven Capital Partners (diverse)
- Emerald Technology Ventures (cleantech)
- Clyde Blowers Capital (engineering)
- Epidarex Capital (life sciences)
- Kelvin Capital (biotech)
- Braveheart Investment Group (diverse)
- Scottish Equity Partners (diverse)

Hybrids

- Scottish Co-investment Fund
- Scottish Venture Fund
- Scottish Loan Fund
- Energy Investment Fund
- Scottish European Growth Co-Investment Programme
- Low Carbon Infrastructure Transition Programme
- Maven UK Regional Buyout Fund
- Scottish Investment Fund
- Scottish Edge
- LendingCrowd
- Scottish Microfinance Fund
- West of Scotland Loan Fund
- East of Scotland Investment Fund
- Business Loans Scotland
- Circular Economy Investment Fund
- Edinburgh Technology Fund Ltd.
- Scottish Social Growth Fund

Source: Author.

policy asymmetries can be best studied by focusing on specific policy sectors. Fourthly, in the sector of entrepreneurial finance and VC Quebec and Scotland developed into "sponsor states," thereby drifting away from Canadian and British LMEs and toward the SME variant. Finally, I contend that Québécois and Scottish nationalisms provide a crucial explanation for such policy autonomy and divergence.

Economic Nationalism

As the writing of this book began, an important contribution to the literature on regional VoC was published by University of Toronto's Rodney Haddow (2015), who compared, notably, economic development policies in Quebec and Ontario since 1990. Noting that levels of public spending in this field remained much greater in Quebec, Haddow argued that while Ontario, along with Canada, can be classified as a LME, Quebec diverges as much from Ontario and the RoC as European CMEs diverge from LMEs (2015, 265–71). Therefore, Quebec was described as a "hybrid" VoC (45), lying between coordinative and liberal models. Most importantly however, Haddow explicitly *rejected* the notion that Québécois nationalism could still explain this divergence.

Recognizing that nationalism was a crucial motive behind state intervention from the 1960s onward, Haddow's argument is that since the 1990s it has had, at best, *indirect* effects on economic policymaking. Québécois nationalism is thus said to *have had* direct impacts on the mutually reinforcing "institutional mechanisms" that henceforth explain higher levels of intervention in Quebec. Drawing from the VoC literature, Haddow (2015, 26–30) identifies three such mechanisms: (a) the "collaborative" and "concerted" intermediation of socioeconomic interests in Quebec, stemming in good part from greater unionization levels; (b) Quebec's "multidimensional" party system, with a relatively low polarization on economic issues between major players (until then, the PQ and PLQ); and (c) its comparatively strong and centralized state bureaucracy.

Unlike Haddow, I contend that nationalism still exerts direct impacts on economic policymaking. Given that minority nationalism is an "ideational" variable, however, its direct effects on policymaking can only be identified by investigating "legislative intent" and the meanings actors involved in the elaboration or implementation of policy attach to their activities. To do so, detailed process-tracing and qualitative analysis must be performed. Because Haddow considers, however, that nationalism is a "non-outcome oriented public sentiment"

(2015, 15), he adopts a mostly institutional and statistical perspective, studying the field of "economic development" at large. Against such a generic policy field, the effects of nationalism can only appear indirect; but if the same analysis had been dedicated solely to the VC industry, for instance, perhaps nationalism would have been found to be more "outcome-oriented."

Haddow, in addition, employs a limitative definition of Quebec's economic nationalism – "fostering a Francophone business class" (2015, 165) – which allows him to argue that "the original nationalist impetus [is] now disputed and secondary" (165), and to confirm his hypothesis that "policies will not be discussed and formulated mainly in relation to explicit province-level 'national' objectives" (61). Yet even this impetus remains a central motivation of public intervention, as attested by the growing importance paid to business succession in Quebec and by the establishment of state-backed funds such as the Fonds Relève Québec (FRQ)[7] or the Fonds d'investissement pour la relève agricole (FIRA). There is even an argument to be made that Quebec's entrepreneurial finance ecosystem as a whole is structured to favour local and thus predominantly Francophone entrepreneurs, even though this is no longer explicitly stated as the objective.

CRCD, for instance, developed a specialization in business succession. Not only did it contribute to both the FRQ and FIRA, but business transfer is a very important aspect of its own investment activities. Gérald St-Aubin, VP for Strategic Investments & Partnerships at CRCD, explains how this generally works (personal interview):

> *Autre activité qu'on peut faire et qu'un fonds privé aura beaucoup de difficulté à faire: on a acheté plusieurs sociétés. Je vais t'en donner une en exemple, qui est à Thetford Mines: Industries X. 300 employés, belle société qui pourrait être et qui sera en croissance. Le propriétaire, Monsieur X., a dans les soixante-quinze ans environ. Il veut vendre et a été approché par plusieurs compétiteurs américains. Mais lui, il vient de Thedford Mines. Il est né là-bas, il a fondé sa société dans son garage, il a grandi avec ses employés. Alors vendre sa société et mettre plusieurs millions dans ses poches, si ces gens-là ont de fortes chances de perdre leur emploi dans le futur, il ne veut pas ça. Nous, ce qu'on fait, c'est qu'on achète la société à 100%. On s'entend avec Monsieur X.: on lui fait une offre, qui est probablement inférieure à ce qu'un stratégique pourrait offrir, mais qui comporte d'autres avantages. Dans Industries X, le management en place était très fort. Alors on fait la transaction avec le management en place, puis en plus on va impliquer les employés dans notre transaction: on regroupe les employés soit sous la forme d'une coopérative de travailleurs actionnaires, soit sous celle d'un régime de participation à l'actionnariat qui est avantageux pour les employés. Notre objectif*

dans le temps, dans dix, quinze ans ou un petit peu plus selon la croissance de la société, est de retransférer la propriété au management et aux employés. Un coup que la société appartient à ses employés, elle est enracinée dans sa région. Plus personne ne sera capable de la délocaliser.[8]

Quebec nationalists and policymakers do not use the language they did in the 1960s and 1970s because the "Francophone business class" is now well established and has different needs. This does not mean economic nationalism no longer exists; it has instead been adapted to those needs, taking on new forms. The objectives of economic nationalism can thus evolve, just as they can be plural at any given time. When Quebec and Scottish governments dedicate great amounts of public resources to the strategic development of their aerospace or food and drink industry, for instance, they certainly do so with national objectives in mind. Economic nationalism thus isn't necessarily and only about favouring an ethno-linguistic group over others, but also about using political tools and public resources to benefit domestic firms, industrial clusters, and supply chains.

My contention is that economic nationalism should not simply be conflated with protectionism or the ethnic division of labour. Instead I follow Helleiner and Pickel, for whom "economic nationalism should be understood simultaneously as political action in a specific historical context, rather than as economic doctrine in a universal context of ideas" (2005, 8). I therefore approach economic nationalism as *ideology, policy, political action,* and *structure* (Pickel 2005, 12). Investigating economic nationalism as both ideology and policy, first, allows for a better understanding of the way economic policies, even if not protectionist or ethnically biased, can be devised based on strategic national objectives. When the SNP government, for instance, justifies the establishment of a state-owned Scottish Business Development Bank (SBDB)[9] to try and mitigate the fact that "Scotland has a lower proportion of medium-sized enterprises than other independent European countries such as Germany, Austria, Finland and Sweden" (Scotland 2015a, 44), it merges nationalist ideology and policy.

If the basic ideological tenet of nationalism is that *political* and *national* "units" should be congruent (Gellner 1983), then at the core of economic nationalism is the idea that *economic* and *national* units should also be as congruent as possible. In the case of minority nationalism, this involves policy asymmetry both in order to gain autonomy and to craft regional economic strategies based on what are perceived to be "national" interests. This is where economic nationalism becomes political action: when the Canadian government, for example, unilaterally decided to eliminate the federal tax credit allocated to LSIFs,[10] a model differentiating Quebec's investment ecosystem from the RoC's, Quebec's government was forced to act given, notably, the major discontent this decision created in the VC industry. Jack Chadirdjian, ex-CEO of Réseau Capital, Quebec's peak VC and private equity association, describes the situation (personal interview):

> La déception de l'ensemble de l'industrie, y compris évidemment du FSTQ et du FACSN, concerne le manque de compréhension du gouvernement par rapport à notre écosystème. Simplement parce que ce système n'a pas fonctionné ailleurs au Canada, cela ne veut pas dire que ça n'a pas fonctionné au Québec. Cela fonctionne au Québec. Est-ce que tout est parfait ? Non, il y a des ajustements à faire. Mais de là à éliminer le crédit d'impôt complètement … La grande déception au sein de l'industrie, ça aura vraiment été l'indifférence du gouvernement fédéral face aux nombreuses interventions de nos membres lui disant qu'il est en train de tuer quelque chose qui fonctionne.[11]

In Quebec's 2015–16 budget, therefore, the annual cap on the issuance of shares was lifted for both the FSTQ and the FACSN, the CRCD was allowed to issue an additional $150 million in shares for 2015, the provincial tax credit applicable to FACSN shares was increased from 15% to 20%, and all three funds were asked to increase their annual investments in Quebec's SMBs by 5%.[12] This process was a clear instance of economic nationalism in the form of political action, state intervention, and the upholding of policy divergence.

Economic nationalism, finally, can operate as a *structure*. It can be approached as a set of economic ideas that become "institutionalized" and, as such, central to national identity. Québécois and Scottish nationalisms indeed comprise sets of economic ideas relating to (a) shared narratives about the distinct history, challenges, and traditions of economic development in these regions; (b) perceptions of particular economic or commercial interests; and (c) widely shared and organizationally embedded – i.e., "institutionalized" – wisdom about the necessity and legitimacy of government intervention. Such sets of ideas can be deemed "institutionalized" when acquiring meanings central to collective identity, thereby producing "lock-in effects" leading to *path dependency* and the reproduction of economic policy "traditions" or "paradigms" (Hay 2011, 68–9). Economic nationalism is thus also about the institutionalization, through policy and organizational embeddedness, of sets of ideas that amount to a collective "economic identity."

When "institutionalized," such ideas can indeed turn into "normative frames" (Surel 2000) or "policy paradigms" (Hall 1993), making it very difficult for policymakers to implement significant changes in economic strategies, policies, or institutional "ecosystems." This can help explain, for instance, continuity in Scotland's interventionist model and the preservation of long-standing Scottish organizations – such as the predecessor of Scottish Enterprise (SE), the Scottish Development Agency (SDA) – in the face of the radical policy shifts that took place under Thatcherism in the 1980s and 1990s. As a long-time SDA and SE senior official remarked,

> one of the def nitions of Scotland is that it's been through traumas in structures and changes in policy, U-turns on policy right and left of centre, but that the kind of wide scale cutting back of economic development as it came to other parts of the UK and many other parts of Europe hasn't really affected Scotland. So, the "Scottish model" still has got remnants of traditional regional economic development models going back in history.[13]

This also leads to continuity in economic policy across partisan cycles. When a certain set of policy paradigms define national identity, it becomes politically hazardous for governments of various economic tendencies to implement fundamental changes. That is in part why, even though the PLQ has long been promoting public retrenchment in economic affairs, on occasions it has even imposed economic nationalism on PQ governments. When the latter created Investissement Québec (IQ) in 1998, for instance, its key goal was to centralize the public prospection of foreign and private investment (Québec 1998a). However, since IQ would incorporate the pre-existing Société de développement industriel (SDI), which had the more general mandate to "promote Quebec's economic development," the Liberal opposition insisted on amending the IQ Bill in order to integrate this larger mandate (Québec 1998b), and this amendment has since allowed IQ to play a much larger role in economic development.

   To summarize, economic nationalism can be conceptualized as being, simultaneously, an *ideology*, a set of *policies*, a basis for *political action*, and an *institutional frame*. In regional contexts such as Quebec or Scotland, its ideological core relates to policy asymmetry: it rests on the belief that these nations can be best served if their governments pursue regionally specific economic objectives through either policy divergence or autonomy. As political action, economic nationalism highlights the co-extensiveness of identity politics and economic policymaking. Hence the widely shared opinion, in Quebec and Scotland, that the government has a duty to prioritize and uphold regional interests even if that entails a deepening of policy asymmetry with the rest of the country.[14]

As an institution, finally, economic nationalism points to the economic "content" of national identity, and to path dependencies induced by the embeddedness of that content – a certain set of economic ideas – into concrete policies and organizations.

Minority nationalism, I argue, offers a crucial explanation for the level of policy asymmetry and government involvement that characterizes the Quebec and Scottish "models." It has driven these regions to extend and/or refine that involvement since the 1990s by insisting that domestic firms and sectors, for strategic as well as for nation-and-state-building purposes, be "sponsored" in order to achieve growth and competitiveness *while retaining local ownership*. Nationalism has had as an effect the promotion of policy autonomy *and* policy divergence through public involvement, leading to similar policy outcomes even though Quebec and Scotland have been evolving in very different institutional contexts. Where LMEs such as Canada and the UK, and other wealthy regions within these countries – Ontario and South East England, for instance – generally favour national-level collaboration, market mechanisms, and private sector leadership, nationalism has impelled Quebec and Scottish governments to influence, leverage, and steer the market and private sector actors in strategic directions, in the name of regional-level "national objectives." Accordingly, in short, I argue that in Quebec and Scotland economic nationalism takes the following forms:

(a) perceived needs for policy asymmetry and strategic planning;
(b) political imperatives to uphold such asymmetry and strategies;
(c) forms of path dependency – ideational and institutional – underpinning those political imperatives;
(d) a tendency for governments of different economic inclinations to intervene, based on those prevailing ideas and institutions.

In most of the recent literature on economic nationalism,[15] authors generally agree with Helleiner that "economic nationalism can be associated with very diverse economic policies," and that "the goal of research should be to explore the diverse and complex influences that nationalism and national identities have on economic policy and processes" (2005, 225). The policy effects of economic nationalism are thus *context-specific*. This is particularly evident when considering *minority* nationalism, and therefore the only way to study such "diverse and complex influences" is to focus on a small number of cases and policy sectors, in order to gain deep knowledge. This is the approach I have chosen.

Scope and Case Selection

Two caveats regarding the scope of this book need to be mentioned at this point. First of all, my intent is not to provide a critical assessment or an evaluation of policy effectiveness but to uncover, with as much detail as possible, the political and ideological underpinnings behind the design and evolution of VC ecosystems in Scotland and Quebec. Underlying this book is the view that policy intent and policy design are interesting and worthy of analysis in and of themselves, irrespective, to a certain extent, of subsequent policy effectiveness. Although evaluations of specific policies and programs are sometimes referred to for information purposes, I generally do not engage with questions such as whether public intervention in VC has benefited or harmed the Quebec and Scottish economies. That said, serious theoretical and empirical research has been devoted in recent years to the strengths and weaknesses of public VC and R&D schemes across cases: the works of VC and innovation policy experts Josh Lerner (1999, 2002, 2009, 2010) and Mariana Mazzucato (2014, 2016)[16] are perhaps among the most instructive in this regard.

On the whole, and even though there seems to be no strong consensus regarding the general merits of public intervention in these sectors, there is a common opinion among analysts that what matters most in terms of long-term efficiency probably revolves around *policy design*: in other words, government programs and public investment schemes can either be economically beneficial or detrimental, "crowd out" private capital or leverage it, and fuel entrepreneurship and innovation or hinder them depending on the ways in which they are organized, implemented, and managed. Still, major disagreements remain as to the basic roles of the public sector: while some experts would contend that a common trait of successful state-backed VC initiatives is to "let the market provide direction" and therefore focus on *leveraging* private investment (Lerner 2009, 183), others argue to the contrary that the ambition of such government programs should be to "shape and create markets," and thus to *steer* private investment toward strategic and priority sectors (Mazzucato 2014, 8). This fundamental difference explains, in part, why analysts also differ in their choice of the relevant *indicators* of policy success. This book leaves such questions open in the absolute but aims to uncover the ways in which Quebec and Scottish governments have perceived their roles over the years.

Second, although the relationships I unveil between minority nationalism and government involvement in VC could perhaps also be found in other regions where nationalism or "autonomist regionalism" is present (Keating 1997c, 24), as well as in other policy sectors, the potential "generalizability" of my arguments is not substantiated. This book is therefore mostly useful in generating hypotheses *about* and methods to assess *for* the effects of minority nationalism on economic policymaking. Following political scientist Arend Lijphart's typology, my contribution could be described as lying between *interpretation* – "generalization applied to a specific case with the aim of throwing light on the case rather than of improving the generalization" – and *hypothesis generation* – "starting out with a more or less vague notion of possible hypotheses, and attempt[ing] to formulate definite hypotheses to be tested subsequently among a larger number of cases" (1971, 692).

The cases of Quebec and Scotland indeed allow us to isolate minority nationalism as an independent variable, and thereby to circumscribe its economic effects. That is because Scotland and Quebec diverge on many other variables that could explain convergence in economic policy. To simplify the demonstration, we can refer to the three main variables used by Haddow (2015) to explain divergence between Quebec and Ontario: collaborative interest mediation (driven by union density), a multidimensional party system with low polarization on economic issues, and a strong and centralized bureaucracy. For each of these indicators, differences between Quebec and Scotland are in fact equally, if not more, significant than those between Quebec and Ontario, or Scotland and the RoUK. Union density, for instance, stood at around 38% in Quebec for 2017, against 27% in Ontario. The same rates were 28% in Scotland and 22% in England. Divergence in union density between Quebec and Scotland is thus equally or more important than between Quebec and Ontario, or Scotland and England. Moreover, while union density has remained relatively stable in Quebec since the mid-1990s, it receded significantly in Scotland, by 11% between 1995 and 2017.[17]

While it is true that the Quebec and Scottish party systems are multidimensional, with major parties positioned on both economic-distributive and constitutional issues, in Quebec all MNAs are elected on a "first-past-the-post" (FPTP) basis, whereas the Scottish MSPs are elected based on a mixed-proportional "additional member system" that allows citizens to vote in both their constituency and, choosing from party lists, their region. Whereas Quebec's system (shared by Ontario) is known to favour majority governments and two-party dynamics, the Scottish system was adopted to favour coalition governments and foster the growth of smaller parties. As a result, Scotland was governed in turn by a SLP-SLD coalition (1999–2007) and by SNP minority governments (2007–11; 2016–21).

Third, state bureaucracy would be the weakest explanation for a convergence of Scotland and Quebec. Invoking higher levels of public spending to explain greater government involvement in economic development is partly tautological, except perhaps from a path dependency perspective. In turn, if public sector employment as a proportion of total employment in 2017 was similarly higher in Quebec (22%) and Scotland (21%) than in Ontario (19%) or England (16%), the gaps are relatively narrow.[18] Most importantly, for nearly 300 years before the re-establishment of a Scottish Parliament in 1999, Scotland did not even have a government of its own but only enjoyed limited administrative autonomy through the Scottish Office, a department of the UK government. Since the devolution of 1998–9, moreover, Scotland still lacks much of the very large fiscal and economic autonomy that Quebec enjoys as part of the Canadian federation (Rioux 2016).

Finally, differences in economic profiles are also worth mentioning: while Quebec's economy is significantly larger than Scotland's, with the Scottish GDP[19] equivalent to around $306 billion (£170 billion) for 2018 against $435 billion for Quebec's, sectoral dissimilarities are notable as well. While SMBs were responsible for around 60% of Scotland's private sector employment in 2016, for instance, the same proportion stood at over 90% in Quebec.[20] Such dissimilarities make policy convergence in financial support to SMBs all the more puzzling, if and only if economic nationalism is overlooked.

Methodology

My challenge with this book, it should now be clear, was to uncover the political rationales justifying specific VC policies and strategies and to evaluate whether nationalism was a significant part of such rationales. Discourse analysis and policy analysis are thus conducted simultaneously, insofar as possible. I also assess for the way decisions that depart from nationalist frames engender political and/or institutional resistance. In addition to previous academic research, my sources thus include but are not limited to: electoral platforms, budget speeches and budgets, parliamentary debates and commissions, bills and legislation, annual reports and publications from economic ministries, reports of special committees on economic development, annual reports and strategic plans from state agencies and public or government-backed investment funds, newspaper archives, opinion polls, and elite interviews (see Appendix).

The approach for this book is modelled on Charles Tilly's (1995, 2001, 2008) "prospective" process tracing strategy. I consider economic nationalism to have causal effects on policymaking through three main mechanisms: *ideological, political,* and *institutional.* It is through such "nationalizing mechanisms" (Pickel 2006) that institutional disjunction (i.e. policy asymmetry) developed between Quebec, Scotland, and their respective countries. Starting from the early 1990s, I identify particular processes – elections, parliamentary debates, consultations and commissions, drafting of bills, adoption of new laws, launching of new economic strategies and budgets, establishment of new funds or agencies, publication of annual reports, economic downturns and crises, etc. – on which the impacts of these causal mechanisms are assessed. In this way I can uncover if, why, and how nationalism caused these two regions to move further down particular policy trajectories while alternative paths were available.

Outline of the Book

At this point, a review of my main hypotheses is in order. Four hypotheses form the framework against which this book's findings can be evaluated:

> *Hypothesis 1:* Minority nationalism affects economic policymaking
> just as it affects other policy sectors. The causal inf uence of nationalism
> on economic development can be established through the use of
> prospective process tracing approaches, having been mediated
> through ideological, political, and institutional mechanisms.

> *Hypothesis 2:* In Quebec and Scotland since the 1990s, nationalism
> favoured policy asymmetry (involving both autonomy and
> divergence) and greater government intervention (compared with
> other regions in Canada and the UK) in economic development,
> thereby fostering the emergence of autonomous "sponsor states" in
> these two regions.

> *Hypothesis 3:* The effects of nationalism on the sponsoring activities
> of Quebec and Scottish governments are manifest in the specif c
> sector of entrepreneurial f nance and the subsector of venture
> capital, where they offer crucial explanatory complements to classic
> economic justif cations for state intervention.

> *Hypothesis 4:* Given the mixed ideational-institutional nature of
> economic nationalism, I expect its effects to be constant since
> 1990, giving way to both ideational and institutional path-
> dependency. Therefore, the development of regional "sponsor
> states" in Quebec and Scotland – through policy asymmetry and

state activism – will have persisted regardless of the alternation between secessionist (PQ, SNP) and non-secessionist (SLP-SLD, PLQ, CAQ) governments.

What I am looking for is evidence linking specific VC policies, organizations, and strategies to past ones and/or to political rationales presenting regional-level national traditions, needs, and interests as distinct and thus requiring policy asymmetry. If such evidence can be found in the legislative intent of policymakers as well as in the discourse and activities of concerned actors, and if it can be established that such policy choices involved autonomy and/or divergence as well as active public involvement, then a plausible case will have been made with regards to hypotheses 1, 2, and 3. In turn, a differentiated analysis of secessionist and non-secessionist governments' platforms, programs, budgets, bills, economic strategies, and policies will allow me to verify my fourth hypothesis. In this case, I expect the PLQ, CAQ, and SLP-SLD to be a little less prone than the PQ or SNP to use public resources, centralize activities, and/or favour policy asymmetry, but if my hypothesis is correct, this should not have had a significant impact on the general process of institutional disjunction ongoing since the 1990s.

Chapters 3 to 6 will be devoted to this process tracing effort. In chapters 3 (Quebec) and 4 (Scotland), I first assess for economic nationalism's impacts from the early 1990s to the early 2000s. Each chapter is structured in a chronological fashion, divided into sections covering particular governments: the third chapter covers periods corresponding to the Bourassa/Johnson (1989–94), Parizeau/Bouchard (1994–8), and Bouchard/Landry (1998–2003) governments in Quebec; chapter 4 focuses on Scotland from the years preceding parliamentary devolution (1990–7) to the end of the first SLP-SLD mandate (1999–2003). Chapters 5 and 6 follow the same model: in Quebec's case (chapter 5), the Charest I (2003–7), Charest II (2008–12), Marois (2012–14), Couillard (2014–18) and Legault (2018–19) administrations are investigated; in Scotland's case (chapter 6), the McConnell (2003–7), Salmond (2007–11), Salmond II (2011–14), and Sturgeon I and II (2014–16; 2016–19) governments are covered.

Before getting there however, the second chapter offers a more thorough overview of the policy sector under discussion. The existing literature on state intervention in the VC sector is weighed against the development of this industry in Quebec and Scotland from the 1960s onward. The objective is to establish and illustrate the extent to which common market-based explanations for government involvement apply, and the extent to which economic nationalism offers a better explanatory potential. In the field of VC, many arguments have been used to explain cross-national divergence in the use of public resources: gaps in funding chains, information asymmetries, the cyclical nature of VC, geographical imbalances, and so on. In all cases, however, I contend that such explanations are, by themselves, unsatisfactory when it comes to Quebec and Scotland.

Chapter Two

Explaining Public Involvement in Venture Capital: Theoretical and Historical Overviews

To this day, VC has almost exclusively been studied from economic, financial, or managerial perspectives. Very few social or political scientists, even among those who specialize in political economy or economic development policy, have conducted research on the VC sector. Even when it comes to government intervention, therefore, it is nearly impossible to acquire adequate knowledge of this sector without reference to specialized journals such as *Venture Capital, Small Business Economics*, the *Journal of Business Venturing, Economic Development Quarterly*, or the *Journal of Corporate Finance*. The most notable exceptions are studies in economic geography, found in journals such as *Regional Studies* or the *Journal of Urban Economics*. In this chapter, I bridge this gap and clarify how this book adds to existing knowledge.

Explaining Public Sector Involvement in VC

If one was to date the advent of major policy interest in start-up businesses and their funding needs, the mid-to-late 1970s would be most accurate. Oil shocks, stagflation, plant closures, production rationalizing / downsizing and offshoring, R&D outsourcing, technological developments, financialization, and shifts toward the services sector were all part of the picture. By the late 1970s, economists such as David L. Birch (1979) thus started arguing that SMBs, rather than large corporations, had been for some time and in the foreseeable future would be the prime job creators and "innovators." Although arguments such as Birch's were later criticized on various grounds (Neumark, Wall, and Zhang 2011), SMBs henceforth became a central focus of economic policymakers. This led to a diversity of approaches, however, as there are many ways to support SMBs and boost "business birth rates."

Over the past decades, the VC industry fueled this policy shift toward "innovation-led growth," as VC "booms" took place in the late 1960s/ early 1970s, early 1980s, and late 1990s (Gompers et al. 2008, 2). Given that start-ups and early-stage companies, by definition, lack established credit histories or significant cashflows, debt financing can indeed prove problematic and banks reluctant to lend. This problem is particularly acute for start-ups and SMBs operating in high technology sectors, where risks and "information asymmetries" – i.e., the gaps between a product's value and possible lenders' understanding of it – are greatest. VC, a particular type of private equity, is a form of investment tailor-made for this kind of business:

> VC refers to investments provided to early-stage, innovative, and high-growth start-up companies. Typically VC investments are seed-stage investments whereby f nancing is provided to research, assess, and develop an initial concept before a business has reached the start-up phase. Also, depending on perspective, VC investments are start-up investments (f nancing provided to companies for product development and initial marketing) ... other early-stage investments (f nancing to companies that have completed the product development stage and require further funds to initiate commercial manufacturing and sales) ... and expansion-stage investments ... used to f nance increased production capacity, market or product development, and/or to provide additional working capital. (Cumming 2012, 1)

Various players engage in this investment sector: individuals related ("love money") or unrelated ("crowdfunding") to the investee; high-net-worth individuals (business angels); corporations; "institutional" investors such as pension funds, sovereign wealth funds, banks, or credit unions; private investment funds (VCs); and governments and their agencies. In most countries, including Canada and the UK, institutions, corporations, VCs, and angels are by far the most significant investors, with governments playing a supporting role. Historically, however, the public sector (including tax-advantaged investors such as the LSIFs) has been particularly active in Quebec and Scotland, playing a very central and strategic role.

By the turn of the century, Scotland accounted for around 7% of registered private businesses in the UK. Yet, it was attracting up to 15% of the total number of VC deals in the UK, second only to the South East England/London region (table 2.1). Scotland, accordingly, was by far the UK's leading region in terms of the proportion of private businesses receiving VC investments, at between 0.105% and 0.125%

Table 2.1. Regional economic weight and share of VC deals, 2000–2001

2000–1	% of UK GVA / Canadian GDP	% of VC deals[a] in UK / Canada (≈)
Scotland	**8%**	**15%**
South East England	14.5%	20%
Quebec	**24%**	**49%**
Ontario	39%	31%

Souces: For Quebec and Ontario: Statistics Canada (n.d.a), Macdonalds & Associates (2001); Québec (2003a); Suret (2004). For Scotland and South East England: BVCA (2001); Don and Harrison (2006); Mason and Harrison (2002a); Mason and Pierrakis (2013); United Kingdom (2012).
[a] By number.

against 0.056% for the RoUK.[1] Scotland's VC "location quotient"[2] thus stood at least at 1.53 in 2000, way ahead of any other UK region. Most interestingly, the public sector was present, in one form or another (direct, co-investments, limited partnerships), in 50% of investments made in Scotland against less than 20% in South East England. This proportion kept increasing, furthermore, and reached 70% on average (against less than 35% in South East England) between 2000 and the 2008 financial crisis, when it peaked to almost 100% (Mason and Pierrakis 2013, 1166–7; see graph 6.2).

By the year 2000, similarly, Quebec accounted for 49% of the total number of VC deals in Canada, way ahead of every other province, including Ontario at 31% (table 2.1).[3] At the time, Quebec's venture capital industry could raise capital equivalent to 1.3% of the province's GDP in a year, a proportion far superior to most developed countries', and the amount of venture capital available per head in Quebec was more than three times larger than in the RoC (Carpentier and Suret 2005b, 9–10). This would have been inconceivable without the contribution of Quebec's public, tax-advantaged, and labour-sponsored funds. In 2000, more than 55% of the total amount of VC invested in Quebec came from tax-advantaged funds, LSIFs, institutional investors such as the CDPQ, or government funds.[4] It was later estimated the public sector was, in one form or another, behind 70% (Québec 2003b) and up to 90% (Suret 2004) of all VC invested in Quebec in the early 2000s.

The literature on VC provides five classic explanations for such public sector involvement in this sector: (a) the existence of "market gaps" in SMBs' funding chains; (b) the use of public resources as "counter-cyclical" tools; (c) the need to mitigate for the "centripetal" tendencies of VC investments; (d) the "positive externalities" flowing from VC investments; and (e) the "leveraging" effects of public investments. Cumming (2007), for instance, has been among those arguing that governments mostly intervene when and where clear gaps exist in businesses' funding chains, due to the private sector's lack of interest.[5] Such gaps typically open where the potential upside of small VC investments (under $100,000, for example) in seed or very early-stage businesses is largely nullified by the risks, administrative costs, or long-term perspective associated with such deals.

For entrepreneurs, however, small investments can make a very large difference, and therefore the lack of profitability perceived by private sector investors can be said to amount to a "market failure," leading to lower rates of business creation or survival. As market gaps typically open for small, seed, or early-stage investments, a popular type of public involvement developed over the last twenty years that consists in promoting and supporting investments from business angels, who tend to invest smaller amounts at earlier development stages, and to adopt a more "hands-on" approach to their investments, working directly with investee companies to improve management, ensure profitability, and secure follow-on funding opportunities (Harrison and Mason 2000b; Harrison, Botelho, and Mason 2016; Landström and Mason 2016; Lerner 1998; Mason and Harrison 1997).

Gaps in SMBs' funding chains are also related to macroeconomic variables largely out of the control of entrepreneurs, investors, or even governments. Notably, recessions and economic crises tend to have a direct and negative impact on VC investing and bank lending, especially in high-risk, high-cost sectors and at seed or very early stages of business development (Block, De Vries, and Sandner 2012, 48). Two examples of such impacts were provided by the 2008 financial crisis and the 2001 dot-com bust: in each case, VCs absorbed significant blows both in terms of fundraising and returns on previous investments, therefore becoming more risk averse and moving up to larger investments in well-established businesses or traditional sectors (Block et al. 2012, 42–3). The argument has therefore been made that governments should intervene to mitigate for VC gaps created during economic downturns, and to build permanent or quasi-permanent pools of capital that can be used as counter-cyclical tools. Some researchers, focusing on Europe, even observed that mere slow growth can drive public involvement (Manigart and Beuselinck 2001, 12).

The fact is now also well-known that VC – both investments and investors – tends to concentrate in specific regions, where large cities, important industrial clusters, or well-developed financial hubs are

present.[6] However, in addition to factors relating to investment opportunities, spatial concentration of VC activity also stems from investors'
own preferences for proximal deals. This tendency has been referred to
as VC investors' "home bias" (Jeng and Wells 2000) and inclination for
"proximity capital" (Crevoisier 1997). Another key motive for governments to intervene in the VC sector is thus to counteract such centripetal forces, so as to fill funding gaps experienced by businesses outside
VC hubs and to stimulate local development by spreading VC to remote
or lagging regions. Similarly, governments can intervene to strengthen
traditional activities in such regions and promote, via the generated
spillovers, diversification and the advent of new, geographically concentrated industries (Porter 1998).

Speaking of spillovers, governments also frequently intervene in the
VC sector to stimulate activities – notably R&D – generating greater benefits for the society as a whole than for any particular investor or business. Such "positive externalities" or "social returns" thus justify public
intervention when and where private actors have little incentive to invest
in costly undertakings promising very slight or no short-term yields, but
which potentially have significant upsides from a societal perspective
(Lerner 1999, 2002, 2009). Renewable energy is a perfect example of an
industry where governments have been called to "start the wheel" (Duru-
flé 2010, 14), as outlays for private investors can often be prohibitive but
positive externalities sizable (Mazzucato 2014, 113–63). Research shows,
besides, that R&D – corporate or academic – is very closely related to VC
availability and effectiveness: where a VC ecosystem is lacking, lower
levels of firm founding and patenting will emerge from R&D, and vice
versa (Samila and Sorensen 2010, 1349). Hence, governments can have an
interest in financing either R&D, VC, or both.

This raises the related issue of public/private interaction, which is
at the core of another largely acknowledged purpose of state intervention. The argument is often made, especially since the late 1990s, that
public VC can serve as a "priming pump" for private VC. Public VC can
"leverage" private VC, first, because it has a "certifying effect," which
raises private investors' attention toward particular businesses or sectors, attesting to the government's trust *in* and focus *on* those (Lerner
2009; Lerner and Watson 2008). This "stamp of approval" argument,
also referred to as the "demonstration effect" or "signaling mechanism,"
has been widely used to explain the recent multiplication of hybrid co-
investment schemes.[7] The other reason why governments can stimulate private or institutional VC is obviously that co-investment splits
risks and costs. In the case of hybrid funds, this can be done through
"profit distribution and compensation structures" maximizing private

partners' returns (Jaaskelainen, Maula, and Murray 2007), or through "downward protections" minimizing their losses (Karsai 2004, 7).

Aside from these classic economic justifications, however, very few authors have provided *political* explanations for differing levels of public involvement in VC. In a series of articles, economic sociologists Kevin T. Leicht and J. Craig Jenkins (1994, 1998; Jenkins and Leicht 1996) compared public intervention in VC across the US states between the 1970s and 1990s, trying to uncover why some states became involved on a larger scale. Their finding was that "the main forces behind investments in these [VC] programs are inner-circle business elites, professionalized legislatures, and a class compromise rooted in peak bargaining and capital/labor political representation" (Jenkins and Leicht 1996, 318). To this neo-corporatist explanation were added secondary variables such as "structural pressures from deindustrialization, fiscal dependence on corporate taxes and declining federal revenues" (Leicht and Jenkins 1998, 1339). In short, their arguments depicted policymakers as *reacting* and *responding* to "external" economic, political, and bureaucratic pressures; ideology, in the sense of a genuine *preference* of policymakers for strategic state intervention, was not part of the equation.

Remarks

To what extent do such explanations apply to our cases up to the 1990s? Many of the explanations actually refer to the "influencing" role of governments, either substituting themselves for private actors (*faire*) or pushing them in directions they might not have taken otherwise (*faire faire* and *faire avec*). What distinguished Quebec and Scottish governments' influence from that of others in Canada or the UK, however, was its early manifestation, magnitude, permanent character, and autonomous (i.e., specifically regional) unfolding. By themselves, the main rationales provided in the VC literature cannot account for such policy asymmetry. Yet it could be argued that the aforementioned arguments are mainly post-hoc rationalizations and/or prescriptive tools; most cases, therefore, would fully conform to neither when studied in detail. It should therefore be reiterated that what this book seeks to explain is not public intervention per se, but *policy asymmetry*. The main point is not that market rationales for state involvement apply imperfectly to our cases – as they would in most cases – but that alternative arguments are needed to explain policy asymmetry and the greater *scale* of public intervention in Quebec and Scotland as compared with the RoC and RoUK.

Jenkins and Leicht's political take more or less subordinates *ideological preferences* for public intervention in VC to *institutional* mechanisms and variables: the size of state bureaucracies, unionization levels, and concerted interest mediation. As for the "structural" pressures they contend favour public intervention, their impacts are already taken into consideration by economic accounts such as the counter-cyclical argument in the case of declining fiscal revenues, or the centripetal and positive externalities arguments in that of deindustrialization. An alternative approach is therefore needed to better understand, from an inductive perspective, the legislative intent behind the establishment of public organizations involved in VC in Quebec and Scotland, the ideas that informed it, and how the actual investment activities of such organizations align with government strategies beyond market imperatives.

The Evolution of Public Sector Involvement in Quebec, 1960s–1990s

That state intervention from Quebec's "Quiet Revolution" to the 1990s carried sociopolitical as well as economic objectives has been well established (Bourque 2000). This was especially true in the sectors of entrepreneurial finance and VC, where the nationalist content of such objectives was most transparent and where Francophone entrepreneurs were given preference to subvert their dependence on Anglo-Canadian capital (Smith 1994). Language-based preferential policies in the realm of business financing were implemented in a context where, up to the late 1960s, Francophones represented more than 80% of Quebec's population but owned less than a quarter of manufacturing businesses and managed around 25% of the province's financial institutions, mostly Desjardins credit unions (Fraser 1987, 85). From the 1960s to the 1990s, state intervention was notably aimed at the establishment of a Francophone entrepreneurial finance ecosystem, specifically linked and devoted to Francophone-led businesses and industries (Bélanger and Lévesque 1994).

The progressive transformation of Quebec's industrial structure was also an overarching objective of government activism up to the 1990s (Fournier 1979, 1987; Tremblay 1979; Tremblay and Van Schendel 2004, 76–81). Four main goals were pursued: (a) the replacement of interprovincial trade by international exports; (b) the reduction of foreign ownership in primary industries; (c) the reorganization of Quebec's manufacturing sector through technological improvement and the merger of small family businesses; and (d) a move away from traditional manufacturing toward new, high-value-added clusters. Such a

multifaceted, structural transformation required both long-term strategic planning, as evidenced by major policy statements like the epochal
'Le Virage technologique' (Québec 1982), and therefore and most
importantly significant intervention by the state.

The Société générale de financement

Created by Quebec's Liberals in 1962, the Société générale de financement (SGF) was the province's first state corporation devoted to economic development and business financing. The justifications given for
this new fund, as well as the act incorporating the SGF, offer no indication that market rationales for state involvement in VC were central to
its establishment. In the 1962–3 budget speech, PM Jean Lesage argued
Quebec simply had, henceforth, to take the lead in economic development policy:

> *Nous vivons à une époque où, dans notre pays comme ailleurs, les juridictions
> régionales ont à accomplir un rôle bien précis en matière de politique économique …
> Nous sommes prêts à accepter ce rôle difficile; mais encore faut-il qu'on nous laisse
> la possibilité de l'exercer; plus exactement, je devrais dire: encore faut-il que nous
> prenions les moyens de l'exercer.*[8] (Québec 1962a, 6)

The new government considered passive economic policy to have
diverted Québécois' savings and profited "foreign" interests in the past:
"*L'ancien gouvernement a laissé le champ libre à des intérêts privés, canadiens
ou étrangers, et au gouvernement fédéral, de telle sorte qu'on est venu chercher
nos épargnes disponibles pour s'en servir à des fins qui souvent ne nous prof-
itaient pas*" (Québec 1962a, 36).[9] Beyond entrepreneurial finance in the
form of VC and private equity, a key mandate of the SGF would thus be
to channel those savings toward Francophone companies. This is why,
until its reform in 1972, the SGF was structured as a hybrid fund, half of
whose shares were owned by the government and the other half mostly
by Desjardins credit unions (Bourque 2000, 43). The 1962 act incorporating the SGF defined its two core mandates as such:

> The objects of the company shall be: (a) to stimulate and promote the for-
> mation and development of industrial undertakings and, accessorily, of
> commercial undertakings in the province so as to broaden the basis of
> its economic structure, accelerate the growth thereof and contribute to
> full employment; (b) to induce the people of Quebec to participate in the
> development of such undertakings by investing a part of their savings
> therein. (Québec 1962b, 233–4)

This "first" SGF (1962–72) was thus born out of conscious efforts to lay the foundations of an indigenous corporate funding ecosystem built around coordination between the state and the Desjardins movement. This can be extrapolated based on Desjardins's participation in the capitalization of the SGF, but also on the basis of (a) Desjardins's very active financial support, throughout the 1960s and 1970s, of Francophone businesses facing takeover threats from Anglo-Canadian or American interests; (b) the setting up of Quebec's first institutional VC fund, the Société d'investissement Desjardins (SID), through special legislation (Québec 1971a); and (c) the very pivotal role the SID played throughout the 1970s and 1980s, investing in local businesses and sponsoring VCs alongside the SGF (Bourdeau, Noël, and Tououse 1994; Lévesque, Mendell, and Van Kemenade 1996; Lévesque, Malo, and Rouzier 1997).[10]

At first, the SGF operated as an industrial holding, launching new companies and acquiring majority shares in ailing Francophone businesses facing bankruptcy or takeover. Its role as an investment fund really took off in the 1970s, after the government bought back Desjardins's shares in the wake of the establishment of the SID. The SGF then took on the role of an investment bank, increasing medium businesses' cashflow and funding mergers to generate larger Francophone companies (Fournier 1979). Operating under the umbrella of the Ministère de l'industrie et du commerce (MIC) since 1975 (Bourque 2000, 51), the SGF kept playing this role throughout the 1980s, regrouping expansion-stage SMBs and funding large companies in strategic supply chains and sectors (Fournier 1987, 24). On the MIC's lead, the SGF officially adopted a sectoral investment approach from the mid-1980s onward, preparing the table for the consolidation and concertation roles it would play in the "industrial clusters" strategy of the early 1990s (Bourque 2000, 95, 143–4).

An argument could be made the SGF was thus intended to address "gaps" in Francophone SMBs' funding chains, engaging public resources to "leverage" private investments from, notably, Desjardins shareholders. Yet this would be to overlook the strategic and national objectives behind its advent and activities. The intent behind the establishment of the SGF can be brought back to three core motives: a perceived need for the provincial government to take the lead in economic development policy in order to foster autonomy; the attendant objective to increase Francophone ownership in key industrial sectors by channelling Québécois' savings toward local businesses; and the strategic aim to establish an indigenous entrepreneurial finance ecosystem capable of allocating, through coordinated action, large sums of money to fund the expansion of existing SMBs into medium-to-large, internationally competitive Francophone companies.

The Caisse de dépôt et placement du Québec (CDPQ)

The inception of the CDPQ in 1965, like that of the SGF, emanated from a need for policy asymmetry aimed at the strategic channelling of Québécois' savings (Québec 1965, 1). It was established – by partial emulation of France's Caisse des dépôts et consignations – to manage and invest the assets of the new Régime de rentes du Québec, a public pension plan put in place in the wake of Quebec's "opting out" of the Canada Pension Plan (Rioux 2014, 59). While the CDPQ was thus crafted as a fiduciary, it was also intended to act as a powerful institutional investor, including in VC:

> *Les intérêts des Québécois ne s'arrêtent pas, après tout, à la sécurité des sommes qu'ils mettront de côté pour assurer leur retraite. Des fonds aussi considérables doivent être canalisés dans le sens du développement accéléré des secteurs public et privé, de façon à ce que les objectifs économiques et sociaux du Québec puissent être atteints rapidement et avec la plus grande efficacité possible. En somme, la Caisse ne doit pas seulement être envisagée comme un fonds de placement au même titre que tous les autres, mais comme un instrument de croissance, un levier plus puissant que tous ceux qu'on a eus dans cette province jusqu'à maintenant.* (Québec 1965, 2)[11]

In his 1965 speech on the advent of the CDPQ, Quebec's premier specified that the government's industrial strategies and the CDPQ's investment activities would have to be "coordinated" and "synchronized," notably via the latter's board of directors, nominated by the premier (Québec 1965, 4–5). As an investor the CDPQ was to coordinate not only with government policies, but also with other major players such as Desjardins and the SGF. In fact, it was specifically mandated to support and complement SGF initiatives and, as such, the CDPQ was allowed to allocate up to 30% of its assets to equity investments, including up to 7% in seed and early-stage VC (Québec 1965, 17–19).

As until the 1980s very few Francophone businesses were listed on stock exchanges, private equity quickly became a vital tool through which the CDPQ became involved in economic development (Brooks and Tanguay 1985, 108). Moreover, as planned, private equity investments were often completed alongside the SGF and/or Desjardins, as the CDPQ shared their objectives to solidify Francophone businesses' funding chains and support their expansions or mergers (Pelletier 2009, 62). The nationalist impetus behind CDPQ investment activities also extended to large, pan-Canadian or American companies: in such cases, the objective was to extend Francophone presence in key industries and businesses, through board nominations (Fournier 1979, 32).

From the mid-1970s onward, CDPQ activities in private equity and VC accelerated. Smaller deals multiplied[12] and the CDPQ, in addition to its $10 million investment in the SID, started sponsoring private VCs – such as Placements Innocan (1973–4) and Novacap (1980–1) – through partnerships with the SGF and other banking institutions (Pelletier 2009). That said, the CDPQ continued to be aggressive in large, expansion-stage deals in strategic sectors, as shown by participations taken in Vidéotron (ICT), Gaz Métropolitain (energy), Domtar (pulp and paper), Canam Manac (steel products), and Noranda (mining) between 1979 and 1982, in a context of economic contraction. To observers outside of Quebec, therefore, the sheer size of the CDPQ's investment portfolio, its coordination with the government's industrial policies, and its strategic interest in expanding Francophone presence in large corporations were increasingly disturbing.

When the Canadian Pacific railway company feared a concerted takeover by the CDPQ in late 1982 (Pelletier 2009, 117), the federal government threatened, with Bill S-31, to limit provincial participation in any pan-Canadian transportation company to 10% of voting shares (Brooks and Tanguay 1985; Tupper 1983). The CDPQ, it was feared, had become an instrument of the nationalist PQ government. Yet the firm rejection of S-31 by most of Quebec's business class revealed broad support for the CDPQ's activities. For instance, Serge Saucier, Chairman of Montreal's Chamber of Commerce, explained: "We agree that the concentration of economic power in government hands is wrong. However, the absence of French-Canadians in real decision-making is worse. Of the two evils, we choose the lesser of the *Caisse*" (cited in Tupper 1983, 24). Ultimately, Bill S-31 was abandoned, not least because worries regarding the PQ/CDPQ relationship were ill-advised and rested on an erroneous conception of Quebec's economic nationalism (Brooks and Tanguay 1985, 118).

Far from restricting the CDPQ's role in economic development and VC, the PLQ government elected in 1985 actually oversaw the CDPQ-led consolidation of Quebec's entrepreneurial finance ecosystem through increased coordination with the SGF, SDI, SID, Banque Nationale, and FSTQ (Pelletier 2009, 154–6). First, a more streamlined process for investee businesses was established, where the CDPQ was able to offer not only financial assistance but also technical and managerial counselling to help SMBs navigate through Quebec's funding chains. Second, from 1988 onward and with direct financial support from the government the Sociétés régionales d'investissement (SRI) were launched; these were regional VC funds specialized in early-stage financing and capitalized by the CDPQ, SID, Banque Nationale, and FSTQ. Finally, alongside other public, institutional, and private investors, new hybrid VC funds operating in the ICT sector, such as Capitech (1990) and TechnoCap (1993), were capitalized (Bourque 2000; Pelletier 2009).

It would be difficult to apply any of the classic market rationales for public involvement in VC to the evolution of the CDPQ. By the 1990s, the CDPQ was investing significant amounts of VC across all deal sizes and stages, in a wide range of industries in and outside of Quebec. Similarly, its counter-cyclical activities of the mid-1970s and early 1980s took place by default rather than design. As with the SGF, the CDPQ was born out of a political preference for policy asymmetry and intended to channel Francophones' savings in order to increase their control of key industries and businesses. Doing so, it played a central role in consolidating Quebec's entrepreneurial finance ecosystem, a strategic objective of successive governments up to the 1990s.

The Société de développement industriel (SDI)

A third state corporation devoted to economic development was established in 1971 as a complement to the SGF and CDPQ. To be sure, the SDI was intended to fill gaps for early-stage SMBs, offering loans or equity deals as small as $100,000. Both the act incorporating the SDI and the debates preceding it confirm, however, that it was given much broader mandates. First, it should be noted the SDI stemmed from a perceived need for policy divergence: as then-Minister of Industry Gérard D. Lévesque explained, its focus on loans and equity was a way to compete with Ontario, which had established a program of industrial subsidies in the 1960s, and to complement federal programs already offering grants and tax credits for regional development purposes (Québec 1971b, 892).

Distinguishing the SDI from the SGF and CDPQ, Minister Lévesque assigned it three main responsibilities: (a) creating new jobs, especially in the services sector, through support for start-up businesses; (b) promoting the advent of new production technologies and high-value-added products to help transform Quebec's industrial structure; and (c) encouraging entrepreneurial initiatives in peripheral regions (Québec 1971b, 889–90). In reality, from its inception the SDI was used by the MIC as a financial arm to support any project deemed relevant. According to its incorporating act, the SDI would have to "carry out any mandate entrusted to it by the Government to promote a project of major economic importance for Quebec by granting the assistance defined by the Government" (Québec 1971c). As for its centrifugal roles, throughout the 1970s 80% of SDI's loans and investments were still made in Montreal and Quebec City, where most of the investment opportunities could be found (Fournier 1979, 61).

The nationalist inclinations of the SDI, on the other hand, were obvious. After 1975, financial support for larger businesses, including foreign-owned companies, was granted in coordination with the SGF and CDPQ with strict conditions favouring local and especially Francophone SMBs: purchase of raw materials, equipment, and services from local suppliers; R&D spending quotas; and the inclusion of a given percentage of Francophones among executives and board members (Fournier 1979, 55–63). SDI activities also expanded rapidly under the PQ government: from 1976 to 1979, the number of businesses receiving financial help skyrocketed from less than 170 to more than 420 (Tremblay 1979, 8). Rodrigue Tremblay, then head of the MIC, explained: "*Le rôle que joue chez nous la SDI nous rappelle quotidiennement et ce, dans chaque dossier que l'on fait progresser, combien notre développement industriel découle de notre propre initiative*" (1979, 3).[13]

Following the PQ's launch of a four-year (1982–6) industrial strategy based on the development of new clusters in electronics and biotechnology (Fortin 1985), SDI activities were then partly reoriented toward R&D financing and high-technology sectors (Bourque 2000, 61). In addition to an existing SDI program supporting investments in "modern technology" manufacturing, the PQ's strategy led to the creation of a new SDI-led initiative, the Programme d'aide aux activités de recherche et d'innovation, financing up to 90% of businesses' R&D spending via interest-free loans repayable through royalties on commercialized innovations (Fortin 1985, 30). This focus sharpened under the Liberals after 1985, as the increase in ministerial mandates and the SDI's new self-financing requirements pushed it further toward equity (Bourque 2000, 92–3). Targeted investment strategies also multiplied in the late 1980s under the lead of Gérald Tremblay, head of the SDI from 1986 to 1989, and increased authority was granted to sectoral portfolios for Tremblay's[14] clustering policies of the early 1990s.

The SDI was thus always a semi-autonomous investor and a financial tool that Quebec's MIC/MICT[15] used to carry out government strategies. Even though the SDI partially corresponded to classic explanations for public involvement in VC, the way it was crafted and the extent of its activities did not. The SDI's focus on loans and equity was imposed to further policy divergence, and its investment niche was first defined to complement the SGF and CDPQ. A substantial majority of its investments were moreover always made in Montreal and Quebec City rather than in peripheral regions. For many of its large-scale investments, especially in the case of foreign-owned companies, the SDI collaborated with both the SGF and CDPQ, as its overarching goals were to both increase Francophone presence in large businesses and maximize their reliance on indigenous supply chains.

The Fonds de solidarité des travailleurs du Québec

The establishment of the FSTQ in 1983, finally, seemingly confirms explanations for state involvement present in the VC literature. First, the FSTQ was founded in the wake of the economic downturn of the early 1980s and at least partially crafted with a counter-cyclical intent. Second, the FSTQ emanated in part from the "peak bargaining" event of April 1982, the "Quebec Economic Summit" (Tanguay 1980, 1990), where the Fédération des travailleurs du Québec (FTQ) suggested the setting up of a VC fund. Part of the FTQ's rationale for such a fund, underpinned by full employment objectives, was rooted in a nationalist perspective, however: already in 1981, the FTQ's President had been arguing in favour of the "nationalization [of private pension plans] and the channeling of savings" toward SMBs and farms (Morin 2012, 90).

As well, if it is true that the fund's origins lay in the severe 1982 recession (Morin 2012, 91), the economic downturn was in turn aggravated by Quebec's 1980 referendum on secession and thus had a political and ethno-linguistic complexion: between 1976 and 1985, 100,000 Anglophones and a hundred corporate headquarters left the province, mainly for Ontario (Fraser 1987, 103). The PQ government, by backing the establishment of a VC fund sponsored by the FTQ, aimed to compensate for what was perceived as a *political* unwillingness of large (mostly Anglophone-owned) financial institutions to invest *in* or lend *to* Francophone SMBs. Invoking the example of a medium-sized manufacturing business from Bedford, the PQ's sponsor of the FSTQ Bill, Robert Dean, remarked:

> *Tous les amis du Parti libéral d'en face, tous les grands financiers du monde de la rue Saint-Jacques ne trouvent pas de capitaux de risque pour aider l'entreprise des travailleurs d'Exeltor et leurs employeurs qui cherchent des investisseurs ... Cette entreprise risque de tomber en faillite si elle ne trouve pas des capitaux de risque parce qu'elle est sous-capitalisée comme bon nombre d'entreprises québécoises.* (Québec 1983a, 2713)[16]

Legislative debates surrounding the establishment of the FSTQ indeed revealed a lot about the motivations of the PQ government. Three key drivers were expressed (Québec 1983a, 2690–1): (a) a need for policy asymmetry, Quebec being perceived as hardest hit by the recession because of its industrial structure and of federal monetary policies; (b) a continuing resolve to channel Québécois' savings toward their own industries and businesses, FSTQ shares being eligible for substantial tax credits when used as part of registered savings plans (in addition to credits applicable to the buying of the shares themselves); and (c) a strategic imperative to coordinate, as much as possible, FSTQ investments with the government's sectoral industrial objectives.

The MIC therefore not only subsidized the setting up of the FSTQ, but also provided it free access to in-house industrial research services, "to better prepare the fund's investment decisions" (Québec 1983a, 2692). To these three main goals were added, from the FTQ's perspective, job creation and safeguarding, the improvement of working conditions in investee businesses, the respect of French as the language of work, and the financial education of workers. To make sure it would play its role as Quebec's largest "private" VC fund, it was established that the FSTQ had to invest, annually, at least 60% of its net assets from the preceding fiscal year in "eligible enterprises," defined as businesses with assets of under $25 million and a net equity under $10 million, the majority of whose employees, moreover, had to be "resident in Quebec" (Québec 1983c; Suret 1990, 246).

This would differentiate the FSTQ from other LSIFs later established in Canada, and in Ontario in particular.[17] Most importantly, Ontario only required "at least 50% of salaries/wages [to be] paid to employees from a place of employment in Ontario" (Osborne and Sandler 1998, 573). Another crucial divergence consisted in the mandatory holding period (572): in Ontario, as in the case of federal LSIFs, shareholders had to keep their shares for a minimum of eight years; in Quebec, they had to hold on to those shares until they reached retirement age (sixty-five years old). This rule was introduced not only to ensure the FSTQ would serve its purpose as a savings vehicle, but also to allow it to provide "patient" VC, by extending the duration of deals and convincing co-investment partners to do the same (Québec 1983b, 6826). Thanks to such provisions, unlike other provinces' LSIFs the FSTQ quickly became a centerpiece of Quebec's entrepreneurial finance and VC ecosystems,[18] investing in businesses and other funds such as the SRI, Capitech (ICT), BioCapital (biotechnologies), AéroCapital (aerospace), EnviroCapital (green engineering), and TechnoCap (Bourdeau et al. 1994; Canada 1995, 33).

The FSTQ would probably not have been established were it not for the relatively close relationship between the PQ government and the FTQ in the late 1970s and early 1980s. Although the FSTQ was partly intended as a counter-cyclical tool, the demand for an LSIF would probably never have emerged without a widespread belief in (a) the existence of a *political* funding gap relating to the PQ's nationalist inclinations, and (b) the necessity of public intervention and policy divergence to mitigate this gap. The mandates and guidelines imposed on the FSTQ in return for government sponsorship extended far beyond the mitigation of market failures, and instead were consistent with strategic, long-term objectives: the channelling of Québécois' savings into local businesses; job creation and safeguarding through support for both ailing and start-up companies; the provision of "patient" VC subordinating high returns to development objectives; and the consolidation of an indigenous investment ecosystem capable of buttressing the government's industrial strategies.

Remarks

From the 1960s to the 1990s, Quebec evolved from one of Canada's smallest VC markets to by far the largest. In no more than fifteen years, from 1980 to 1995, Quebec's share of the Canadian VC market jumped from less than 10% to over 50% (Canada 1995; Lévesque et al. 1996, 1). Moreover, around 60% of all VC investments in Quebec were by then made by public or tax-advantaged funds, against more or less 30% in Ontario (Canada 1995, 52). Public initiatives such as the SGF, CDPQ, SDI, and FSTQ were thus central to the development of Quebec's VC ecosystem. Common explanations for public involvement in VC all applied in some way and at some point: the "market gaps" and "leveraging" arguments to the SGF and SDI, and the "neo-corporatist" and "counter-cyclical" arguments to the FSTQ and CDPQ for instance. These cannot, however, explain the very active and dominant role the public sector came to play in the distinct "Quebec model" that was formed and institutionalized by the early 1990s (Bourdeau et al. 1994). It can be argued, instead, that the fundamental motivations of policymakers for the 1960–90 period were linked to economic nationalism, through:

(a) perceived needs for asymmetry in economic/industrial policy;
(b) long-term, regional-level strategic objectives aiming to transform Quebec's industrial structure and support the advent of new, competitive, and high-value-added clusters (including the VC cluster itself);

(c) attempts to maximize the channelling of Francophones'
    savings toward local SMBs and entrepreneurs, and to increase
    Francophone presence in major businesses and key industrial
    sectors;
(d) political imperatives to intervene based on those needs and
    objectives, i.e., to build a coordinated, provincial investment
    ecosystem facilitating the implementation of Quebec's industrial
    strategies; and
(e) both an ideological and a "path-dependent" preference for the
    perpetuation and refinement of the "Quebec model" of active
    public involvement, as seen notably in the relative continuity that
    characterized the Liberal period from 1985 to 1994.

The Evolution of Public Sector Involvement in Scotland, 1960s–1990s

Throughout the 1960s, Scotland was in a similar situation, economically
and relative to England, as Quebec in Canada. Scotland's economy was
becoming increasingly peripheral due to the decline of heavy manufacturing clusters organized around shipbuilding and the increasing
concentration of financial capital in London. For historical and cultural
reasons not unlike those prevalent in Quebec at the time, this meant
expanding foreign ownership of large businesses and new industrial
sectors, such as electronics or oil and gas (Moore and Rhodes 1974;
Devine et al. 2005). Scotland's precarious economic position was therefore central to the mounting nationalist pressures for policy asymmetry
emerging during the 1960s and 1970s (Hechter 1999, 302).

Comparing this drive for economic policy asymmetry with Quebec's
can be hazardous, as Scotland did not have a "government" of its own
before devolution in the late 1990s. Still, many organizations specifically
devoted to Scotland already existed at the turn of the 1960s. First and
foremost, the Scottish Office[19] (SO) was a department of the UK government responsible for Scottish affairs, which managed the implementation of British policy in Scotland, crafted Scottish policies in certain
domains, and lobbied Scottish MPs, the central government and other
departments for policy initiatives or additional resources (Keating 2010,
21). Another was the Scottish Council for Development and Industry
(SCDI), a networking association bringing together businesses, private
sector groups, unions, local authorities, public institutions, universities,
and civil society representatives to lobby and advise policymakers on
Scotland's economic development.

One early manifestation of the perceived need for asymmetry came with the publication of the Toothill Report in 1961, commissioned by the SCDI with the SO's support. This report of the Committee of Inquiry into the Scottish Economy highlighted Scotland's low levels of firm formation in "new industries," concentrated in South East England (SCDI 1961, 183–5). Central to its recommendations was the establishment of "an economic unit to advise on the general measures needed to ensure the health and growth of the economy, on the implications for Scotland of national economic policies, on the broad issues of investment policy, [and] on the economic implications of the programmes of public investment" (SCDI 1961, 191). By 1962, a new Scottish Development Department had accordingly been created, and put under SO responsibility.

The Toothill Report "stated that policy should not aim to prop up inefficient or dying industries. It called for a widening and strengthening of the country's industrial structure through the development of science-based industries, the newer capital goods industries and engineering-based consumers' industries" (Peden 2005, 252). Under the impulse of the SCDI, SO, and Scottish Development Department, massive new public investments flowed into Scotland for such purposes. While public spending in Scotland was already 12% higher than the British average in 1960–1, this gap reached 27% in 1972–3 (Parry 1983, 100), following a 900% increase between 1964 and 1972 (Devine 2008, 148). By 1975, Scottish public expenditures devoted to "industry and employment" were 107% higher than the British average (Parry 1983, 104). This can be explained, in part, by the establishment and investment activities of new economic development agencies.

The Highlands and Islands Development Board (HIDB)

The creation of the HIDB in 1965 was a clear illustration that policy asymmetry was perceived as necessary by Scottish representatives and SO officials. Secretary of State for Scotland (SOSS) William Ross, head of the SO, remarked: "It has become obvious to everyone who studies the problem that after all the commissions, reports and surveys … what really has been needed is an authority with executive powers to deal comprehensively with the problems; not to deal one at a time, but comprehensively. For this reason we have decided to establish the Highland Development Board" (Hansard UK 1965, cc. 1080–1). The advent of the HIDB also had a lot to do with the UK's 1964 elections, in which the strongly devolutionist Liberal Party made important gains in the Scottish Highlands.

In their Manifesto, the Liberals advocated "the decentralisation of power and wealth from London" and the advent of a Scottish Parliament, "so that Scottish domestic affairs receive the informed attention which Westminster cannot provide" (British Liberal Party 1964, n.p.). This vote in favour of a devolutionist party did not go unnoticed, especially since close to 50% of Scottish voters also supported the Labour Party, promoting "regional economic planning" and the establishment of "regional planning boards" in Scotland, Wales, and Northern Ireland (British Labour Party 1964). As pointed out during parliamentary debates, local authorities – hitherto responsible for business support – in the Scottish Highlands had already come out in favour of the HIDB (Hansard UK 1965, cc. 1153–4). They expected such an agency would bring more resources to the Highlands, and they were right.

Although public expenditure by the SO in the Highlands had already almost tripled between 1955 (£13 million) and 1965 (£33 million),[20] the advent of the HIDB had a noticeable impact in that by the end of the 1960s the proportion of government spending in Scotland dedicated to the Highlands (10%) rose to double the region's demographic weight (Newlands 2005, 170). The Highlands thus started reaping an increasing proportion of the rapidly rising industrial expenditures in Scotland, which had grown by more than 300% – and 100% more than the British average – between 1966 and 1969 (Parry 1983, 101). This was not due solely to the advent of the HIDB, but it certainly contributed.

The 1965 act establishing the HIDB clarifies the objectives it was intended to pursue. First, the SOSS and by extension the SO would retain great influence over the HIDB. The chairman and deputy chairman would be appointed by the SOSS, as would all board members (UK 1965, 2). Interestingly, the first appointments were two renowned Scottish devolutionists: the chairman, Robert Grieve, had been the SO's Chief Planning Officer for Scotland since 1960 and would later be an influential member of the Campaign for a Scottish Assembly (CSA) in the late 1980s; its deputy chairman, John M. Rollo, was an entrepreneur and the founder of Oban-based Rollo Industries, who would also advocate in favour of a Scottish parliament for most of his life. The fact that HIDB leaders were named by the SOSS thus allowed not only close coordination with the SO but also the appointment of managers dedicated to policy asymmetry.

The SOSS and SO retained the power to "give the Board directions of a general character as to the exercise and performance of their functions" (UK 1965, 2). Moreover, the HIDB had to submit to SOSS's approval the main strategies and activities it intended to pursue (UK 1965, 3). In other words, the HIDB became the financial arm of the SO for this part of Scotland. Asymmetry in development policy for the Highlands was thereby secured, and the main players involved in this domain – commercial banks and private funds, local authorities, unions, universities, businesses, etc. – had to coordinate, henceforth, as much with the HIDB as with central government departments (Hughes 1982, 1059).

The HIDB was set up with a large economic development remit, including research and advisory tasks, urban regeneration, environmental preservation, transport, tourism, the acquisition of land or industrial buildings, and the launch of new businesses (Hughes 1980), alongside "the general function of preparing, concerting, promoting, assisting and undertaking measures for the economic and social development of the Highlands and Islands" (UK 1965, 1). To execute such tasks, the HIDB was given the power to issue loans and grants, as well as to invest in private equity. As J.T. Hughes, ex-head of the HIDB's Policy and Research Division, put it,

> the Board's activities have been described as a "merchant bank with a social purpose." As compared with other regions of the UK the Board is a means of injecting capital into businesses in an underdeveloped area on more favourable terms and over a much wider spread of industries … Board projects are also intended to create development in areas where the normal business risk is so great that, even with Board assistance, private enterprise would not be expected to operate. (1980, 2)

At the time, no other regional agency in the UK administered financial assistance programs. Although financial assistance was one of many HIDB functions, it quickly monopolized most of its budget. Leveraging was, besides, a clearly expressed objective of the HIDB, as mentioned in its first annual report: "We are planning to seek a meeting with the general managers of the joint stock banks so that our combined efforts to promote development in the Highlands and Islands can reinforce one another" (HIDB 1967, 12). Over the next five years, more than £9 million were spent by the HIDB, leveraging £11 million in private investments.

Although HIDB investments definitely had leveraging effects, it should be remembered that the HIDB was intended to invest where, "*even with Board assistance*, private enterprise would not be expected to operate." Clause 6 of the 1965 act thus purposely allowed the HIDB to take over existing businesses or to create new ones *in the absence of private capital* (UK 1965, 4). The point could also be raised that the HIDB was set up as a centrifugal tool, to counter the concentration of entrepreneurial finance and VC in Scotland's "Central Belt." This was partly true, given the peripheral position – geographic, economic, and cultural – of the Scottish Highlands. Upon further analysis however, it appears the strategies pursued by the HIDB contradicted the "spatial" argument.

Although the HIDB considered financial assistance requests from any industrial sector and any region of the Scottish Highlands, a specific strategy, the Moray Firth Development Scheme, was adopted from the onset and consisted in generating industrial "growth points" along an arc from the cities of Nairn and Elgin in the southeast to Tain in the northwest, by way of Inverness (HIDB 1967, 16). Therefore, the HIDB would contribute to the geographical concentration of investments around three specific cities (HIDB 1975, 109): between 1965 and 1975 a third of all grants, loans, and equity investments were made in Inverness county, with another 40% shared between the Dingwall (Ross-shire county) and Inveraray regions (Argyll county). The most convincing explanations for the establishment of the HIDB thus remain the perceived needs for policy asymmetry and the building of an investment ecosystem specific to the Scottish Highlands, based on the idea that economic development had to be managed locally (Danson et al. 1990).

By the mid-1970s, the HIDB was allocating £5 million in grants, loans, and equity each year, a fivefold increase since 1966 (HIDB 1975, 33). Moreover, despite the advent of large-scale oil extraction in the Scottish parts of the North Sea in 1974, few investments were made in this sector, as most of the HIDB's funding was still directed at indigenous SMBs and start-ups, for industrial diversification purposes (HIDB 1975, 33). From 1973 onward, the HIDB concentrated on developing the emerging ICT and electronics clusters, funding small ventures to strengthen American and Japanese plants' supply chains (HIDB 1975, 38–45; Peden 2005, 260). The HIDB's Finance Division had also, by then, been reinforced with a Management Services section helping investee businesses find follow-on funding from other sources within Scotland, thereby strengthening funding chains and underpinning a Scottish investment ecosystem.

The HIDB was both a vector of policy autonomy, as the financial arm of the SO, and an example of policy divergence, as no other regional agency in the UK had ever been granted direct investment responsibilities. Although it was crafted in part as a centrifugal tool, the intent behind its establishment and the scope of its activities extended far beyond this. The most crucial role of the HIDB was to palliate for the private sector's incapacity to generate an investment ecosystem strong enough to underpin economic diversification in the region, to increase Scottish ownership in key sectors, and to facilitate entrepreneurship without generating too much indebtedness. These were all long-standing challenges that became central parts of the development strategy for the region. The HIDB was born out of the perceived necessity of public intervention and policy asymmetry to face such challenges.

The Scottish Development Agency

The establishment of the SDA in 1975 also took place against the background of mounting nationalism in Scotland. It was "a case study of the influence of political circumstances on a significant institution. SDA in part was an outgrowth of the concern by the established political parties about the electoral support for the SNP and the demands for political separation of Scotland or for increased devolution in the UK" (Rich 1983, 272). In addition to the slight victory in the UK's October 1974 election of a Labour Party promising parliamentary devolution for Scotland and Wales (British Labour Party 1974), mounting nationalist pressures for economic decentralization emanated from Scotland, with the SNP reaping an historic 30% of the regional vote. Combined with the rising unemployment and hyperinflation (27% in 1975) plaguing Scotland, the SNP's performance clearly was aided by debates during the summer of 1975 surrounding the adoption of the SDA Bill.

SOSS William Ross then remarked: "The SDA marks the creation of a uniquely Scottish approach to industrial development in Scotland ... A more direct approach is needed if we are to transform and modernise the structure of Scotland's older industries and help home-based Scottish industry to develop" (Hansard UK 1975, cc. 465–6). Most of the deliberations between Labour, SNP, and Liberal MPs concerned how much power, budget, and, especially, autonomy the SDA should have. The SNP was concerned that the SDA would be subordinated to the new National Enterprise Board (NEB), a similar body established at the UK level. On this issue also, the importance of policy asymmetry as a guiding principle was reiterated by the SOSS: "The agency will in no sense be a creature of the NEB. It will be responsible to me as Secretary of State ... It will have its own funds and take its own decisions. These will be decisions about Scotland taken in Scotland" (Hansard UK 1975, cc. 474).

In fact, a division of labour developed between the NEB and the SDA. The "SDA proposed an aggressive policy of industrial development that would absorb a large proportion of the budget – initially 40% and later at least one third – in loans and equity for small and medium-size industrial firms, while the NEB was responsible for handling the public ownership of major companies such as British Leyland and

Rolls-Royce" (Rich 1983, 278). The NEB would thus act as an industrial holding, while the SDA would mainly operate as a public VC fund supporting Scottish start-ups and SMBs. The SDA Bill – and the act that followed in November 1975 – notably specified the agency would absorb the pre-existing Small Industries Council for the Rural Areas of Scotland (SICRAS), which had until then managed a portfolio dedicated to SMBs of small Scottish towns (UK 1975, 15; Hood 2000, 317).

Like the HIDB, the SDA was given a large economic remit: "Furthering economic development; the provision, maintenance or safeguarding of employment; the promotion of industrial efficiency and international competitiveness; and furthering the improvement of the environment" (UK 1975, 2). Its prime function, however, was "providing or assisting in the provision of finance to persons carrying on or intending to carry on industrial undertakings," to which was added the ability to launch or acquire businesses, with or without private partners (UK 1975, 2). The SOSS would nominate the chairman, deputy-chairman, and chief executive, and give the SDA "directions of general or specific character as to the exercise of [its] functions" (UK 1975, 2–4). Around the time the SDA was created, besides, the executive responsibility for "selective industrial assistance" – that is, for the allocation of grants, loans, and equity investments to Scottish businesses – was transferred from the UK's Department of Industry to the SOSS, making the latter, in effect, Scotland's "industrial Minister" (Fairley and Lloyd 1995, 58; Hansard UK 1975; UK 1975, 5).

The provision of financial assistance to Scottish SMBs quickly became the SDA's main activity, despite mediocre investment performances during the 1970s. High returns were not among the three primary goals. The first was the expansion and consolidation of entrepreneurial finance and VC ecosystems in Scotland, as "in spite of its sophistication in many other regards, the Scottish financial sector was historically slow in giving birth to institutions specialising in either development or venture capital" (Hood 2000, 315).[21] As the SDA's first chief executive commented, "short-term borrowings are in general well provided for, chiefly by the clearing banks, and it is equity, risk-taking capital in the broadest interpretation of the term, that is the main area of need, and on which the Agency should concentrate" (Robertson 1978, 24).

The second main goal, as was also the case in Quebec at the time, was the transformation of Scotland's industrial structure away from traditional manufacturing and toward technology-intensive industries: "Scotland has some vigorous and efficient firms in technologically advanced industry but relative to the UK as a whole, it has a disproportionate share of older industries, some of which are in static and some in declining markets. So we need to improve the balance, and increase the proportion of modern, often science-based, industries" (Robertson 1978, 23). Industrial diversification in electronics and financial services had been underway since the early 1960s, but had taken place and continued to deepen mostly thanks to foreign investment (Rich 1983). In fact, aside from the HIDB and SDA initiatives, "from 1945 to the early-1990s the primary mechanism for revitalising the Scottish economy was viewed as the attraction of inward investment" (Brown and Mason 2012, 19). Therefore, the third main objective of the SDA was to "encourage the further development of indigenous industry and an increase in the proportion of Scottish-based companies" (Robertson 1978, 23), in an effort to compensate for the largely foreign ownership of most of the largest employers in Scotland's high-tech industries (Brown 2002; Turok 1993).

From 1977 onward, the SDA was assigned responsibility for the Glasgow Eastern Area Renewal (GEAR) project, aimed at the regeneration of Glasgow through investments in infrastructure and local businesses (Wannop 1984). Such "area projects" also became a central part of the SDA's activities, with additional ones launched in Clydebank, Motherwell, and Dundee between 1979 and 1982 (Gulliver 1984). The SDA concentrated on investment in growth sectors, and indeed particularly on the electronics cluster in Scotland's Central Belt, from Glasgow in the east to Dundee in the northwest, later referred to as "Silicon Glen." This mix of sector-based and area-based investment had no counterpart elsewhere in the UK and was then characterized as "the closest British equivalent to comprehensive industrial planning on the French or Japanese model" (Rich 1983, 283). By the time the Thatcher administration took office in 1979, thus, Scotland was already engaged not only on a path of policy autonomy but also of policy divergence.

The SDA's status as a public agency allowed it to pursue regional-level, national objectives: the sponsoring of indigenous start-ups and SMBs contributed to increase Scottish ownership in high-value-added industries but also helped strengthen the local supply chains of large businesses and the funding chains of smaller ones, facilitating the commercialization of Scottish innovations (Rich 1983, 283–4). Sponsoring included financial support *and* active technical and managerial assistance. Such hands-on involvement contributed to the deepening of policy divergence between Scotland and England. The SDA was aiming at the advent of a new Scottish business class, therefore focusing on SMBs' long-term viability and performance. As England already possessed well-established locally owned businesses in key sectors, the focus was rather put, up to the early 1980s, on medium-to-large businesses and on employment targets (Moore and Booth 1986).

The advent and evolution of the SDA was thus reminiscent of the HIDB's. Investment activities were part of a larger economic mandate, but became the main focus and monopolized the largest part of the budget early on. The political context was also similar, with a serious resurgence of nationalism and devolutionism in Scotland. As with the HIDB, therefore, the motivations behind the SDA initiative cannot be reduced to common market rationales. Strategic policy intents were straightforward and plainly expressed by both the SOSS and SDA executives. They consisted in (a) accelerating and consolidating, along-side the HIDB, the development of a regional investment ecosystem in Scotland; (b) supporting the SO's efforts to transform and modernize Scotland's industrial structure; and (c) increasing Scottish ownership in new industries' supply and value chains, to counterbalance growing foreign investment.

The "Scottish model" and Thatcherism

Outside of Scotland, the 1970s in the UK were characterized as a "policy-off" decade in terms of support to start-ups and SMBs (Greene, Mole, and Storey 2004, 1208). This changed after 1979, with the Thatcher Conservatives' new focus on entrepreneurship (Riddell 1989; Kava-nagh 1990; Gamble 1994; Stewart 2009). Four main programs aimed at entrepreneurship and entrepreneurial finance were introduced at the UK level in the early 1980s: the "enterprise zones" in 1980, the Loan Guarantee Scheme (LGS) in 1981, the Enterprise Allowance Scheme (EAS) in 1982, and the Business Expansion Scheme (BES) in 1983. In all four cases, the government's intent clearly was to "maximise the numbers of people starting a business on the grounds that this would directly reduce unemployment" (Greene et al. 2004, 1209).

The enterprise zones "experiment" reflected the ideological shift operated under Thatcher and mainly consisted in the establishment of circumscribed areas – mostly in disadvantaged regions – where busi-nesses were allowed to set up and operate free of capital, property, and income taxes (Stewart 2009, 56). Three were launched in Scotland in the early 1980s (Clydebank in 1981, Invergordon and Tayside in 1983) and another one in 1989 (Inverclyde). Although the zones were relatively successful in boosting business birth rates, it should be noted that the Clydebank and Tayside (Dundee) zones were situated in active SDA area projects, and the Invergordon zone in an area already covered by the HIDB's "growth points" strategy. "The enterprise zone experiment in Scotland benefited, therefore, from a certain degree of local momentum and indeed from a massive injection of public sector investment" (Danson and Lloyd 1992, 213).

The three other UK-wide initiatives were all quickly revealed to be out of touch with Scotland's needs, reinforcing the perceived necessity of policy asymmetry. Through the LGS, the British government would back 80% of the value of bank loans (up to £75,000) made to start-ups and SMBs (Stewart 2009, 57). Yet, unlike in England, Scottish SMBs' access to bank loans wasn't much of a problem (Robertson 1978, 24). Throughout the 1980s Scottish banks proved better prepared than England's to lend to start-ups, and "Scottish bank customers were significantly less likely to be required to provide collateral to borrow against" (Clay and Cowling 1996, 118). Therefore, between 1981 and 1994 Scottish businesses only received around 5% of LGS-backed loans, against 34% for South East England (Cowling 1997, 11).

The EAS, in turn, granted £40 per week in additional unemployment benefits to individuals setting up a business. To be eligible, however, participants had to contribute at least £1000 on their own, in effect paying for the first twenty-five weeks of the scheme (Greene et al. 2004, 1209). The BES, finally, entitled British citizens to tax credits – and after 1986, untaxed capital gains – when investing in unlisted businesses either directly or through specialized investment funds (Harrison and Mason 1989, 149). Although the BES was relatively successful in providing English start-ups additional VC investments, its problem in Scotland was the same as the EAS's. Namely, Scotland had one of the worst rates of new firm formation in the UK because it had "low levels of wealth as proxied by home ownership, a socioeconomic structure under-represented in education and in managerial and professional skills, and a plant structure which to some extent militated against workers gaining experience of small firms" (Ashcroft, Love, and Malloy 1991, 404).

On the whole, Scots simply didn't have enough money or entrepreneurial knowledge and experience to reap the benefits of initiatives such as the EAS and BES. As a result, like the LGS, both programs simply reinforced the imbalances favouring English and especially southeastern SMBs (Ashcroft 1988). This was particularly evident in the case of the BES, as Scotland's share of investments (by value) always remained much lower than its economic weight in the UK, and declining. In 1983–4, Scotland reaped under 5% of BES investments, against 40% for South East England; by 1985–6 Scotland's share had dropped to only 1.6% while South East England's had skyrocketed to 72% (Mason and Harrison 1989, 40).

By the early 1980s, besides, the HIDB and SDA were already the centrepieces of the Scottish investment ecosystem, therefore overshadowing new initiatives in the eyes of entrepreneurs and private investors. By 1983, the SDA could boast a 3.5 leverage ratio (Gulliver 1984, 330), and by the mid-1980s the HIDB was investing over £20 million per year, leveraging close to £60 million in private investments (HIDB 1986, 4). The Thatcher administration was thus forced to recognize the importance and success of public involvement for Scotland's economic development, as it was already producing the leveraging effects the LGS and BES aimed at. But while institutional path dependency certainly had a lot to do with the persistence of policy asymmetry, ideational and political variables also played significant roles throughout the 1980s.

Organizations such as the Scottish Trades Union Congress, SCDI, HIDB, SDA, and SO all pressured the Thatcher government to safeguard Scotland's investment ecosystem. In 1980, "despite the anti-interventionist and one nation rhetoric, Scottish Office ministers were well aware of the need to fight Scotland's corner at Whitehall [and] Scotland continued to be marketed as a separate entity" (Barber 1982, 180). By 1981, the SDA's new chairman, Robin Duthie, was denouncing the Conservatives' ignorance of the Scottish economic situation and the SO was pushing for the SDA to remain the key VC fund in Scotland (Barber 1982, 170; Stewart 2009, 57). As a result, although SDA resources were reduced after 1979, the agency's role was actually further refocused toward entrepreneurial finance, and a specialized VC division, Scottish Development Finance (SDF), was added to the SDA structure in 1982.

The advent of SDF signalled a shift that brought the SDA closer to the contemporary "Scottish model," based on hybrid co-investment. An SDF advisory board was set up to include entrepreneurs and private sector VC specialists, and the SDA proved ever more active in collaborating with VCs and financial institutions. As ex-SDA official and University of Strathclyde's Professor Neil Hood later remarked, "in large measure due to strong and effective leadership throughout the 1980s, and against a background of a dominant *laissez-faire* philosophy under Margaret Thatcher as PM, the SDA had managed to evolve into the (almost) acceptable face of economic development interventionism in Scotland" (2000, 322).

Remarks

By the late 1980s, both policy autonomy and policy divergence in economic development were thus entrenched in Scotland's political culture and institutionalized, notably, through the SDA/SDF and HIDB.

An indigenous investment ecosystem had by then been established in Scotland, structured around these public agencies. One further indication of this was the creation of Scottish Financial Enterprise in 1986, a peak organization representing Scotland's financial services cluster. Another was that, by the early 1990s, Scotland had become the UK's second VC market after South East England, in terms of total amounts invested and number of investee companies. Scotland had also become the UK's leading region, by far, in the proportion of businesses receiving VC (BVCA 1999, 51–3).

As was the case in Quebec, classic market justifications for public intervention in VC applied at some point and to some extent: particularly, the "spatial" argument applied to the HIDB and the "leveraging effect" and "positive externalities" rationales to the SDA/SDF. Still, these cannot really help understand the core motivations of policymakers or the fact that, by the turn of the 1990s, the HIDB and SDA were present in all deal stages, deal sizes, and industry sectors. It can be argued instead that minority nationalism played a very central role in generating:

(a) perceived needs for policy asymmetry and, especially, executive responsibility in the realm of entrepreneurial finance;
(b) long-term, regional-level strategic objectives aiming to transform/ diversify Scotland's industrial structure and purposely support the advent of new, competitive high-value-added clusters (including the VC cluster itself);
(c) attempts to increase Scottish presence and ownership in key industrial sectors and major economic centres, through f nancial and managerial sponsorship of start-ups and SMBs forming part of foreign companies' supply chains (particularly in the electronics sector);
(d) political pressure, coming from economic organizations such as the SCDI and SDA/HIDB but also from SO representatives and Scottish MPs, to intervene based on those needs and objectives; i.e., to build and sustain a specif cally Scottish investment ecosystem, more responsive to regional needs and interests; and
(e) ideological and institutional dynamics leading to the preservation of the "Scottish model" of active public involvement in entrepreneurial finance and VC, as seen in the activities of the HIDB, SDA, and SDF throughout much of the 1980s, under the free-market oriented Thatcher administration.

Now, a reasonable argument could certainly be made that this focus on "increasing Scottish presence and ownership in key industrial sectors" was, for most of this period, directly contradicted by Scotland's reliance *on* and promotion *of* foreign investment. Many experts have indeed pointed this out (Brown 2002; Brown and Mason 2012; Turok and Richardson 1991; Turok 1993, 1997), although some of their arguments regarding Silicon Glen's "footloose" character and lack of "embeddedness" in the Scottish economic structure were later qualified by others (McCann 1997; McGregor, Swales, and Yin 2001). However, the point, ultimately, is this: to the extent that the attraction of foreign investment was necessary for the industrial reconversion of Scotland, the development of public investment tools geared toward the multiplication and growth of locally-owned SMBs operating in emerging, technology-intensive sectors was precisely an attempt to create and support the local linkages deemed lacking between multinational corporations and the Scottish economy. In that sense at least, HIDB and SDA activities were not inconsistent with Scottish economic development policy more generally. Quite the opposite is true, given that the sponsorship of local SMBs was thus required to mitigate for the adverse effects of inward investment on Scotland's corporate ownership structure.

Chapter Three

Quebec, 1990–2003

The fact that Quebec's heavy government involvement in business financing since 1960 both stemmed from and furthered nationalist objectives has been widely recognized, including by Haddow (2015, 38–9). As economic liberalization and North American free trade took root in the late 1980s and early 1990s, however, and as much of the new Francophone business class – "Québec Inc." – embraced these transformations, it has been argued that the sway of nationalism on Quebec's economic policymaking receded significantly, while market-oriented rationales gained influence:

> Nationalist ideas motivated economic intervention in Quebec during the 1960s and 1970s. A desire to promote francophone entrepreneurship, even in the face of uncertain short-term economic logic, justif ed an activist state there, just as a wish to overcome late industrialization earlier encouraged state-led growth elsewhere. But by the 1990s intervention was institutionally embedded, and its initial goal of fostering a French business class was largely fulf lled. Nationalism was now very much contested as a motivation for intervention. The PQ still sometimes justif ed policies in nationalist terms, but not the Liberals. By the end of our period [2010] even the former party usually relied on economic arguments: state intervention was needed to ensure long-term economic growth. The original nationalist impetus now was disputed and secondary. (Haddow 2015, 165)

Yet this argument relies on a restrictive definition of economic nationalism, one that mostly focuses on ethno-linguistic considerations. It obscures the fact that, in particular policy sectors, "economic arguments" used to justify public involvement from the 1990s onward were themselves underpinned by nationalist motivations. In the case of VC, numerous new government-backed initiatives were implemented in

Graph 3.1. Evolution of Quebec's VC industry, 1990–2003

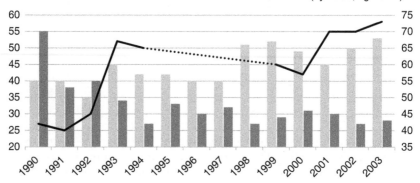

Sources: Macdonalds & Associates Limited (1990–2004).
Notes: Approximate figures. Includes investments from government (SGF, SDI, IQ, etc.), LSIF (FSTQ/FACSN), institutional (CDPQ), corporate (CRCD), and a proportion of "other" (angels, etc.) sources. Information on investor type for the years 1995 to 1998 was unavailable.

Quebec from the late 1980s onward, which could hardly be explained strictly by market-oriented rationales.

In fact, Quebec's VC industry and the role of the provincial state within it both kept progressing, in relative size, during the 1990s and early 2000s (graph 3.1). In 1990 the province reaped around 40% of Canadian yearly investments, still well below Ontario at 55%. This proportion reached over 50%, well over Ontario at 28%, by the time the PLQ came back to power in 2003. Clearly, this had a lot to do with a steep progression of government involvement, which did not culminate in the late 1980s but actually grew at a faster pace than Quebec's VC industry itself during the 1990s. From around 40% in 1990, the proportion of publicly backed and/or tax-advantaged VC investments in Quebec, by value, skyrocketed to over 70% in the early 2000s while the same proportion in Ontario never surpassed around 30%.

A good indication that nationalist logics present before 1990 persisted long after can be found in graph 3.1. While the recession led to a rapid increase in government involvement between 1991 and 1993, public intervention in VC never receded once counter-cyclical measures came to an end, in 1993–4. That is because, in addition to temporary measures, throughout the 1990s new public investment tools were created dedicated to strategic, regional-level national objectives. Among those were the SRI, Fonds de développement technologique (FDT), Fonds québécois de dévelppement industriel (FQDI), Sociétés Innovatech, Sociétés locales d'investissement dans le développement de l'emploi (SOLIDE), Fonds régionaux de solidarité (FRS), FACSN, Centres locaux de développement (CLD), Fonds locaux d'investissement (FLI), IQ, La Financière agricole (FA), CRCD, and La Financière du Québec (FDQ). As I show throughout this chapter, minority nationalism continued to impact such policy initiatives through ideological, political, and institutional mechanisms.

The Bourassa II and Johnson Administrations (1989–1994)

The first half of the 1990s in Quebec saw (a) the most severe recession since the early 1980s; (b) the coming into effect of North American free trade; and (c) the constitutional crisis following the Meech Lake (1990) and Charlottetown (1992) failures, leading to the 1995 referendum on secession. This combination led to a mix of counter-cyclical measures, renewed emphasis on business support, and increased asymmetry. Evidence of all three tendencies can be found in successive budgets from 1989 to 1994, but also in the investment strategies of government-backed funds. A look back at measures taken in the last two years of the 1980s – i.e., before the recession – is also quite informative.

Two major developments took place in 1988–9 that directly impacted subsequent policies: the establishment of the first three SRI, and the setting up of the FDT in the wake of the ratification of the Canada-US Free Trade Agreement (CUFTA). In both cases, perceived needs for policy asymmetry and public intervention were linked to strategic objectives necessitating compensation for trade liberalization and "inadequate" federal policies. A look back at the late 1980s thus allows for a better understanding of the mechanisms through which nationalism, government strategies, and investment activities became ever more closely intertwined.

The Sociétés régionales d'investissement

The first three SRI – Capidem Québec, Capital de l'Estrie, and Investissements Mauricie-Bois-Francs-Drummond – were launched in 1988–9 by the CDPQ to increase its presence in local, early-stage SMBs and to bring Quebec's financial institutions together, thereby helping manu-facturing businesses face the challenges of continental free trade and a rising Canadian dollar (CDPQ 1989, 6). The CDPQ was also calling for the coordination of Quebec's VC institutions to sustain and boost entrepreneurship in secondary urban centres: Quebec City (Capidem), Sherbrooke (Capital de l'Estrie), Trois-Rivières and Drummondville (Investissements Mauricie-Bois-Francs-Drummond). The centrifugal argument therefore applies only partially to this initiative, devoted to the consolidation of existing "sectors of excellence" in three industrial hubs outside of Montreal.

The "market gap" rationale, by contrast, was at the centre of the SRI initiative, as the CDPQ recognized a lack of deals under $500,000 for start-ups and SMBs (CDPQ 1989, 16). This was only part of the motiva-tion, however. Were it not for its intention to extend and refine early-stage businesses' funding chains, the CDPQ could have acted on its own, given the depth of its resources (CDPQ 1989, 16). Instead, the SRI were capitalized – with around $10 million each – in equal parts by the CDPQ (20%), FSTQ (20%), SID (20%), Banque Nationale (20%), and regional authorities (20%). Not only did the SGF, SDI, and regional authorities play a key role in their advent, but the provincial government itself subsidized the SRI by covering part of their starting and administrative costs (Bourque 2000, 147). The SRI were perceived as an integral part of Quebec's approach to regional development, heavily oriented toward entrepreneurship and entrepreneurial finance (Québec 1989, 13).

The SRI were thus a truly integrated initiative, mobilizing Quebec's investment ecosystem to pursue three strategic objectives: (a) the promo-tion of entrepreneurial centres outside of Montreal; (b) the sponsorship of small manufacturers and exporters in the new context of CUFTA; and (c) the widening of those businesses' funding chains through enhanced coordination between major financial institutions. Over the next five years, the CDPQ and its partners capitalized seven other SRI to cover entrepreneurial hubs around strategic areas (CRISES 2000, 41). In total, close to $100 million were devoted to the SRI between 1988 and 1994, a large amount considering the small size of target investments, between $50,000 and $500,000.

The Fonds de développement technologique

Similar logics animated the government's intervention in high-technology sectors and R&D. The key political drives were to palliate for a lack of federal investment in Quebec and to catch up with Ontario in terms of technological competitiveness (PLQ 1989, 22). Direct state intervention, in the context of North American free trade, was perceived as a strategic necessity. In the late 1980s, the SDI's investment activities in high technology were increasingly taking the form of equity loans issued on mandates from the MICT: by 1989, the yearly value of ministerial mandates issued to the SDI far exceeded its autonomous investments (Bourque 2000, 92; SDI 1990).

In this context, the FDT was launched to complement the SDI by funding marketable R&D conducted in concert by industry and universities. The creation of the FDT in late 1988 was specifically intended to complement tax credits promoting R&D, as well as programs of the SDI and Agence québécoise de valorisation industrielle de la recherche (AQVIR). Quebec's government referred to this as an "integrated R&D strategy," with FDT grants supplementing fiscal deductions, loans, and equity investments imparted to "mobilizing R&D projects." The FDT thus became part of a funding chain coordinating many players in Quebec's investment ecosystem (Québec 1989), and its activities were intended to generate positive externalities by offsetting the high costs of R&D. Yet the FDT was also crafted to meet perceived needs for policy autonomy.

The PLQ (1989, 22) notably argued that the addition of the FDT to existing measures was necessary because the federal government was spending, by the late 1980s, almost five times more in Ontario's R&D projects than in Quebec's. In addition, the FDT was a direct response to the setting up of the Ontario Technology Fund in 1987, capitalized with $1 billion over ten years (Bourque 2000, 101; Ontario 1987). The establishment of a billion-dollar fund made a great impression on Quebec's government: its response was the FDT, endowed with a five-year $300 million budget. Although the FDT was, in absolute terms, smaller than Ontario's tech fund, it represented a much larger injection of new money, relatively speaking, into Quebec's R&D. Partly as a result, from the early 1990s onward Quebec caught up to Ontario with regards to government spending in R&D (graph 3.2). The numerous measures put in place in the 1989 budget led to noticeable yearly increases up to 1995, while Ontario stagnated. By the early 2000s, Quebec's government was injecting more money in R&D, in absolute terms, than Ontario's despite a provincial GDP almost 50% smaller.

Graph 3.2. Provincial government's R&D spending, Quebec vs. Ontario, 1990–2003 ($ millions)

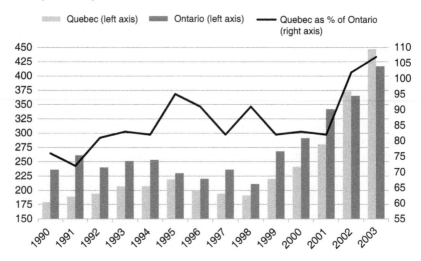

Source: Statistics Canada (n.d.b).

The counter-cyclical budgets

The 1990s, however, opened with an economic slump that turned into a recession by the end of 1990, with Quebec experiencing negative GDP growth in 1991 (−2.5%) and slow growth (0.3%) for 1992 (Statistics Canada n.d.a). As regards entrepreneurial finance and VC, the budgets of the early 1990s thus contained economically driven, counter-cyclical policies, but also politically driven initiatives reflecting perceived needs for asymmetry and state intervention. This contrast helps understand how the effects of economic nationalism persisted under the PLQ government up to 1994. It illustrated the institutional embeddedness of economic nationalism, with the SDI and FDT being extensively used in the early 1990s as vehicles reconciling short-term economic needs with long-term, regional-level national objectives.

By April 1990, with businesses experiencing a sharp decline in profits, revenues from corporate taxes started to retreat.[1] Federal transfers to Quebec were also receding, dropping from a 4.3% increase in 1989–90 to 0.3% in 1990–1 (Québec 1990b Annexe B, 5). Furthermore, interest rates were maintained far too high for Quebec's Minister of Finance's liking: "*Je continue de maintenir que les taux d'intérêt sont inutilement élevés, qu'ils menacent la croissance économique et qu'ils contribuent à maintenir le taux de change du dollar canadien à un niveau qui mine la capacité concur-rentielle de nos entreprises"* (Québec 1990b, 22).[2] In this context, the need for counter-cyclical strategies heralded a range of measures designed to help businesses, and especially SMBs, uphold their cashflow and capacity to invest.

Among those were two new SDI programs, adding $45 million to its investment budget. One was temporary and counter-cyclical, while the other was intended to promote long-term, strategic changes in Quebec's industrial structure. The first, with a two-year budget of $30 million, issued equity loans to manufacturing businesses experiencing depleting cashflows. The other was in turn dedicated to the consolidation of small businesses with under $25 million in assets, an effort to create continentally competitive medium-to-large companies in the context of CUFTA:

> *Dans de nombreux secteurs, les entreprises québécoises se caractérisent par leur petite taille et la multiplicité des unités de production. Comme le marché se définit de plus en plus sur une base continentale, il est devenu impératif de favoriser le regroupement d'entreprises de production afin de permettre la mise en place de firmes plus compétitives.* (Québec 1990b Annexe A, 9)[3]

In this case, the main rationale was strategic and aimed at helping Quebec SMBs compete with larger Ontarian and American companies. This new SDI program was allotted $15 million, and investments also took the form of equity loans covering the costs of mergers and acquisitions. While both additions to the SDI fulfilled economic purposes, in the new business consolidation program state intervention was not limited to short-term, reactive logics but also responded to a long-term and strategic need to adjust to CUFTA and compete with Ontario.

Substantial new public resources were also directly engaged in Quebec's businesses through the FDT, as $50 million was assigned to a new investment division covering green technology ventures (Québec 1990b Annexe A, 34–6). Merely a year after its inception, the FDT was thus mobilized by the government for strategic purposes, to kick-start the emergence of technologies which could give Quebec a competitive edge in a context of rising environmental concerns (Québec 1990b, 15).[4] Two initiatives were then introduced in 1991 whose justifications also extended well beyond immediate economic imperatives: the establishment of the FQDI, and the addition of yet another division to the FDT, the R&D-PME division.

In the first case, the need for policy autonomy was explicitly stated and stemmed from a disengagement of the federal government from large-scale industrial development and the attraction of foreign investments (Québec 1991 Annexe A, 38). The FQDI was intended to provide financial support to "major industrial projects" involving expenses of $10 million or more and susceptible to attract foreign investments in high-tech sectors. A sum of $200 million was allocated to the FQDI, out of which it could fund up to 20% of admissible projects' costs. This nationalist drive for policy autonomy and state intervention also factored into the new FDT initiative. The R&D-PME division was granted an initial budget of $20 million to subsidize very high-tech, early-stage ventures and SMBs. It was thus specifically crafted to promote the advent of Quebec-based suppliers for projects covered by the FQDI.

Projects admissible for R&D-PME support, in addition, had to be "conducive to a substantial improvement in the competitiveness of same sector businesses or other economic sectors in Quebec" (Québec 1991 Annexe A, 40). Although subsidies were limited to $5 million, nothing indicates that R&D-PME was intended to fill a particular funding gap. Instead, state intervention was justified in structural, strategic terms (Québec 1991 Annexe A, 40):

> La structure industrielle du Québec repose pour l'essentiel sur les PME et comporte encore trop peu d'entreprises dans les secteurs de haute technologie … Pour élargir la base des entreprises québécoises appartenant au secteur à haute intensité technologique, il est donc important d'accroître le soutien gouvernemental aux activités de recherche des PME qui œuvrent dans le domaine des technologies de pointe.[5]

These initiatives had concrete, durable effects on Quebec's investment ecosystem. Notably, the proportion of early-stage investments (smaller, but high-risk) as a percentage of total VC deals in Quebec increased substantially, from around 30% in 1992 to 50% in 2003 (graph 3.3). As a result, while Quebec was reaping a growing number of investments every year, their average size was decreasing. By 2000, the average size of VC transactions made in Quebec was below $2.2 million, while the same average exceeded $7.5 million in Ontario (Macdonald & Associates Limited 2001).

The years 1992 and 1993 were also particularly important, as two new public VC funds were created: the Société Innovatech du Grand Montréal (SIGM) in 1992, and the Société Innovatech Québec & Chaudière-Appalaches (SIQCA) in 1993. The SIGM was to be the centerpiece of a plan to make of Montreal a locomotive for the technological modernization of Quebec's industries. Granted a five-year budget of $300 million, the SIGM would support marketable R&D in Montreal and act as yet

Graph 3.3. Evolution of Quebec's VC industry II, 1992–2003

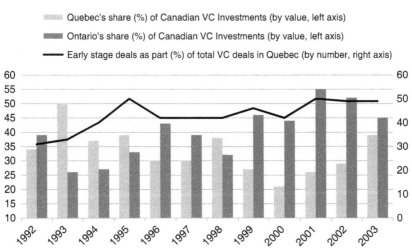

▨ Quebec's share (%) of Canadian VC Investments (by value, left axis)

▬ Ontario's share (%) of Canadian VC Investments (by value, left axis)

━ Early stage deals as part (%) of total VC deals in Quebec (by number, right axis)

Sources: Macdonalds & Associates Limited (1994–2004).
Note: Approximate figures.

another financial arm of the MICT. The president of the board and its nine members were nominated by the government, with two coming from the ministry itself. It was thus made clear that SIGM's activities would take place "within the framework of governmental orientations," as any investment greater than $5 million required ministerial approval (Québec 1992).

To boost its leveraging effect, the SIGM was allowed to invest with public or private sector partners. With few exceptions however, all initial partners for 1993 had direct ties to the public sector: the SDI, CDPQ, FSTQ, SID, one SRI, and AéroCapital (Québec 1993b, 3855). The SIQCA was then created almost by default in December 1993, along the exact same lines but with a smaller budget of $60 million. This was a good example of path dependency: once Montreal was given such a fund, it became politically hazardous not to grant Quebec City one (Québec 1993b, 3842). Various economic organizations indeed lobbied for it throughout 1993 (Laplante 1993; Déry 1994), and by 1994 similar groups from Estrie (Sherbrooke) and Montérégie (Longueil) were also asking for their own Innovatech.

The establishment of the SIGM and SIQCA thus add to the evidence that the early 1990s by no means witnessed a waning of economic nationalism. Policymakers' appetite for government involvement, policy asymmetry, and the pursuit of strategic, regional-level national objectives even sharpened. All these initiatives, besides, were part of a larger trend in Quebec, of which the government's "clusters strategy" and FSTQ activities would become centrepieces from 1992 onward.

Clusters & LSIFs: Quebec vs. Ontario

In December 1991, Quebec's MICT launched an industrial clustering strategy. As Bourque remarked (2000, 131–2), this represented a nationalist "renewal" of Quebec's approach to economic development. The clusters strategy aimed to develop competitive advantages in key industrial sectors through the establishment and funding of "neo-corporatist" consolidation, coordination, and partnership mechanisms between same-sector businesses, unions, regional authorities, and the provincial government (Bourque 1995). Not only were the policy ideas behind it cast in nationalist terms (Tremblay 1993a, 4), but the strategy itself was based in part on import-substitution objectives:

> *L'une des retombées de la mise sur pied de tables de décideurs dans le cadre de la stratégie des grappes industrielles est la découverte par nos donneurs d'ordres de nombreux fournisseurs québécois capables de produire des biens et services de qualité à prix compétitifs … Au Québec, nous avons les compétences et la capacité pour innover et développer des produits originaux de haute qualité, qui autrement devraient être importés.* (Tremblay 1993b, 4–6)[6]

Twenty-one clusters were identified and targeted, for which the state would act as a "catalyst" to strengthen existing synergies or help create new ones (Tremblay 1991, 5). Apart from its nationalist content, however, this strategy was interesting for two other reasons: first, because Ontario tried and mostly failed to replicate it, and second, because the provision of VC was identified as one of its crucial components.

In 1992, the Ontario government introduced its Industrial Policy Framework, which included sectoral clustering as a key objective. The centrepiece of this framework was the Sector Partnership Fund, set up with a three-year, $150 million budget to promote and finance interfirm cooperation in specific sectors (Hall 1998, 208–17). The government also tried to establish the Ontario Development Corporation in 1993, modelled after the CDPQ, to funnel billions of dollars from public sector pension funds toward businesses. However, facing refusals from most pension funds, including the biggest – OMERS (Ontario Municipal Employees Retirement System) and the Ontario Teachers' Pension Plan (Haddow 2015, 186) – Ontario was forced to rely on private sector partners and ended up creating the Ontario Lead Investment Fund in 1994, a very small $70 million, 10-year fund to which the government would contribute 40%.

In the end, the whole clustering aspect mostly failed: "The SPF underspent its allocation in every year it existed and at the time it was terminated, in July 1995, less than half the initial allocation had been committed" (Wolfe and Gertler 1999, 21). When the Conservatives dissolved both the Ontario Lead Investment Fund and the Sector Partnership Fund in 1995, "major Ontario business associations approved; lower taxes and freer markets were a higher priority for them" (Haddow 2015, 187). Arguably, the failure of Ontario's New Democratic Party (NDP) to implement interventionist economic policies can be explained by the province's "adversarial industrial relations" and the adequate provision of capital by private funds (Haddow 2015, 187). The contrast with Quebec, however, also suggests that the absence of nationalism as an ideology producing this capacity for tripartite partnership and cooperation was perhaps a more fundamental issue, upstream of Ontario's "adversarial" industrial culture.

Another illustration of this contrast was provided by the launch of tax-advantaged LSIFs by the NDP government in 1992. Again, policy emulation would prove highly problematic (Osborne and Sandler 1998, 510–11). While Quebec's LSIF regime was then restricted to a single union federation, Ontario opened its regime to any union, employee association, or professional association (Ayayi 2002, 9). This allowed for "an unlimited number" of LSIFs and a very scattered, loosely coordinated system unsuited for the carrying out of economic strategies (Osborne and Sandler 1998, 522). It also revealed the lack of a partnership culture between the provincial government, unions, and industry. The NDP government was, in fact, forced to allow for an unlimited number of LSIFs precisely because there was no FTQ-like union willing to cooperate with the government in supporting Ontario businesses (Osborne and Sandler 1998, 523–4).

Many LSIFs were thus created primarily to access tax credits, and small unions or associations were often paid to "rent" their name to such funds. Ontario's "rent-a-union" problem meant that LSIFs never became strategic partners with which tripartite coordination could be achieved. In Quebec by contrast, the FSTQ had long been a proponent of such an approach: "*L'objectif n'est pas seulement d'intervenir en cas de coups durs ou de garder la propriété de nos entreprises ici grâce à des noyaux d'actionnaires qui formeront des blocs de contrôle; il est aussi de planifier des opérations conjointes ayant des effets structurants sur l'économie québécoise*" (Fournier 1991, 240).[7]

The contribution of the FSTQ to Quebec's clustering strategy, for instance, took three main forms: (a) a 20% participation in the SRI; (b) the resources granted – in partnership with the CDPQ, SGF, and Innovatechs – to hybrid VC funds in key clusters such as forestry (Fonds Agro-Forestier), ICT (Capitech & TechnoCap), biotechnologies (Bio-Capital & GeneChem), aerospace (AéroCapital), environmental technologies (EnviroCapital), and computer software (Logisoft); and (c) the network of local funds (SOLIDE) it established in partnership with the provincial government and local authorities after 1991. Although these SOLIDE were to be focused on providing minor loans (under $50,000) to very small businesses, they proved strategic in facilitating the implementation of Quebec's industrial policies.

First, they were established in the province's Regional County Municipalities (Municipalités régionales de comté [MRC]), thereby organizing economic development around key localities. Second, they strengthened coordination dynamics within "local production systems" and, through their links with the SRI and FSTQ, gave local businesses access to regional and provincial investment ecosystems (Lévesque 2000, 16–17). Third, the SOLIDE provided, like their FSTQ sponsor, "patient capital" as well as managerial support and workplace training, thereby enriching an approach to local economic development based on long-term considerations. They also filled funding gaps ($5,000 to $50,000) and complemented Quebec's VC ecosystem by focusing on seed-stage "micro-businesses" (CRISES 2000, 43). Finally, they strategically increased the presence of provincial investors at the local level, until then mostly served by federal funds (Lévesque et al. 1996, 31).

For these reasons, although the SOLIDE were a joint initiative of the FSTQ and MRC, Quebec's government supported them both financially and administratively. The state granted between $100,000 and $150,000 to each of the province's MRC so that they could set up local funds – the Fonds d'investissement local – that would work and invest alongside the SOLIDE (CRISES 2000, 43–4; Lévesque 2000, 3). The first SOLIDE was launched in April 1993, and following the government's intervention thirteen others were established before the end of 1994.

This intervention also confirmed, along with the SRI and Innovatechs, a trend favouring the extension of Quebec's investment ecosystem to regional and local levels. Between 1989 and 1994, seventy-five state-backed regional and local funds were set up (Lévesque et al. 1996, 18–22). Although such funds played centrifugal roles, the rationale behind government support could hardly be reduced to that: by 1996, Quebec's peripheral regions had much better access to state-backed entrepreneurial finance than at any point in the past, but Montreal and Quebec City still enjoyed similar levels of public funding, thanks notably to the Innovatechs (Lévesque et al. 1996, 22–4).

The Parizeau and Bouchard Governments (1994–1998)

The PQ then regained power in 1994 on an electoral platform calling for a reinforced reliance on the provincial state as an economic actor (PQ 1994, 3). This stance was underpinned by a conviction that Quebec had long been disadvantaged by Canadian economic policies and a lack of federal investments, notably in R&D, compared to Ontario (8, 25). These beliefs obviously warranted state intervention and policy asymmetry, as illustrated by the party's pledge to more systematically use institutions such as the SDI and Hydro-Québec to fund and support high-tech ventures in coordination with VCs and banks (21–2).

Rodney Haddow is thus quite right in noting that "the change in government did not result in a significant change in policy, in spite of the fact that the new PQ industry minister, Daniel Paillé, quickly announced the end of Tremblay's clusters strategy" (2015, 175). The PQ government indeed continued to rely on sectoral and peak-level concertation mechanisms, as attested by the economic summits of late 1995 and late 1996, the creation of a standing committee of state corporation executives, and the regrouping of many of those corporations under the banners of the SGF and IQ after 1998 (Bourque 2000, 190–200).

The "Plan Paillé," the SISQ, and the FACSN

Even before its first budget, the Ministère de l'industrie, du commerce, de la science et de la technologie (MICST) of the PQ government launched the Programme d'investissement en démarrage d'entreprises, rebranded as the "Plan Paillé." This plan consisted in a refocusing of state aid to Quebec's SMBs, building on the SDI program of loan guarantees. It was meant to strengthen clustering through an aggressive *faire faire* policy, aimed at getting Quebec's financial institutions more deeply involved in the funding of seed-stage and early-stage ventures perceived as the future bedrock of provincial clusters. In this sense, the Plan Paillé was consistent with the previous approach, focusing on the advent of local supply chains in key sectors. The whole idea behind the Plan was for the state to sponsor young entrepreneurs by acting as an endorser.

A $300 million budget was managed by the SDI and spent on loan guarantees for start-up businesses likely to create at least three new jobs over three years (Québec 1997a). Entrepreneurs made their own demands for loans, and banks or credit unions were responsible for the evaluation of projects. Any time a loan of $50,000 or less was awarded, the SDI guaranteed 90% of potential losses as well as the first year's interests on the loan. The MICST evaluated that the average loan would be around $30,000; with a budget of $300 million, the creation of 10,000 new businesses and 30,000 new jobs over three years was thus expected. In less than six months, between December 1994 and June 1995, close to $250 million was engaged in over 4,500 ventures. An additional $100 million was then injected into the program, and guarantees were reduced to 80% of potential losses.

Given the program's popularity, the list of admissible sectors was reviewed so that by early 1997 eligible start-ups had to operate in high-value-added sectors such as environmental technologies, ICT, or business services. In this sense also, the Plan Paillé was a *faire faire* sponsoring strategy, aimed at getting private institutions to support seed-stage ventures in high-value-added, strategic sectors. The Plan was devised after consultations in 1994 unveiled a funding gap for seed-stage businesses looking for $50,000 or less (Paillé 1994). A nationalist motivation also underpinned this plan, however: it was devised to provide an alternative – both for entrepreneurs and financial institutions – to the federal Small Business Loans program which, since mid-1993, guaranteed 90% of eligible start-ups' potential losses on loans of up to $250,000. As much as it was about funding gaps and leveraging, the Plan Paillé was thus also about policy autonomy.

Moreover, the Plan was part of a larger set of complementary VC initiatives. The 1995–6 budget introduced new programs for high-tech SMBs and R&D, since Quebec was still getting less than 20% of federal R&D spending, against more than 50% for Ontario (PQ 1994, 8). A five-year, $50 million Fonds des priorités gouvernementales en science et en technologie was first set up to support R&D projects identified as "priorities" by the MICST (Québec 1995a Annexe A, 111). Then, the PQ government created a third Innovatech, the Société Innovatech du Sud du Québec (SISQ), covering the Estrie region and the entrepreneurial hubs of Sherbrooke, Magog, and Granby (Québec 1995d). The SISQ was granted a five-year $40 million budget and was modelled after the other Innovatechs.

This was yet another example of path dependency, both ideational and institutional: not only were government-backed VC funds consistent with the PQ's stance on state intervention, but the success of the SIGM and SIQCA had brought about mounting pressures – notably from Sherbrooke and Gatineau/Hull – for additional Innovatechs. For the same strategic reasons invoked by the PLQ in 1992 and 1993 however, including the proximal relationships between Innovatechs, the MICST, and the SDI, the PQ actually went further and finally extended the geographical mandates of the three Innovatechs to all of Quebec (Québec 1995d).

Another major move made in 1995 was the creation of a second LSIF (Québec 1995a, 8). This didn't come as a surprise, given the PQ's long-time support of the FSTQ and its need to muster CSN support for Quebec's sovereignty (Québec 1995b). The PQ had always been convinced of the strategic advantages provided by LSIFs, and one of Jacques Parizeau's first economic announcements as PM in November 1994 was the uncapping of annual contributions to the FSTQ, which had been fixed at $100 million by the previous government (Parizeau 1994). Both the PQ and CSN, however, wanted this new fund to be different and to act as a complement to the FSTQ, rather than as a competitor.

The FACSN, accordingly, was to support cooperative and/or "worker-controlled" SMBs, with the objective of extending these models to new sectors. Two permanent members of its board would therefore be named by the Desjardins movement, to promote coordination with Quebec's largest cooperative institution (Québec 1995e). This specific role of the FACSN ensured it would complement rather than duplicate the activities of the FSTQ, CDPQ, SDI, and other VCs (Québec 1995b). That said, the PQ expected Quebec to draw the same advantages from the FACSN as it did from the FSTQ. Most importantly, it was argued that LSIFs promoted mutual understanding and partnership between employers and employees as well as a "sense of belonging" among Quebec workers, both crucial issues from a nationalist perspective (Parizeau 1994; Québec 1995c).

Like the FSTQ, the FACSN would have to invest, annually, at least 60% of its assets in eligible Quebec businesses having a majority of employees resident of Quebec and net assets of under $100 million (Québec 1995g). Of this 60%, at least 40% would have to be invested in smaller businesses with under $50 million in assets. In exchange, a 20% tax credit for FACSN's shares (in addition to a 20% federal tax credit) was applied, and subscribers were restricted from selling their shares before retirement age to allow for the provision of "patient capital." This (and the same applied to the Plan Paillé and SISQ) was a clear indication of the government's dedication to policy divergence and the perpetuation of Quebec's model, combining *faire* and *faire faire* sponsoring strategies. The rationales underpinning such initiatives were thus never limited to market imperatives, but included nationalist political preferences, strategic objectives, and path dependency dynamics.

With the FACSN, the PQ added a major player to an already robust VC ecosystem: one month after the launch of its operations in January 1996, the FACSN had raised close to $8 million from 5000 depositors (Beaulieu 1996, 75); by the end of 2003, it had over 50,000 subscribers and its assets exceeded $300 million. Yet the very numerous initiatives taken since the late 1980s came under criticism by 1995 after a report by Quebec's Auditor General (Québec 1995h). Mostly focusing on MICST programs (including the Plan Paillé), the auditor denounced frequent duplication, especially in the case of small-size early-stage funding. Although this report didn't condemn state intervention per se, it deplored long bureaucratic delays as well as an inadequate monitoring of results. Some recommendations regarding program harmonization and tighter coordination with regional authorities thus directly informed the PQ's subsequent policies, such as the establishment of the CLD and the setting up of IQ.

The FRS and CLD

In its 1994 electoral platform the PQ notably advocated a decentralization of decision-making to regional authorities. This didn't mean the provincial state would retreat from regional development, however, as one of the PQ's central pledges was to capitalize new "regional development funds" (PQ 1994, 30). Soon after the election, discussions were thus initiated with the FSTQ, whose regional roots ran deep thanks to the SRI and SOLIDE. The PQ's lift of the ceiling on contributions to the FSTQ, mentioned earlier, was part of a deal in return for which the FSTQ would sponsor the new regional development funds with some of the additional money raised (Parizeau 1994; Québec 1995a, 7).

By early 1995, the government and the FSTQ reached an agreement: sixteen Fonds régionaux de solidarité (FRS) would be created,[8] each endowed with an investment budget of over $6 million – the largest, such as the FRS Île de Montréal, would get double or triple that amount – for a total of $135 million, 90% of which came from the FSTQ, and 10% from the Banque Nationale. The government would also contribute to the set-up and administrative costs for each FRS. This contribution amounted to a little less than $2 million per fund over five years, for a total of over $32 million (CRISES 2000, 40). While the FRS were crafted as centrifugal tools, every region in Quebec was involved, including existing VC hubs. There was, therefore, much more to this initiative than spatial considerations.

The FRS stemmed from two key objectives. The first was to expand the LSIF model to Quebec's regions. The FRS would not only provide

VC and support regional development, but also ensure management and worker training, thereby promoting tripartite collaboration between regional authorities, business owners, and labour: "89% of businesses in which the FRS invested are not unionized. The FRS thus bring regional stakeholders a different vision of investment ... By promoting partnership and concertation both at the business and regional scales, the funds show that the economic sphere is not limited to competition alone" (CRISES 2000, 42).[9]

This extension of the LSIF model through the FRS allowed for the recruiting of new FSTQ shareholders, as workers of investee businesses were encouraged to subscribe. It also facilitated coordination with FSTQ investment strategies at the regional level, and at the local level through the SOLIDE. FRS investments would serve a market niche in between the SOLIDE and FSTQ, although the FRS could also invest alongside the FSTQ in bigger projects requiring regional expertise. Finally, the FRS would coordinate with the FSTQ on sectoral investment strategies (CRISES 2000, 32). In sum, they were a way to promote regional concertation between governments, businesses, labour, and financial institutions (Canada 1995, 60).

The second key objective behind the FRS was to help kick-start the government's own regional development policy, launched with a White Paper in April 1997 (Québec 1997b). In this paper, the regional scale was presented as a conveyor belt between the national and local scenes, best suited for concertation and coordination purposes (Québec 1997b). The idea – which led to the establishment of the Ministry of Regions in late 1997 (Québec 1997c) – was to decentralize decision-making, notably in the realm of business support and entrepreneurship, while making sure that planning mechanisms remained coordinated with the strategic frameworks and policies adopted at the national level. The FRS were a good fit for such a policy, decentralizing additional resources while ensuring coordination with national-level strategic objectives. The true centerpiece of the PQ's reform, however, was the establishment of the CLD, business support centres engaging in development planning and capital investment.

The mandates of the CLD were (a) to devise development plans at the local/MRC level; (b) to act as "one-stop-shop" service centres for entrepreneurs, offering business planning assistance for start-ups, management support for development-stage SMBs, and guidance to help business owners navigate through Quebec's funding chains; and finally (c) to provide financial aid through grants, loans, guarantees, or equity investments. Each CLD was funded by the provincial government (around two-thirds) and the MRC (one-third), and was to dedicate a significant part of its annual budget to direct financial support to businesses. Every CLD would be responsible for three distinct funding tools (Québec 2001a): the Fonds Jeunes promoteurs, offering grants to entrepreneurs less than 35 years old; the Fonds de développement des entreprises d'économie sociale, subsidizing cooperative and social economy enterprises; and most importantly the Fonds local d'investissement (FLI).

The FLI was the largest investment tool available, through which the CLD invested over $35 million between 1998 and 2000, leveraging more than $385 million in investments from other sources (Québec 2001a, 36). The CLD and their investment funds thus quickly became major players in regional and local development: over a hundred CLD were established between 1998 and 2000, and almost 5,000 local businesses were supported as a result. The $75 million invested in total by the CLD over these three years, moreover, leveraged around $730 million from other sources, for a total of over $800 million invested in Quebec's local economies (Québec 2001a).

The CLD would also cooperate closely with other local actors, such as the SOLIDE, FRS, credit unions, and chambers of commerce (Québec 2001a, 18–19). The FRS and the CLD were thus consistent parts of a strategic effort to extend Quebec's model of development, based on public involvement and multipartite concertation, to regional and local levels. This was clearly part of a longing for policy asymmetry but also for policy autonomy, as Quebec tried to replace the federal government as the main provider of funds for regional development, as specified in the 1997 White Paper (Québec 1997b; Lévesque et al. 2003). In 1996, the federal government was the main provider for 26% of regional and local investment funds operating in Quebec, against 37% for the provincial government and FSTQ combined; by 2002, Quebec's government and the FSTQ had become leading providers for 49%, against 16% for the federal government (Lévesque et al. 2003, 12).

Objectif emploi and Investissement Québec

This reform of regional and local development showed the PQ government's inclination for state involvement did not prevent it from reorganizing the Quebec model. The new economic strategy introduced in the 1998 budget was another illustration, involving important changes while remaining explicitly interventionist and nationalist. The strategy was notably informed by a report published in the nationalist review *L'Action Nationale*[10] in 1996, which showed that a significant portion of Québécois' savings was still exported rather than reinvested locally because of the peripheral position Quebec still occupied in Canadian mutual funds' portfolios.

This report, of which a second part was published in 1997,[11] made a deep impression on the PQ government:

> Recent, thorough research, notably that conducted by the Action nation-ale, has revealed that a large portion of our savings are managed outside Quebec ... Various ref ections have led to a change in attitude and instilled greater awareness among certain f nancial decision-makers, who have already begun to repatriate to Quebec capital managed elsewhere for no apparent reason ... We must manage in Quebec a larger portion of our savings. (Québec 1998a, 29)

The numbers were indeed alarming. Based on the annual reports of over 900 Canadian mutual funds, representing over $145 billion in assets, the 1996 study established that only $5.8 billion were managed by Quebec-based funds in 1995, a meagre 4% of the total, against over $115 billion (79%) for Ontario. Quebec barely reaped 5.5% ($7.9 bil-lion) of investment portfolios despite contributing around $29 billion to those funds (20% of their assets). Of this $29 billion, besides, over $20 billion was subscribed by Francophones; in return, Francophone-owned businesses received only $3 billion in investments (2% of total assets). The situation did not improve much in 1996: out of $240 billion in assets, studied funds only invested $14 billion in Quebec (6%) and of the $5.4 billion invested in Quebec's businesses by Canada's ten larg-est mutual funds, only 35% went to Francophone-owned businesses.

These reports shed a disturbing light on Quebec's peripheral posi-tion. Given such bleak findings, the PQ introduced a new economic strategy, Objectif emploi (Québec 1998a), the importance of which has not always been fully recognized despite its ambitious aim to increase private investment in Quebec, in partnership with public corpora-tions and agencies, by $20 billion over five years. This goal, besides, was only one of the strategy's two main parts. The second consisted in the "Action Plan to Promote the Development of the Financial Sector" (Québec 1998c, 1998d), focused on the active promotion and support of Quebec-based mutual funds. The government notably decided to offer substantial tax breaks for new Quebec-based funds established before 2000 (Québec 1998c, 1998d). The most significant measure was taken by the CDPQ, however, another good example of the close coordination between public investors and the state. Following major equity invest-ments in Quebec's financial services industry, the CDPQ launched the Services financiers CDPQ subsidiary in September 1997, which would have as a mandate to invest in Quebec-based mutual funds and to increase by $15 billion the pool of assets managed in the province by 2002 (CDPQ 1998, 27).

Between 1997 and 1999, Services financiers CDPQ built a portfolio of almost $500 million in Quebec (Pelletier 2009, 253) and partnered with Desjardins to create a new series of mutual funds, the Fonds Cartier. The CDPQ's involvement, besides, was only one manifestation of its late-1990s activism. Since 1995, it had considerably increased its investments in Quebec, through a number of new VC and equity subsidiaries (Pelletier 2009, 214): Accès Capital (a network of regional funds regrouping the ex-SRI), Capital CDPQ (specialized in small, growth-stage businesses), Capital d'Amérique CDPQ (focusing on medium-sized companies), Capital Communications CDPQ (investing in ICT), Sofinov (high-tech), and T^2C^2 (biotechnologies, electronics, and multimedia). Together with Services financiers CDPQ, these funds built a portfolio of over $6 billion and were investing over $2.5 billion per year by 1998 (CDPQ 1999, 30–1).

This increased effort was highly consistent with the other main component of Objectif emploi, which aimed to increase private investments by using the state's leveraging power. This part of the strategy had already been launched with the introduction of the Fonds pour l'accroissement de l'investissement privé et la relance de l'emploi (FAIRE) in 1997, which had leveraged, in combination with other measures, $3.5 billion in private investments over eighteen months (Québec 1998e, III). The overarching objective in this case was to leverage $19 billion in private investments over five years (1998–2002), building on Quebec's public corporations and agencies (Québec 1998e, 18).

In order to increase these public corporations' capacities and their coordination with government strategies, the PQ also merged the SGF with pre-existing sectoral state holdings. The new SGF was assigned the five-year objective of generating $10 billion in private investments and would henceforth, in partnership with the private sector, buy equity stakes in companies of ten key sectors (Québec 1998e, 24–5). Another basic principle of Objectif emploi, in turn, was to "systematically promote Quebec-based technological innovations" through public sector support, outsourcing, and procurement. A new $50 million Société Innovatech Régions-Ressources (SIRR) was thus added to the Innovatech network to foster technological improvements in remote areas. The capital stock of the SIGM, SIQCA, and SISQ was finally increased by $75 million, bringing the Innovatech network's total to $525 million (Québec 1998e, 30).

Graph 3.4. Contributions of the Innovatech network, 1998–2003 ($ millions)

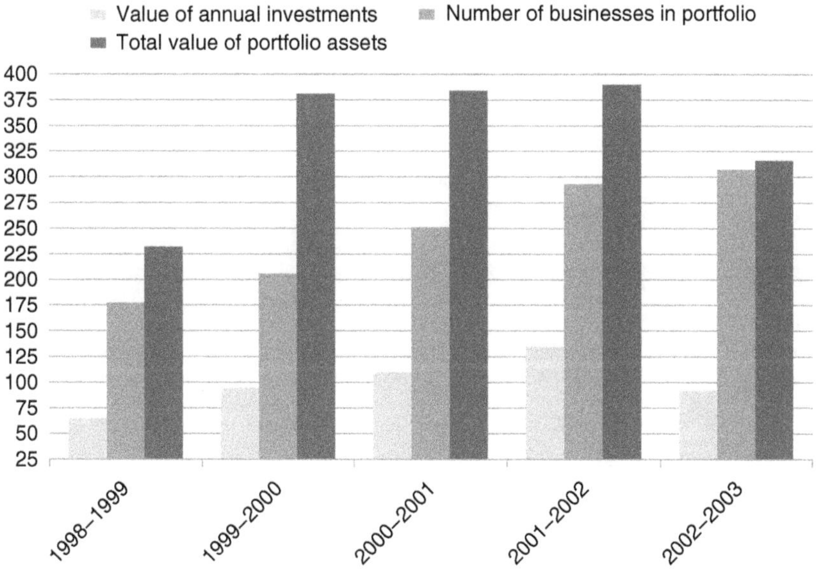

Source: Québec (2003b, 45).

The main initiative taken in the wake of Objectif emploi, however, was the establishment of the new public development agency Investissement Québec, merging the SDI with the MICST's foreign investments directorate (Québec 1998e, 45). The SDI thus ceased to exist as a separate entity, although its key program of loan guarantees was safeguarded and transferred to the IQ subsidiary Garantie-Québec. Aside from guarantees, two main roles were assigned to IQ: one of "coordination," and one of "prospection" (Québec 1998e, 45–8). In the first case, IQ would act as a "one-stop-shop" for local and foreign investors seeking government support for major investment projects, mobilizing the appropriate departments and involving other public or hybrid investors to offer administrative, managerial, or financial accompaniment.

As a "prospector" of foreign and domestic investments, IQ would also actively work to "brand" Quebec as an investment destination, acting as a complement to the province's *commercial attachés* – which focus mainly on export promotion and outward FDI – by identifying and lobbying potential foreign investors. Finally, IQ would encourage new investments domestically, offering support for businesses'

Graph 3.5. Contributions of IQ, 1998–2003 ($ millions)

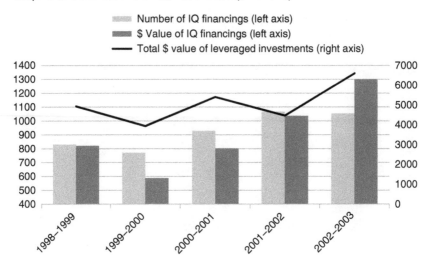

Sources: IQ (2000–3), annual reports.

expansion or modernization projects, notably to "avoid the closing or moving of decision units outside Quebec" (Québec 1998e, 48). The case of IQ is thus particularly interesting, because it turned out to be much more than an investment prospector, promoter, or coordinator, instead becoming a very dynamic (equity) investor itself.

Although this had not really been planned at the time, it can notably be explained by a small but significant amendment to the original IQ Bill. Although articles 27, 28, and 35 of the bill, as introduced in May 1998, already established that IQ would administer government financial aid programs or mandates and that it could invest in VCs, article 25 detailing IQ's mission initially limited it to the *promotion* of investment. Yet during committee work Liberal MNA Robert Benoit pointed out that since IQ would absorb the SDI, its mandate ought to recoup SDI responsibilities, which included "economic development" and "jobs creation" (Québec 1998b). An amendment was thus passed that reframed article 25, so that IQ would have as its missions not only to "facilitate the growth of investment in Quebec" but also to "contribute to the economic development of Quebec and the creation of employment opportunities" (Québec 1998e).

This allowed it to play a more encompassing role. As remarked in IQ's first annual report, the agency's mandates, notably with regards to the implementation of government strategies and the "creation of employment opportunities," required continuity in the provision of entrepreneurial finance (IQ 1999, 3). By 1999, IQ had thus already built a $1.7 billion portfolio, including over $600 million in government "priority projects" and close to $500 million in equity, leveraging $5 billion in prospective investments (IQ 1999, 30; IQ 2000).

The cases of Objectif emploi and IQ showed there was still a perceived need to channel a larger part of Québécois savings' toward local (and especially Francophone) businesses, a core objective of Quebec's economic nationalism since the early 1960s. Their impacts on public investors such as the CDPQ, SGF, and SDI also revealed a concrete effort to refine coordination and strengthen the capacities of Quebec's investment ecosystem. This signalled the importance bestowed to this ecosystem in what was, otherwise, a context of public sector retrenchment (Imbeau and Leclerc 2002; Graefe and Rioux 2017). Finally, the ambitious leveraging objectives imposed on the SGF, Innovatechs, and IQ denoted a strategic shift which would only deepen in the 2000s: the increased reliance on a *faire faire* approach of co-investment with institutional, hybrid, and private funds.

The Bouchard and Landry Governments (1998–2003)

Five months after the act establishing IQ was voted, the PQ was returned to power as a majority government. This was Lucien Bouchard's first election as head of the PQ, and Jean Charest's first as head of a "new" PLQ, critical of the Quebec model and advocating drastic state retrenchment (PLQ 1998; Charest 2000; Jérôme-Forget 2000). The reorganization of the SGF, as well as the establishment of IQ, were openly criticized as a costly reshuffling of "structures," for which tax reductions and regulatory relief should be substituted. The PQ, instead, promoted a refinement of the *faire faire* approach combining the intensification of IQ's prospection activities with enhanced provision of VC for SMBs (PQ 1998, 9–12).

The decentralization of economic development initiated between 1996 and 1998 was also to be reinforced, as new resources were to be injected in the CLD and other regional/local VC funds (PQ 1998, 16). In short, the PQ offered continuity without refraining from major new initiatives, as the cases of the CRCD and FDQ would show. This second mandate would however also be marked by major external shocks: the dot.com bust of the early 2000s, the 9–11 attacks in 2001, and the economic downturn that followed.

The budgets of continuity

The year 1999 opened with a major dispute between Quebec and Canada over the Social Union Framework Agreement (SUFA) signed by the federal government and all other provinces in February (Gagnon 2000). The stumbling blocks concerned the recognition and modalities of federal government spending in areas of provincial jurisdiction (Rioux 2014, 16–17). Although this agreement mainly applied to social policies, it also had implications for economic development, as this "spending power" extended, historically and as part of the new agreement, to R&D (Tremblay 2000). It is in part against this background[12] that new measures were taken as part of a plan to "accelerate research and innovation" (Québec 1999a), aimed at solidifying Quebec's autonomy in R&D: (a) the establishment of the Valorisation-Recherche Québec (VRQ) agency, endowed with $100 million to promote and subsidize R&D valorization; and (b) the creation of an adjoining $75 million public investment fund, Innovation Québec (INNQ), put under direct responsibility of the new Ministère de la recherche, de la science et de la technologie (MRST).

This budget was the extension of Objectif emploi: given its success in generating private investments, $300 million in additional resources were injected in the strategy (Québec 1999b, 18). IQ programs were topped-up, with the FAIRE receiving $50 million to initiate a program of exchange rate guarantees for exporting SMBs, too dependent on a "weak and volatile" Canadian dollar (Québec 1999b, 21). The main initiatives, however, were the VRQ and INNQ (Québec 1999a, 1). Objectif emploi's R&D component was directly inspired by the "national systems of innovation" approach developed by economist Christopher Freeman. In a subnational context, this approach necessitated policy asymmetry as it focused on the importance of closely knit, interconnected networks between businesses, government bodies, research institutions, and VC funds (Québec 1999a, 12–13). As part of a two-year, $400 million effort to accelerate R&D, the MRST, VRQ, and INNQ would thus fund tripartite (government/businesses/universities) research partnerships and the commercialization of their fruits.

Of the INNQ's $75 million budget, $20 million was notably dedicated to government-defined "priority R&D projects," and another $4 million to fund seed-stage ventures (Québec 1999a, 49, 77). Out of the VRQ's $100 million budget, in turn, half would be spent on subsidies to support the commercialization of university research (Québec 1999a, 75). While Quebec's government was creating the MRST, VRQ, and INNQ, besides, established organizations were already engaging in high-tech sectors at an increasing pace: by 2000, the vast majority of the SGF's VC investments were made in technology-intensive businesses, where it often partnered with the FSTQ, CDPQ, Innovatechs, and hybrid funds like BioCapital (SGF 2000, 19, 39–40). The CDPQ itself was investing hundreds of millions in these sectors, through subsidiaries like Sofinov and T²C². It was also actively helping Quebec keep up with a rapidly evolving ICT sector: in 2000, for instance, the CDPQ partnered with Québecor and invested over $2.2 billion to buy the cable company Vidéotron, thereby perpetuating Québécois ownership by blocking a merger with Ontario's Rogers Communications (Pelletier 2009, 282).

The 2000–1 budget was, in turn, one of regional development. Its most important project was La Financière agricole (FA), merging the pre-existing Régie des assurances agricoles du Québec and Société de financement agricole. The new FA was to offer income stabilization regimes and programs of financial aid for agricultural projects. Quebec's government pledged to inject it with a massive $5.6 billion over seven years to guarantee 100% of potential losses on loans issued to farmers by Desjardins credit unions (Québec 2000b). The FA was also devised to support farm succession in the face of growing indebtedness and international land speculation (Québec 2000a; L'Italien, Nantel, and Bishinga 2014), consistent with the increased focus of government-backed funds on business succession more generally.

The FA highlighted two aspects of the PQ's approach: a perceived need for state involvement to ensure appropriate access to capital, and the close relationship it intended to cultivate with Desjardins as a partner. This was also a prelude to its new regional development strategy (Québec 2001b) and to the launch of CRCD, the province's third tax-advantaged VC fund. The PQ's overarching objectives still focused on ensuring long-term Québécois control in regional economies: on top of efforts to secure farm ownership and succession, both the new regional strategy and the investment guidelines of CRCD would indeed place great emphasis on the development of the cooperative sector, given the high survival rate and the "inalienable" character of its businesses.

Capital régional et coopératif Desjardins and La Financière du Québec

These two initiatives were announced in Quebec's 2001–2 budget. The FDQ was a three-year, $800 million economic development plan targeting Quebec's "régions-ressources." CRCD consisted in the crafting of a new VC fund in collaboration with Desjardins, designed to "funnel risk capital toward regions and cooperatives" (Québec 2001c, 21). The details of both projects were laid out in a policy document in which the main problems affecting the régions-ressources were listed (Québec 2001b). The lack of access to VC was identified, but most interesting were the reasons invoked to explain equity gaps. Acknowledging that large amounts of VC had already been channeled to regions through the SRI, FRS, SOLIDE, CLD, FACSN, and Innovatechs, the PQ concluded that *demand-side* inefficiencies, rather than mere centripetal *supply*, caused problems.

There was a clear lack of investment opportunities given the paucity of high-value-added industries in these regions and their relatively heavy reliance on the extractive sector and traditional manufacturing (Québec 2001b, 31–6). There was also a notable concentration of cooperative businesses – 25% of Quebec's co-ops were situated in the régions-ressources – which, because of their organizational structure, are not particularly well-suited for VC firms that require voting rights and high capital returns (Québec 2001b, 43; Bertrand 2003, 118). The PQ's plan therefore included not only a simple increase and decentralization of VC supply, but a deeper effort of industrial diversification and the channelling of VC to the cooperative sector. The creation of CRCD in 2001 was a key component of this effort. As a tax-advantaged VC fund, CRCD would be allowed to raise $150 million per year through the selling of shares entitling buyers to a tax credit equal to 50% of their value, up to $1,250 per year (Québec 2001b, 126).

In return for government backing, investors would have to keep their shares for a minimum of seven years, and investment guidelines reflecting the state's objectives were imposed on CRCD.[13] At least 60% of its assets were to be invested each year in admissible SMBs and, out of that 60%, 35% had to be invested in SMBs from the régions-ressources and/or in Quebec-based co-ops (Québec 2001b, 127–8). "Admissible" SMBs would have to own under $50 million in total assets and employ a majority of their workforce among residents of Quebec. Eligible co-ops, in turn, had to have their head office in Quebec or at least half their payroll stemming from employees of a Quebec-based establishment (Québec 2001d, 7).

CRCD was thus intended as much more than just another tax-advantaged VC fund: it was created to act as a complement to other regional and local funds (Bertrand 2003, 127, 143–8; Québec 2001e, 2001f), and as a powerful capitalization tool to restructure Quebec's regional economies by supporting high-tech "créneaux d'excellence" in accordance with government priorities (Québec 2002b, 78). The act establishing CRCD was adopted in June, and by December 31st it had already raised upward of $80 million from 35,000 investors (CRCD 2002, 2). As early as 2003, 25% of all CRCD investments had already been made in SMBs from the régions-ressources and in co-ops (Bertrand 2003, 117). Appetite for its shares was quickly revealed to be strong: over its first five years, CRCD built a $650 million capital stock and an investment portfolio of over $415 million. By 2006, CRCD was investing, annually, more than $125 million in Quebec's businesses including over $25 million in régions-ressources and co-ops (CRCD 2007, 4–7).

CRCD also quickly developed an expertise in biotechnologies, ICT, and manufacturing technologies while sponsoring and strengthening the development of the cooperative sector. Following its first year in operation, the government published a major "policy statement on the development of cooperatives" in which their strategic importance for Quebec was made explicit. Noting Quebec's cooperative sector was, by far, Canada's largest, the PQ argued this was a comparative advantage worth cultivating given (a) the much higher survival rates of co-ops as compared with private start-ups, and (b) the inalienable character of their ownership, shielding co-ops from foreign takeovers and ensuring long-term, local rootedness (Québec 2003a, 21–2).

Ambitious objectives for Quebec's cooperatives were thus established, including a 25% increase of investments in the sector over ten years (Québec 2003a, 32). To achieve this goal, a number of other initiatives were launched to complement CRCD's contribution. Among those was the establishment of a hybrid fund of funds in 2001, Fil*action*, in partnership with the FACSN. Mainly dedicated to regional co-ops, Fil*action* would invest small amounts, directly or through subsidiary funds,[14] in the form of loans and micro-loans, guarantees, or equity. New programs were also added to IQ in order to support co-ops and social economy businesses, which were to be administered by IQ's new subsidiary, FDQ, set up in late 2001.

This new IQ subsidiary, replacing Garantie-Québec, was introduced as part of the 2002–3 budget, published following the dot.com bust and 9–11 attacks. In addition to a small stimulus package (Québec 2001g, 26–31), the PQ government took advantage of the economic downturn to introduce new public schemes. The budget was accompanied by a new economic strategy, AGIR, which presented Quebec's government as both a "facilitator" and a "partner" (Québec 2001h, 61). It was to solidify and perpetuate these roles that the FDQ was set up: noting the inefficiency of loan guarantee programs in times of financial downturn, the government wanted IQ to reconnect with *faire* and *faire avec*.

The FDQ would thus continue to offer loan guarantees but would henceforth also act as a public "investment bank" for SMBs, issuing loans, equity loans, mezzanine finance, and equity investments (Québec 2001g, 28; 2001h, 13–15). The importance of the previously discussed amendment to the original IQ Bill – extending IQ's role to economic development at large – was again revealed, as IQ's role shifted from one of *faire faire* to a much larger mandate: "*La FDQ agira en complémentarité avec les institutions financières ou en partenariat avec ces dernières en respectant leur champ usuel d'intervention, mais aussi en récupérant l'espace que ces mêmes institutions cependant délaissent ... C'est ainsi qu'on pourra la qualifier de banque d'affaire des PME québécoises*" (Québec 2001i, n.p.).[15]

Concluding Remarks

All in all, the 1990–2003 period in Quebec witnessed a significant intensification of state involvement in VC. As graph 3.6 demonstrates, Quebec's VC ecosystem grew substantially: from 1997 onward, the quantity of VC raised in Quebec skyrocketed, to reach a high of over $3 billion in 2001. The amount of VC available for investment followed the same pattern, with a 450% increase between 1994 and 2003. Such drastic growth would not have occurred without an even greater increase in the provision of government-backed VC (see graph 3.1). Between 1995 and 2002, while total public resources (including tax expenditures) dedicated to business support grew by 283%, this included an impressive 1511% increase in the value of equity shares acquired by Quebec's state corporations in the province (Québec 2002b, 81).

If the PQ government was thus very active in the realm of entrepreneurial finance and VC, it also perpetuated a trend present under previous PLQ administrations. With initiatives such as the Sociétés régionales d'investissement, Fonds de développement technologique, Fonds québécois de développement industriel, Innovatechs and SOLIDE, the Liberals had already established some of the strategic policy objectives later refined by the PQ. The initiatives of the late 1980s were as much about the coordination of Quebec's investment ecosystem (SRI) and policy emulation (FDT) as they were about regional or sectoral funding gaps. The early 1990s schemes, in turn, had as much to do with strengthening Quebec's high-tech supply chains (FQDI, SIGM) or multipartite concertation (clusters, SOLIDE) as with counter-cyclical imperatives or the leveraging of private investments.

Although, as Haddow contends, the PQ subsequently made strides toward "encouraging more market sensitivity and decentralization" (2015, 175), this in no way signalled a waning of economic nationalism. If decentralization and a shift to *faire faire* approaches did take place under the PQ, this was almost always against the background

Graph 3.6. New VC raised and VC available for investment, Quebec, 1994–2003 ($ millions)

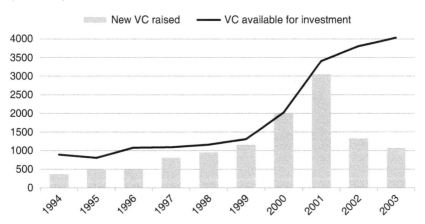

Sources: Macdonalds & Associates Limited (1995–2004).
Note: The very sharp decline in money raised after 2001 can be explained by the economic downturn that followed the dot.com bust and 9–11 attacks.

of perceived needs or political preferences for policy asymmetry: the Plan Paillé was devised as an alternative to the federal regime of loan guarantees, the Fonds régionaux de solidarité and Centres locaux de développement allowed Quebec to replace the federal government as the prime sponsor of regional funds, IQ reinforced Quebec's autonomous prospection of foreign investment, and the FA was designed as a tool to help secure local farm ownership and succession.

The same can be said of the FondAction CSN and CRCD, moreover: while in the first case the idea was to extend Quebec's unique LSIF model, in the second the intent was to bank on Quebec's comparative advantage in the cooperative sector, and notably on the "inalienable" character of its businesses. The advent of the FDQ, finally, was born out of a recognition by the PQ that a *faire faire* approach based on loan guarantees could not ensure the attainment of strategic objectives that required a recourse to the state's sponsoring roles. In short, thus, the 1990–2003 period in Quebec was clearly marked, with regards to state (and state-backed) intervention, by economic nationalism through (a) *ideological mechanisms*, as illustrated by preferences for policy asymmetry and the pursuit of regional-level national objectives; (b) *political mechanisms*, as exemplified by the PQ's reaction to *L'Action Nationale* reports; and (c) *institutional mechanisms* impacting government decisions, notably in the cases of the Innovatechs, LSIFs, and IQ.

Chapter Four

Scotland, 1990–2003

The period stretching from the early 1990s to the early 2000s was a very particular one for Scotland. It saw major reforms to the HIDB and SDA but also mounting nationalist pressures for parliamentary devolution, a winning referendum on that issue, and the establishment in 1999 of the first Scottish Parliament in almost three hundred years. Besides, economic nationalism continued to play key roles, throughout the 1990s, in upholding policy asymmetries developed in Scotland since the 1960s. This can be assessed through an analysis of initiatives such as the Business Birth Rate Strategy, the Scottish Business Shop Network, the Small Business Loan Scheme and Scottish Export Assistance Scheme, the Scottish Equity Partnership, the Technology Ventures system, the Scottish Technology Fund, and perhaps most importantly the Local Investment Networking Company (LINC).

Economic development and technology spending in Scotland was thus maintained at very high levels relative to the UK's during these years (graph 4.1), and the central role the public sector kept playing in Scotland's entrepreneurial finance and VC ecosystems was at the heart of this persisting asymmetry. Major initiatives taken in the wake of devolution, in this sense, represented continuity rather than novelty. Among those were the Business Growth Fund, LINC's Trial Marriage Scheme and Investment Facilitation Grant, SE's clustering strategy, and the Small Business Gateway.

The perceived necessity *of* and ideological preference *for* such policy asymmetry, which underpinned the Scottish devolutionist movement, stemmed from economic nationalism. Nationalism was indeed a crucial drive of policymakers when devising and implementing the abovementioned investment tools, both before and after devolution. Brian McVey, Director of Strategy and long-time senior official at SE,

Graph 4.1. Public spending on economic development and technology,* Scotland vs. UK, 1998–2007 (£ millions)

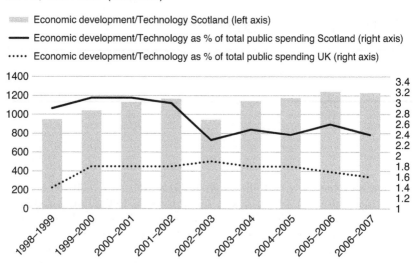

Sources: GERS (1999–2008).
* "Enterprise & Economic Development" + "Science & Technology" categories as % of total public spending (including debt servicing).

probably sums it best when recalling this anecdote from pre-devolution Scotland:

> It was all always there. It was there before devolution, because the Ministers made their names by doing a good job for Scotland. We were always more aggressively competitive. I remember one of my predecessors, Chief Executive at SE, describing a meeting he had in London, where he talked about what he was trying to do to get more inward investment for Scotland and got lectured by his colleague from the Treasury, saying "that's dangerously close to a nationalistic argument you're making there!" And he went: "You're damn right it is!" This guy was a nationalist with a big N. So we've always used that. And it's behind the rhetoric the current government uses.[1]

Strategic Policymaking in Pre-devolution Scotland (1990–1997)

Throughout the 1980s, as explained at the end of chapter 2, the Thatcher government had little choice but to recognize that the increasingly important roles played by the HIDB and SDA were widely perceived, in Scotland and by the Scottish small business community, as both legitimate and necessary. As Scottish journalist Maurice Smith later remarked:

> For all the Brave New World talk of "hands-off" government during the previous decade, Scottish business – indeed, Scottish life – appears to have remained wedded to some kind of consensus thinking as it enters the 1990s ... In this regard, Scottish business leaders have more in common, arguably, with their counterparts in the Irish Republic or some mainland European states, than with those in southern England ... It has been diff cult for leading Conservatives to persuade business that corporatist Labour creations such as the SDA are essentially a bad thing – interventionism, and all that – when so many enterprises have owed their creation, or their survival, in some part to the SDA. (1992, 44)

Yet the UK government had not given up on its attempts to roll back Scotland's public sector. By 1988, a major reform of the HIDB and SDA was initiated, which, although adding to their responsibilities, also decentralized and privatized much of their activities (Danson et al. 1990). In this context, however – as in the early 1980s – Scottish nationalism played key roles in ensuring a degree of continuity and the prevalence of these agencies' strategic, national objectives.

The Enterprise and New Towns (Scotland) Act 1990

The idea of a reform of the HIDB and SDA struck a chord with Thatcher after the general election of June 1987, when Conservatives lost half of their Scottish seats and were reduced to 24% of the popular vote in Scotland, against 42% for Labour (Smith 1992, 50). The proposition of the Confederation of Business Industry – Scotland (CBI Scotland), a merger of training and economic development responsibilities within new structures operating through networks of local, "employer-led" agencies, allowed Thatcher to justify a reform otherwise unlikely to receive support in Scotland. On the one hand, it would mitigate Scottish interventionism, but on the other, it would contribute to Scotland's autonomy by transferring training responsibilities from the UK's Department of Employment to the SO and, from there, to the new HIDB and SDA. In December 1988, the SO published a White Paper detailing this idea and by January 1990 the Enterprise and New Towns (Scotland) Bill had been introduced (Danson et al. 1990).

Both the White Paper and this bill advocated for a rebranding of the HIDB and SDA as Highlands and Islands Enterprise (HIE) and Scottish

Enterprise (SE), but most importantly for the establishment of autonomous Local Enterprise Companies (LECs), which although funded by
SE and HIE would function as private agencies with majority board
representation (at least two-thirds) for local business interests. LECs
would in essence be local, private sector-led subcontractors for SE and
HIE, themselves turned into umbrella organizations coordinating LEC
networks.[2] Training responsibilities and the bulk of business financing
and sponsoring activities were to be transferred to LECs (Hayton and
Mearns 1991, 308). This could have "heralded the start of the most radical change in Government policy toward the sponsoring of economic
development in Scotland for a generation" (Hood 1990, 65), but did not.

Although the integration of training and economic development
policy was a long-standing demand of many business organizations in
Scotland, the UK government saw it as a political opportunity in addition to an economic necessity. It allowed the Tory SOSS, Malcolm Rif-
kind, to present the reform as a devolution of powers toward Scotland:

> I shall explain why the Government and a wide spectrum of Scottish
> opinion believe that to be highly desirable. The f rst and most obvious
> reason – and one that industry has pointed to – is the desirability of a sin-
> gle door for industry with regard to business support and training ... The
> second main ingredient is the transfer of responsibility for training from
> Sheff eld to Edinburgh and from the Department of Employment to the
> SO ... That is of great signif cance. In addition, it is a Scottish solution to
> meet Scottish needs. (Hansard UK 1990, cc. 842)

While the Thatcher government used the language of policy asymmetry to justify the bill, SNP and Labour MPs from Scotland still rejected
it. Nationalists argued that without a much wider devolution of powers to Scotland the proposed reform would be at best inconsequential
(Hansard UK 1990, cc. 886–90). Labour MPs, in turn, worried that the
LECs would give local businessmen excessive economic influence (cc.
845). Both Nationalist and Labour MPs, most significantly, pointed out
that national coordination over economic policy could be jeopardized:
"Even more damagingly, the establishment of SE and the LECs will
destroy the strategic, Scotland-wide analysis of economic development,
leaving a dangerous vacuum at the centre. The central role that the SDA
has carried out successfully will also be lost" (cc. 896).

Between the time the bill was adopted in June 1990 and the com-
mencement of SE/HIE operations in April 1991, it became clear that
such concerns were shared not only by part of Scotland's small business
community (Smith 1992, 55) and local authorities (Danson et al. 1990),

but most importantly by SDA/SE and HIDB/HIE officials themselves, who saw it as their duty to safeguard a capacity for national coordination and strategic planning. This capacity was widely recognized as a major characteristic of Scotland's economic development model, which the LECs were perceived as jeopardizing (Danson et al. 1990, 189).

The LECs were to be responsible for the provision of financial assistance to businesses, a policy sector the HIDB and SDA had used extensively to steer private investment and the Scottish economy in strategic directions. Immediately after the act establishing SE and HIE was passed, thus, internal transition taskforces started working on the elaboration of a system ensuring, via the process of budget allocation, efficient coordination on strategic priorities between LECs and SE/HIE (see figure 4.1). Among such priorities was to improve access to capital for technology-intensive SMBs, so as to "reflect the inherited priorities of the SDA" (Hood 1991, 75).

Neil Hood, a senior manager at the SDA, one of the leaders of the transition team in 1990, and later director of SDF and SE's deputy chairman, painted a clear picture of the necessity to ensure policy continuity:

> Local focus can be blended with national strategy and effective impact at the national level. That this is achieved from the outset is absolutely fundamental. Every endeavor has been made to ensure that the business planning process currently under way within SE and the LECs starts on that footing. But it will need much resolve on the part of all parties, not least through Government's support of the Board of SE to ensure that it remains in synchronisation. The strategy of SE as a network of bodies interrelated by contract has to be driven by overall Scottish interests, not by other imperatives … Substantial, and often heroic, efforts have been made over recent months within many LEC areas to ensure that all these parties remain on reasonably common ground. It is to be hoped that such unity is developed and sustained. (Hood 1990, 66)

This is precisely what is meant by referring to economic nationalism as a "set of institutionalized economic ideas" and as "perceived imperatives" or "ideological preferences" for policy asymmetry and strategic intervention. In the case of the transition from the SDA to SE, such ideas, perceptions, and preferences were mobilized both at a political level, through Scottish MPs, and at the executive level, through senior SE officials. This also applied to HIE, where national programs framing LECs' operations were quickly implemented between 1990 and 1995 (HIDB 1990; HIE 1993, 1996; Lloyd and Black 1993). These efforts to safeguard institutional capacities for coordination and strategic intervention,

Figure 4.1. SE/LECs Strategic Planning Organizational Chart, 1991–1992

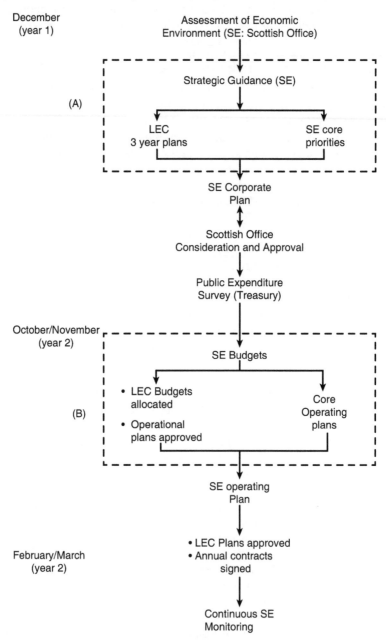

Source: Hood (1991, 72).

moreover, would soon allow for the advent of major, structuring policy initiatives.

The Business Birth Rate Strategy (BBRS)

Most of the business financing efforts of the SDA and HIDB during the 1970s and 1980s had been geared toward an increase of Scottish presence and ownership in key industrial sectors, with a specific focus on SMBs. Among the concerns at SE and HIE was a potential shift in policy focus, operated through the LECs, toward medium-to-large businesses. This concern was quickly appeased, however, as the composition of the preliminary LEC Boards – the "Steering Groups" formed in 1991 – established a balanced representation of SMBs and medium-to-large companies (Hayton and Mearns 1991, 311). The relatively small size of LECs, moreover, meant that they would carry relatively little influence on their own and would be highly dependent upon national structures for funding. By 1992–3, each LEC only accounted for between 5% and 10% of SE/HIE networks' total budgets, except for Glasgow (SE, 12%) and Argyll (HIE, 15%), the larger LECs (Lloyd and Black 1993, 77; SE 1993, 22).

SE and HIE thus retained substantial influence over the LECs, as illustrated by the requirement to get national approval for any investment exceeding £30,000 (HIE) or £250,000 (SE). Both SE and HIE also safeguarded their capacity for strategic planning and policy coordination. In the early 1990s, with Scotland barely coming out of the recession, this capacity was used to boost economic growth through a national effort aimed at increasing entrepreneurial levels in Scotland, so as to promote the advent of locally owned start-ups, strengthening Scottish supply chains and endogenous clusters. This policy notably took the form of a major initiative launched in 1993, the Business Birth Rate Strategy (BBRS), which was to span over ten years and be granted with a budget of £20 million per year (Brown and Mason 2012, 19–23). Many of the organizations constituting Scotland's entrepreneurial finance ecosystem today were established in its wake.

Following the launch of this strategy, SE's Chief Executive Crawford Beveridge commented on the problem it was devised to address: "For some years, perhaps decades, we in Scotland have been aware that as a nation we seem to have lost some of that entrepreneurial drive for which the Scots were once famed … It is apparent that we have a fundamental problem. That problem can be traced back to a simple lack of companies in Scotland" (cited in Dow and Kirk 2000, 28). The BBRS was thus crafted to address the long-standing problem of Scotland's over-reliance on foreign-owned corporations. After all the efforts of the 1970s and 1980s, this was still a major concern: by 1994, Scotland was second-to-last among British regions for the number of registered businesses per capita, lagging the UK average by a wide margin (Dow and Kirk 2000, 31). And yet, "even with poor relative performance, the research showed that new starts accounted for some 125,000 jobs during the 1980s in Scotland, much more than alternative sources such as inward investment or the expansion of larger enterprises" (Hood and Paterson 2002, 238).

A core objective of the BBRS, accordingly, was to catch up to the UK's "business birth rate" average by 2000,[3] through the establishment of at least 25,000 start-ups. The "unofficial" goal, however, was in fact to catch up to South East England/London, the UK's leading region for businesses per capita (Talbot and Reeves 1997, 26; Deakins, Sullivan, and Whittam 2000, 161). According to Dr. Geoffrey Whittam, Reader in Entrepreneurship at the Glasgow School for Business and Society, Glasgow Caledonian University and a leading expert on Scotland's VC ecosystem and entrepreneurial policy, the *economic* rationale behind the BBRS was to reach "normal" levels of business creation, but the *nationalist* ambition was to establish Scotland as a UK leader:

> It was a deliberately political strategy or, to be more polite, a "social-economic" strategy. The problem in Scotland was that new f rm formation was a lot lower than in the south east of England. Now, there's a question about the methodology that was adopted at the time, because new f rm formation in Scotland wasn't really any worse than in the north of England. They chose a more successful region to try and imitate, to increase the number of new f rms. So they were comparing with the best.[4]

To attain such ambitious – perhaps unrealistic – targets, SE established six priorities: (a) promoting an entrepreneurial culture to increase the proportion of Scots having "entrepreneurial intentions;" (b) "improving formal and informal support networks" for entrepreneurs; (c) maximizing access to entrepreneurial finance and VC; (d) "widening the entrepreneurial base" by sponsoring female entrepreneurs; (e) growing the number of start-ups in manufacturing, high-technology, and business services; and (f) widening the proportion of "fast-growing new starts," or *gazelles* (Hood and Paterson 2002, 239; Woods 2006, 1).

Multiple initiatives aimed at seed-stage and start-up-stage ventures, notably implemented through the LECs, would complement each other. As a national strategy therefore, the BBRS aimed to mobilize a wide array of actors: [5] "The strategy seeks to involve the business

Graph 4.2. Contributions of SE and HIE, 1991–1998 (£ millions)

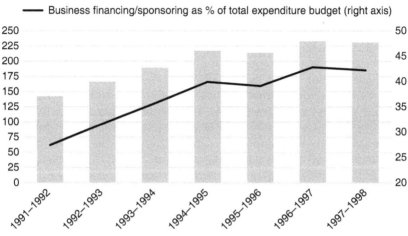

Sources: SE & HIE (1992–8), annual reports and accounts.

community, the media, the financial sector, the education system, and business support networks across Scotland in stimulating the encouragement of entrepreneurship and helping improve the environment for new business start-ups" (SE 1995, 15). Among its first initiatives was the £100 million Small Business Loan Scheme, launched in October 1994. This scheme, aiming to provide Scottish start-ups and SMBs with long-term, preferential loans was established in partnership with banks, to which SE would pay loan interests beyond a pre-established "interest rate cap" (SE 1995, 12). This was a good example of the national concertation mechanisms the BBRS was designed to foster.

The various financial tools launched as part of the BBRS also resulted in a significant increase of SE/HIE networks' spending on business capitalization and sponsoring: from a total of £142 million in 1991–2, it reached over £230 million before devolution (graph 4.2). The proportion of SE/HIE resources dedicated to business financing and sponsoring – as opposed to administrative costs or professional training activities – also grew from 27% to 42% over the same period. Among other BBRS initiatives was, notably, the Scottish Business Shop Network, a partnership with LECs, chambers of commerce, and universities also launched in 1994. The aim in this case was to establish forty "first-stop-shops" across Scotland, offering support to businesses for "training, patents, exporting, opportunities in Europe, franchising, marketing and finance" (SE 1995, 16). Subsidies of up to £30,000 were also made available to exporting SMBs through the Scottish Export Assistance Scheme, crafted in collaboration with LECs and chambers of commerce as part of SE's 1995–2000 Export Development Strategy (SE 1996, 24–5).

Apart from a few regional exceptions, however, the BBRS didn't succeed in generating the targeted improvement in entrepreneurship levels or job creation (SE 1996, 19; Talbot and Reeves 1997; Dow and Kirk 2000, 34; Fraser of Allander Institute 2001; Hood and Paterson 2002, 239–42; Van Stel and Storey 2004). Yet positive impacts were felt in at least three ways: first, it boosted levels of public assistance – financial and managerial – to businesses; second, it triggered concertational practices and established bases for national-level coordination between SE/HIE, LECs, Scottish banks, chambers of commerce, and other players; finally, it gave way to the establishment of new programs and organizations around which the present-day Scottish ecosystem was built.[6] It also initiated a cultural shift in Scotland, leading to significant increases in "entrepreneurial intentions" among Scots and creating "stronger institutional support for business start-ups" (McVey 2000, 35; Hood and Paterson 2002, 240). Thus, "for those who wanted to take the plunge, there was a lot more of a supportive environment than was perhaps the case previously."[7]

LINC Scotland, the Scottish Equity Partnership, and Technology Ventures

As part of this emerging "supportive environment," a new non-for-profit organization was established in 1993 to act as an introductory service between Scottish SMBs and potential individual investors, the so-called "business angels." This kind of service was already offered by many LECs, but no coordinated national effort had yet been initiated. In the wake of the BBRS, the advantages of a centralized system facilitating angel investment were increasingly recognized: angels' "home bias" and tendency to invest small amounts – back then, generally less than £50,000 – in seed and start-up stage ventures were notably sought after (Mason and Harrison 1995, 1997). In partnership with the SO, SE thus led the charge for the establishment of LINC, a national network linking entrepreneurs and angels across Scotland. As David Grahame, then and still its executive director, explains, LINC always enjoyed a special status:

> We were part of the Glasgow LEC, but quickly it became obvious that to get to critical mass we had to be Scotland-wide. So we spun-out in 1993 as

Graph 4.3. Private VC/private equity investees per 1,000 registered businesses, Scotland vs. UK, 1994–1998

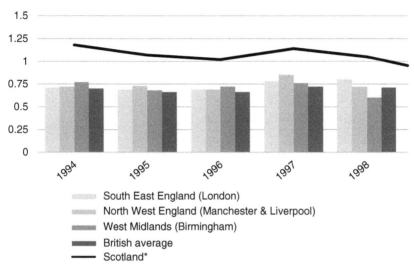

South East England (London)
North West England (Manchester & Liverpool)
West Midlands (Birmingham)
British average
Scotland*

Source: BVCA (1999).
* Because the figures used for this graph are based on the investment activities of BVCA members (SE and most Scottish angels/angel syndicates are not), Scotland's quotient is significantly undervalued for the whole period.

a Scotland-wide agency, and in those days there was, for tax purposes, a thing called "enterprise agency." Enterprise agencies were def ned as private sector, non-prof ts dedicated to entrepreneurial development objectives, and what this meant was that your private sponsors got tax breaks. So we were given enterprise agency status by the then SOSS, and that was hugely important.[8]

For much of the 1990s, Scotland was attracting a disproportionate share of the UK's VC and private equity deals, and a much larger proportion of its businesses were receiving equity investments than was the case elsewhere in the UK (graphs 4.3 & 4.4). Yet most of that capital was invested in expansion-stage businesses and in traditional, low-tech sectors (Murray 1994, 1995; Murray and Lott 1995). A funding gap thus existed for start-ups and early-stage high-tech ventures, which the BBRS and LINC were intended to fill (Harrison and Mason 1996; Mason and Harrison 1995, 1997).

Graph 4.4. Share of private VC/private equity investees in UK total vs. share of registered businesses in UK total, Scotland, 1993–1998 (%)

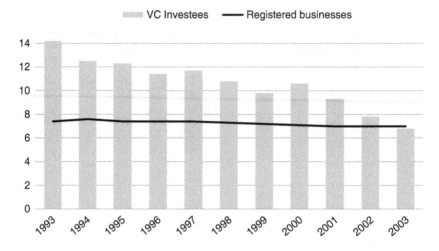

Source: BVCA (1999).

As the only national-level, enterprise agency type tax-advantaged angel network in the UK at the time, LINC was devised to make the most out of Scotland's comparative advantages and therefore deepened policy asymmetry with England (Mason and Harrison 1997, 114). As Dr. Whittam remarked (personal interview), LINC was to capitalize on Scotland's transition away from heavy manufacturing, which had already led, throughout the 1980s and in the wake of the recent Maastricht Treaty, to the closure or relocation of many large corporations:

> A strength of Scotland comes from unintended consequences: you've had a domination of the economy by large multinationals, and when you've had that retrenchment of large multinationals going to Eastern Europe for example, because of the change in the economic structure, a lot of top executives didn't relocate to Poland but stayed and were given big redundancy packages. I met a guy who was Head of Finance for Continental Tires in Scotland: he told me there was no way he was going to move, and there was no way he would be gardening and decorating for the rest of his life. The angels will tell us they want to give something back to Scotland.

LINC was thus crafted in part to harness the investment potential of a growing pool of high net-worth ex-managers keen on investing locally. Moreover, it was to take advantage of Scotland's coordinated, public sector backed economic development model. This initiative, in other words, was specific to Scotland because it would have been inapplicable elsewhere. As per Dr. Whittam (personal interview), Scottish identity played a key role in this sense:

> This is where the "identity" aspect comes to the fore. England is very strange, because what you've got there is London, and then the rest of England. If you look at some of the [angel] syndicates in England, in Yorkshire for example, they will be more "pro-Yorkshire" than pro-London. There's a local sensibility, and that is actually replicated across England so that you don't have the one voice LINC represents in Scotland for the angel network.

LINC was thus able to coordinate much of Scotland's angel activities thanks to the SE/HIE networks, and to effects of scale. In England, however, the angel ecosystem remained much more loosely integrated, as many different networks subsisted. As David Grahame remarks, "with SE, we have had the advantage of a single regional authority for the whole period ... The conventional wisdom suggests a good hinterland size for angel activity is about 5 million; whether here or in Boston, it's the same. England was over 50 million people, far too big for a single national effort to work" (personal interview; see also Mason and Harrison 1997, 119). LINC, besides, was successful from the onset: by 1994–5, LINC's "matching services" were responsible for around half the total value of angel investments in Scotland (SE 1995, 15; SE 1996, 18), and by 2000, close to 400 angels had become members of the network (Mason, Botelho, and Harrison 2016, 327–8).

LINC was not the only BBRS initiative aimed at improving access to VC, however. It was part of a coordinated effort that included the establishment of two other funds. One was the Scottish Equity Partnership (SEP) launched in 1995–6, a £25 million hybrid VC fund co-capitalized by SDF and private partners. The SEP was explicitly intended to leverage private investments and fill funding gaps for early-stage, high-tech businesses (SE 1996, 18). Yet "from a SE perspective, the promotion of SEP had a core economic development rationale, but it was more related to the longer term strategic goals of stimulating leading edge technology and high growth potential SMEs, than to shorter term considerations" (Hood 2000, 326). The SEP was indeed a strategic complement to both SDF and LINC: with an investment range of £100,000 to £500,000 it would provide follow-on funding for LINC's investees, but also occupy a tactical position between SDF investments rarely exceeding £200,000, and VC investments rarely below £500,000 (Harrison and Mason 2000b; Hood 2000, 325; SE 1996, 18).

Then came the Scottish Technology Fund (STF) in 1997, a hybrid VC fund specialized in high-tech university spin-outs and capitalized equally

Graph 4.5. Government-backed R&D* as % of GDP, Scotland vs. RoUK, 1999–2006

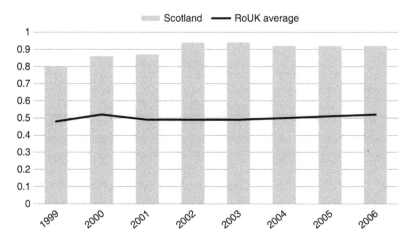

Source: Scottish Government, *Gross Expenditures on Research and Development Scotland* (GERD).
* R&D financed/performed by governmental and higher-education institutions.

by SDF and 3i, the UK's largest private VC investor. This fund aimed to foster the advent of innovative start-ups, and thus of new investment opportunities for LINC members, SDF, the SEP, and 3i (Hood 2000, 326). The STF was managed from within SDF and was in fact born out of another SE scheme, Technology Ventures. Launched less than a year earlier, Technology Ventures focused on the sponsoring of R&D "with the aim to increase the number of spin-out companies from Scottish Higher Education Institutions, [and] to improve the level of understanding of commercialisation more generally within the academic sector" (SE 2013, 7).

Technology Ventures concentrated on the specific sector of nano-technologies, offering grants for R&D and commercialization (SE 1998, 11). The reasons for this focus, in line with previous efforts to build the "Silicon Glen" cluster, were explained at the launch of the scheme in December 1996: "Scotland is a small country and has to prioritise its R&D investments. It was suggested that nanotechnology, or microen-gineering, is an emerging technology of great potential which is well within the capabilities of Scotland's science and industrial base."[9]

In combination with Technology Ventures, the STF would contribute in establishing Scotland as the UK's leader in the public sponsorship of R&D. By 1999, government-sponsored R&D was already accounting, at 0.8% of Scotland's GDP, for almost double the RoUK's average, a gap that kept increasing (graph 4.5). This was another telling example of the way in which, even in pre-devolution Scotland, policy asymmetry persisted and perhaps widened in accordance with the perceived needs of the Scottish economy, and the drive of SE/HIE officials for Scottish-specific solutions and national coordination.

The "Statecraft Phase" (1997–2003)

From this perspective, the devolution process of the late 1990s thus accentuated a trend that was already well underway. It was far from inconsequential, however. As the reforms of the SDA and HIDB had shown, until devolution Scotland's economic development model remained vulnerable. Although largely autonomous, SE and HIE were still answering to an SO subordinated to Westminster. Underpinned by Scottish (economic) nationalism, devolution contributed to a "rescaling" of the UK's political economy, opening new avenues for policy auton-omy and divergence. SE and HIE would henceforth answer to the Scot-tish Executive's Enterprise and Lifelong Learning Department"(ELLD) and to Scotland's Minister for Enterprise, who would "provide SE with overall strategic direction, provide more detailed strategic direction in specific areas, and agree the performance measures" (Scotland 2003, 4).

Between 1999 and 2001, accordingly, a string of new initiatives had direct impacts on the activities and structures of SE and HIE. Notably, the LECs were brought back into the agencies as public sector subsid-iaries in order to homogenize and synchronize local development (Scot-land 2000a). In an essay published after her mandate as head of the ELLD from 2000 to 2002, Wendy Alexander (SLP) confirmed that LECs were always perceived as "balkanising" the Scottish model, a trend against which the state-building efforts of the first Scottish Executive were devised (2003, 10): "The Parliament has unquestionably facilitated Scottish solutions to Scottish problems and aligned Scottish spending much more closely with the wishes of the Scottish people. All this is part of our statecraft phase – the playing out of the transition from the administration of Scotland to her better governance."

Devolution and economic development

In 1995, the Scottish Constitutional Convention (SCC)[10] published its final manifesto in favour of parliamentary devolution, in which the fine print of a Scottish Parliament's functions was laid out. "Scotland's Par-liament, Scotland's Right" (SCC 1995) illustrated how central economic nationalism was to Scotland's devolutionist movement. Among the three components of the SCC's "case for change," along with democratic accountability and regional autonomy, stood the issue of economic asymmetry: "The Scottish economy can be differentiated from those of other parts of the UK, both in its strengths and in its weaknesses ... UK economic policy has, hardly surprisingly, failed to address these circumstances closely, systematically or effectively. Scotland's Parliament, equipped with the sort of powers described in the pages that follow, will be able to do much better" (SCC 1995, n.p.). The economic advantages of devolution were not only presented from a policy standpoint but also from a *political* standpoint:

> Members of the Scottish Parliament will have the advantage of being geographically close to Scotland's business community. This proximity will allow for better contact to be maintained between business and political decision-makers. In comparable circumstances in other areas of Europe with home-rule parliaments or Assemblies this proximity has proved of major economic benef t, allowing a broader and deeper mutual understanding of business and political conditions. (SCC 1995, n.p.)

The opportunity for devolution finally opened in 1997 with the election of Tony Blair's "New Labour," which had pledged to hold a referendum on the question (Denver 1997). This referendum was held only four months after the election, in September 1997, with all the SCC members and the SNP campaigning in favour of devolution (Denver et al. 2000; Surridge and McCrone 1999; Taylor and Thomson 1999). Three-quarters of Scottish voters also supported it, and the formal process was thus set in motion in December 1997 with the introduction of a Scotland Bill closely inspired by the SCC's 1995 Manifesto.[11] When asked what devolution immediately changed for Scotland, experts of entrepreneurial finance point not only to policy asymmetry but also to sociopolitical impacts related to Scottish identity. For Dr. Geoffrey Whittam (personal interview),

> The greater pride in being Scottish should not be underestimated: you're getting more control and more power to make decisions that might impact your own country. If you think of the typical business angels, they're basically looking for investment opportunities, so when Scotland comes much more to the fore, they become more conscious of it and engage in helping businesses in Scotland.

This focus on Scotland and the "power to make decisions" were perhaps particularly important in the case of SE and HIE. As SE's Brian McVey explains (personal interview),

SE as an organization wasn't big on the radars of the SO … The political and parliamentary scrutiny was quite different, because from Westminster, SE was only one of a number of regional agencies, it was a long way away and relatively small against a lot of things scrutinized at Westminster. Suddenly, the Scottish Parliament drew loads and loads of interest into economic development and loads and loads of interest at SE. So all of a sudden we had 128 MSPs hugely interested in this and Parliament's Committee structures became a mechanism for that.

One of the first moves of the SLP-SLD coalition government elected in May 1999 (Denver and MacAllister 1999; D. McCrone 1999; Surridge and McCrone 1999) was indeed to launch a parliamentary inquiry on local economic development – i.e., on the LECs – led by the new Scottish Parliament's Enterprise and Lifelong Learning Committee. Before this committee could even produce its final report, however, the Scottish Executive already concluded that "there [were] evident problems in using what was designed not to be a national delivery machine to deliver national programmes and priorities," and "that greater central control and a more universal approach, concentrating on delivery rather than innovation, was needed" (Bennett and Fairley 2003, 7–8).

This final report, published in May 2000, only confirmed the Executive's concerns. The Committee concluded that there was "congestion, confusion, overlap, duplication, and competition" in Scotland's local development ecosystem, and that this was predominantly harmful to entrepreneurs and start-ups (Scotland 2000a). It was recommended that "the Executive should take the lead in guaranteeing that a simpler, more cohesive structure exists in Scotland for the delivery of local economic development services … and be prepared to penalise publicly-funded bodies who do not co-operate in this process" (Scotland 2000a, Conclusion 5). Therefore, "LECs should significantly change their character. They should change their status from private companies to public bodies; open up their boards to other non-business members; [and] increase the level of transparency in their activities" (Conclusion 13).

Later that year, LECs were indeed reintegrated into SE and HIE as public subsidiaries (SE 2000). The Scottish Executive also created new local bodies – not unlike Quebec's CLDs – designed to streamline business services and allow for enhanced coordination with the Executive's strategies (Bennett and Fairley 2003). The new Local Economic Forums were established in each LEC area and were to regroup LECs themselves, local authorities, and chambers of commerce (Scotland 2000a). Their main purpose was "the achievement of measurable outcomes established by the Executive" in terms of "new business starts, support to small businesses, key local industries, [and] skills training" (Scotland 2000a, Conclusion 10).

Clearly, one of the first impacts of devolution was thus to open the door for this long-desired "centralization of policy through the strengthening of SE and the reorganisation of the Local Enterprise Network" (Bennett and Fairley 2003, 17). Such recentralization, fueled by economic nationalism, further deepened Scotland's policy divergence from England. In good part to reciprocate for the devolution of economic development responsibilities to Scotland, for instance, Regional Development Agencies were established across England in 1999–2000, each endowed with a hybrid Regional Venture Capital Fund by 2002–3.[12] As Scotland was recentralizing business sponsoring activities, economic development in England was thus being decentralized (Harding 2000, 306–7). Unlike in Scotland, entrepreneurial finance and VC in England were still not considered "part of a larger integrated system" (Mason and Harrison 2003, 865).

This centralization of economic development policy through the Scottish Executive, SE, and HIE allowed for the launch of a second phase of the BBRS, this time crafted as a clustering strategy. It was devised in close collaboration with the Scottish Executive, which had just adopted its first manufacturing strategy, "Created in Scotland," crafted in concertation with the newly established Scottish Manufacturing Steering Group of which SE, HIE, Scottish Financial Enterprise, the SCDI, CBI Scotland, and the Scottish Trades Union Congress were all members. In the context of the late-1990s high-tech bubble, Created in Scotland aimed to strike the right balance between continued diversification toward technology-intensive industries, and sustained backing of competitive traditional sectors – such as food and drink or oil and gas – still accounting for much of Scottish employment (Scotland 2000b, 3).

The development, with the state's financial and organizational support (Taylor and Raines 2001, 32–3), of "inter-company alliances and partnerships" in key sectors was to be at the centre of Scotland's new manufacturing strategy (Scotland 2000b, 21, 34). It was to bridge FDI prospection and entrepreneurial sponsorship efforts by developing deeper synergies between large (often foreign-owned) companies and indigenous SMBs acting as suppliers (Botham and Downes 1999; G. McCrone 1999; Taylor and Raines 2001). At the heart of both Created in Scotland and the new BBRS' clusters strategy were ambitious objectives: 40,000 new local start-ups were to be created by 2003, and a total of 100,000 by 2010 (Scotland 2000b, 29). While recognizing that the BBRS had not delivered on such objectives in the past, the belief was that devolution would allow for the development of better adapted,

Scottish-specific tools: "The Scottish Executive aims to use its devolved powers to provide assistance to business to ensure that there is a full portfolio of schemes targeted on specific Scottish problems and tailored to individual circumstances, thereby complementing UK-wide schemes with support measures that particularly reflect the Scottish circumstances" (Scotland 2000b, 23).

These were initiatives of a newly established government "under public pressure to prove itself" and eager to use its new powers and resources to promote policy asymmetry (Taylor and Raines 2001, 28). Yet, the clusters strategy was in fact more than five years in the making. The eight key clusters defined in this strategy – food and drink, biotechnologies, semiconductors, oil and gas, optoelectronics, tourism, forestry, and creative industries – had been identified as early as 1993 by Michael E. Porter's consulting firm, Monitor, commissioned by SE in the wake of the first BBRS (Botham and Downes 1999; Learmonth et al. 2003; Rosiello 2004). Clustering was thus heavily subsidized from the onset, with over £360 million earmarked for the first five years (Taylor and Raines 2001, 14). This represented almost 25% of SE/HIE total contributions to business financing and sponsoring from 1999–2004. Additional Scottish Executive grants and R&D support schemes (Scotland 2000b, 28, 33, 38; Scotland 2008c), aside from new SE-led and LINC-led VC programs, were soon launched as well.

Strategic policymaking in a VC bubble

Devolution took place in the very particular context of the late-1990s dot.com bubble, with VC investments climbing sharply and increasingly targeting very early-stage, high-tech start-ups (Gompers et al. 2008; Lockett, Murray, and White 2002). The scale of the UK's VC boom was impressive: while the entire industry had invested around £1 billion in 1995, it invested over £8 billion in 2000. Much of this bubble was triggered by early-stage investments, multiplied by 575% over the same period (Mason and Harrison 2001, 663). Scotland's businesses clearly benefited from this boom: private VC and equity investments in Scotland soared from a total of £110 million in 1995 to almost £450 million in 2001 (BVCA 1999, 2005). While Scottish businesses were receiving larger amounts of private VC and equity, however, Scotland was losing ground, in relative terms, to South East England (graph 4.6).

As amounts invested in Scotland were climbing, the proportion of Scottish businesses receiving private VC or equity investments was declining, because South East England was reaping an increasingly large share of the smaller – and thus more numerous – early-stage

Graph 4.6. Private VC/private equity investees per 1,000 registered businesses, Scotland vs. UK, 1998–2004

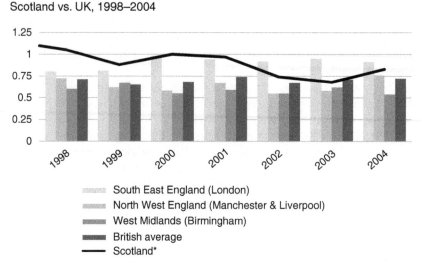

Sources: BVCA (1999–2005), reports on investment activity.

investments. From 1997 to 2000, early-stage VC and private equity investments in South East England rose from £67 million to £414 million, a growth of 525%; over the same period, this growth was "only" 150% in Scotland (BVCA 2005, 74). Between 1998 and 2002, accordingly, South East England increased its share of private VC and equity investments in the ICT sector from 34% to 60%, while Scotland's share dropped from 20% to 4% (by value; BVCA 2005, 77, 81).

If the momentum garnered by Scotland's VC and private equity industry since the early 1990s was thus accentuated by the dot.com bubble, it was lost during the subsequent burst, in 2001–2, as South East England and especially London attracted an growing share of this industry in the UK. This, however, was only part of the picture. Since 1990, Scotland's private VC and equity had been increasingly supplemented by public, hybrid, and angel investment tools, which supported the VC ecosystem during the early-2000s. According to figures compiled by SE (Don and Harrison 2006, 41), 2002 was the only year in which early-stage VC investments receded in Scotland, as annual increases in both the numbers of investee businesses and amounts invested were recorded in 2000, 2001, 2003, and 2004 (graphs 4.7 & 4.8). Accounting only for private and institutional investors, thus, Scotland did lose a lot of ground to South East England in the early 2000s. By adding public,

Graph 4.7. Total number of early-stage VC investments in Scotland, 2000–2004, including foreign, private, institutional, public, hybrid, and angel investors

Number of companies

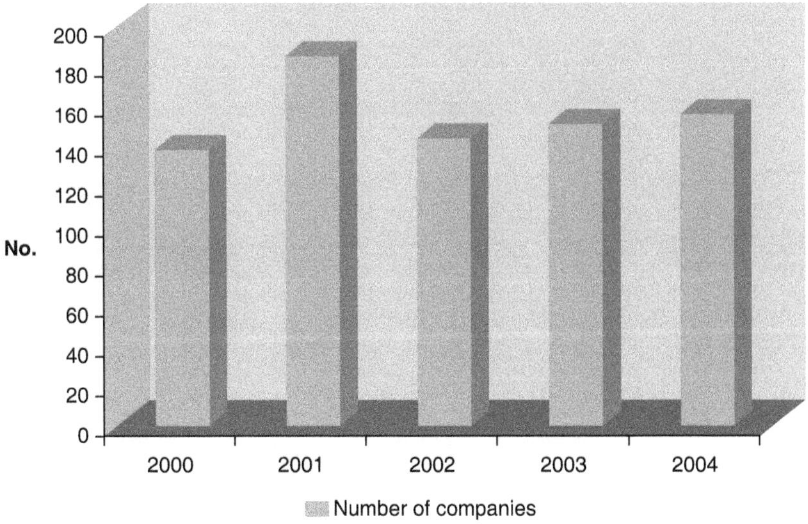

Source: Don and Harrison (2006, 41).

hybrid, and angel investments to the equation, however, a much different picture emerges.

By the turn of the century, Scotland's public sector was involved – either directly through public funds or indirectly through hybrid funds – in 50% of all VC deals made in the region annually. In South East England and London, by contrast, public sector presence was estimated at around 20%. By 2004, the same proportions had reached over 70% in Scotland and around 35% in South East England / London (Mason and Pierrakis 2013, 1167). Scotland's public sector was particularly active in early-stage funding rounds and high-tech deals, for which private capital was now increasingly concentrating in London. While private and institutional VCs invested around £130 million in early-stage Scottish ventures between 2000 and 2004 (BVCA 2005, 74), public, hybrid, and angel investors contributed at least five times that amount. In total, over £840 million in VC were thus actually made available to Scotland's early-stage businesses over these five years (Don and Harrison 2006, 71; graph 4.8).

Clearly, public and hybrid investment tools – angels being very common co-investors in hybrid funds – had a significant impact on the Scottish VC market: by 2004, hybrid investors were involved in almost 60%

Graph 4.8. Total value of early-stage VC investments in Scotland, 2000–2004 (£ millions), including foreign, private, institutional, public, hybrid, and angel investors

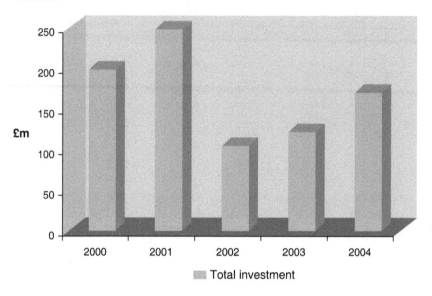

Source: Don and Harrison (2006, 41).

of all early-stage VC deals made in Scotland (graph 4.9), and business angels were providing almost a quarter of all early-stage VC, up from about a fifth in 2000 (Don and Harrison 2006, 72). These three types of investors – public, angel, and hybrid – more than made up for the decline of VCs' role in Scotland's early-stage financing. Looking back, the argument could thus be made that public sector initiatives mostly had counter-cyclical purposes. Yet, while the absolute decline in early-stage, private sector VC really began in 2002, most of these initiatives were in fact launched during the boom between 1999 and 2001 and were thus underpinned by different objectives.

Immediately following Created in Scotland for instance, the Scottish Executive published its first major economic policy statement, the "Framework for Economic Development in Scotland," in which increases in the availability of VC were justified by *faire* and *faire faire* rationales:

In the context of the private sector, the inf uencing agenda [of the Executive] relates to issues in which the Government may feel it has no direct

Graph 4.9. Share of hybrid investments as % of total early-stage VC deals in Scotland, 2000–2004, by number

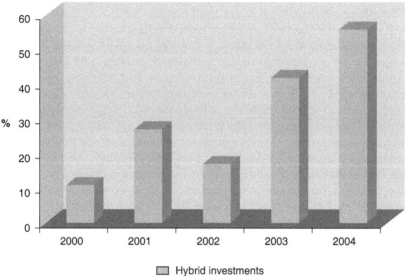

□ Hybrid investments

Source: Don and Harrison (2006, 50).

> policy or expenditure role but, nonetheless, wishes to exhort and catalyse private-sector decision-makers into pursuing particular objectives ... The Executive sees a need more systematically to promote policies and programmes through action-oriented strategic thinking. (Scotland 2000c: xxi)

The £12 million Business Growth Fund (BGF), a collaboration between SE and the Executive, was first devised to accelerate the attainment of business creation objectives. Launched in the summer of 1999, it concentrated on "high growth potential" ventures and complemented angel, STF, and SEP investments by offering loans and equity in the £20,000–£100,000 range (Scotland 2000b, 28). The BGF was also complemented by the expansion of the Business Shop Network in 2000, rebranded as the Small Business Gateway. This publicly-funded service was henceforth to coordinate with central SE and HIE structures – rather than with the LECs – and to focus on seed-stage and start-up stage businesses (O'Hare 2004). Just as LINC provided "matching services" for angels and entrepreneurs, the Small Business Gateway would act as a direct referencing mechanism between young companies and SE/HIE.

Combined with the BGF, it revealed the renewed attention SE/HIE and the Scottish Executive intended to pay high "growth-potential" start-ups (Brown and Mason 2012, 23–5), as well as early-stage businesses' "investment readiness" (Mason and Harrison 2001).

By the end of the 1990s, Scottish policymakers were aware of the fact that, in the context of the dot.com bubble, no "gap" existed in early-stage VC. A vast and growing quantity of private and institutional funds were available to Scottish businesses, and therefore one of the main reasons why Scotland was losing ground relative to other regions of the UK was indeed the lower "attractiveness" of its start-ups. For all kinds of reasons, "many of the businesses which [did] seek VC [were] not *investment ready*. This encompasses all aspects of the business that relate to an investor's perception of its 'investability,' including management team skills, the clarity with which the opportunity is defined, the business model, route to market, governance arrangements and presentation" (Mason and Harrison 2004, 163). Investment readiness was then a big problem in Scotland: by the turn of the century, Scottish VCs sometimes had to return funds to shareholders because of a lack of viable investment opportunities (Mason and Harrison 2004, 162), and LINC members were only able to invest around 10% of their available capital for the same reason (Mason and Harrison 2002b, 2002c).

An important but little-known *faire faire* program was therefore adopted in collaboration with LINC, in order to support businesses that showed potential but were not entirely investment ready. First launched in 1998–9 as the Trial Marriage Scheme, this program was a joint effort of LINC, the SO, the Scottish Executive, and the European Regional Development Fund (ERDF), "created in response to evidence that there was a category of investment opportunities that investors intuitively recognised to have potential (e.g. a good idea, interesting technology, market potential) but required significant additional work to get to the point where they could attract funds" (Mason and Harrison 2004, 166). This scheme was specifically aimed at high-tech start-ups of the "Silicon Glen," and the choice of LINC as a partner reflected this focus on local, "hands-on" investments (Mason and Harrison 2002c).

The whole idea, indeed, was to get angels involved in the management of potential investee companies for several months, something VCs rarely do because of time and cost constraints. Grants of up to £10,000 were thus offered to pay angels working to enhance companies' investment readiness, and if at the end of the process the angels or any other investor decided to invest, the grant then had to be paid back to LINC. The scheme was relatively successful and was relaunched in late 2001 as the Investment Facilitation Grant. Under this revised version, grants reached up to £15,000 and were now equity-convertible: if LINC members decided to invest in a supported company, the grant could be turned into equity and LINC became a shareholder, alongside its own members. Many dozens of grants were distributed through this scheme over the first few years, thereby allowing LINC to build its own small VC portfolio (Mason and Harrison 2004, 169–70).

Beyond investment readiness however, Scotland's slow pace of business creation and high business death rates remained significant problems (Dow and Kirk 2000). The *faire* and *faire faire* approaches implemented through the BGF, Small Business Gateway, and LINC programs were thus complemented by two major *faire avec* tools directly aimed at the advent of a larger number of high-tech R&D spin-offs, and at the provision of follow-on funding for development or expansion-stage SMBs. The first was the next phase of Technology Ventures, launched in January 2000 as Technology Ventures Scotland. The main objectives of the program remained intact but were accompanied by the establishment of the £30 million Proof of Concept Fund in late 1999, a SE-led initiative funding technology licensing, university spin-offs, and seed or start-up stage high-tech ventures. Both Technology Ventures Scotland and its adjoining fund were set up as part of the Scottish Executive's new Science Strategy for Scotland, seeking to "increase the effective exploitation of scientific research to grow strong Scottish businesses" (Scotland 2001, 22).

In August 2000, finally, SDF sold 25% of its SEP shares to private investors, thereby keeping a 25% chunk of the resulting £110 million hybrid co-investment fund rebranded as Scottish Equity Partners Ltd. The objective, according to SE, was to leverage "bigger funds" from private sources that would otherwise not have invested alongside the previous SEP because of its public character (SE 2001, 7; Hood and Paterson 2002, 243). SE's 25% stake allowed it to keep the fund in line with national strategies, however: notably, it would have to focus on technology-intensive, development-stage ventures and on an investment range of over £250,000 to complement public funds and small VCs (Hood 2000, 338–9). As chapter 6 will show, the advent of Scottish Equity Partners marked the development of a new trend in Scotland's VC ecosystem: the multiplication of hybrid co-investment funds devised to complement each other and to ensure coordination between private sector investments and public sector development strategies.

Concluding Remarks

As policy measures of the late 1990s and early 2000s illustrate, devolution indeed gave way to a dynamic "statecraft phase." Between 1999 and 2003, SE and HIE spent a yearly average of £300 million on business

Graph 4.10. Contributions of SE and HIE, 1991–2004 (£ millions)

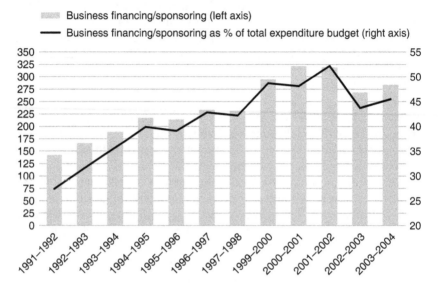

Sources: SE & HIE (1999–2004), annual reports and accounts.

sponsoring and capitalization, as the second phase of the BBRS, the BGF, Small Business Gateway, and Proof of Concept Fund were implemented. Such initiatives monopolized close to 50% of SE/HIE total budgets during these years, up from about 40% for most of the second half of the 1990s (graph 4.10). As with the recentralization and enhanced coordination of local development through the reformed LECs and Local Economic Forums, these were all tools designed to provide "Scottish solutions to Scottish problems" and, in so doing, to enhance the "influencing role" of the new Scottish Executive. The advent of such a statecraft phase after devolution was not particularly surprising: in fact, a careful analysis of the public sector's role in entrepreneurial finance and VC since 1990 proves that such dynamism represented continuity rather than a break with pre-devolution Scotland.

The perceived necessity *of* and ideological preferences *for* policy asymmetry and state intervention already had concrete effects in 1990, as the *political* opposition to the reform of the SDA and HIDB gave way to *institutional* pressures for the preservation of national-level strategic capacities. Without a proper evaluation of the policy roles played by economic nationalism *before* devolution, therefore, one can only attain a partial understanding of major initiatives such as the BBRS and LINC, which had lasting impacts on the Scottish economic model and VC ecosystem.

To say that nationalism underpinned many of the entrepreneurial finance policies implemented in Scotland throughout the 1990s does not mean that market rationales had no role to play: most of the initiatives launched by HIE during these years or even by SE in the early 2000s aimed to counteract the concentration of VC in Edinburgh, Glasgow, or London. Similarly, from the Small Business Loan Scheme to Scottish Equity Partners, the need to leverage private and institutional investments was always present, just like the willingness to mitigate funding gaps for early-stage ventures. In each case, however, such rationales were complemented by political and/or strategic objectives fueled by economic nationalism, without an accurate assessment of which the growing asymmetries between Scotland and the RoUK could hardly be explained. In this regard, Scottish devolution thus represented a symptom rather than a cause.

Chapter Five

Quebec, 2003–2019

By the early 2000s, policymakers were increasingly recognizing that Quebec's entrepreneurial finance ecosystem had to be complemented with investment tools combining *faire faire* and *faire avec* approaches. The high-tech bubble of the late 1990s, the dot.com bust of the early 2000s, and the subsequent economic downturn all drove public investment up, as state-backed funds looked to profit from this bubble and to support businesses struggling to cope with the following burst. This led to significant losses, however, for public investors such as the Innovatech, SGF, and CDPQ. Between 2001 and 2003, the SGF lost over $700 million (SGF 2006, 2) while the CDPQ made negative annual returns (−4.9% in 2001, −9.6% in 2002) and lost billions of dollars in asset devaluations (Pelletier 2009, 290–1, 362, 364). In the context of the PLQ's election in April 2003, this triggered renewed interest for a shift toward *faire faire* and *faire avec*, if not *laissez-faire*.

Such a shift characterized the first PLQ mandate, so that by 2007 the approximate value of state-backed investments as a proportion of Quebec's VC industry had receded to 42%, down from over 70% in 2003 (graph 5.1). The specific way it unfolded, however, with the purposeful mobilization of the government's direct investment tools and tax-advantaged funds, also showed that this shift responded to strategic, national objectives, reinforcing policy asymmetry rather than eroding it. The 2003–7 period, moreover, revealed the resilience of Quebec's model, a testament to the ideological and institutional path dependency dynamics constitutive of economic nationalism. From 2008 onward, the value of state-backed investments stabilized at an average of 47% of Quebec's total, as the province continued to reap a disproportionate (although lately declining) number of deals (graph 5.1).

The 2008–9 crisis and recession also mitigated the trend away from direct government involvement. SGF and IQ investments resumed their

Graph 5.1. Evolution of Quebec's VC industry III, 2003–2018

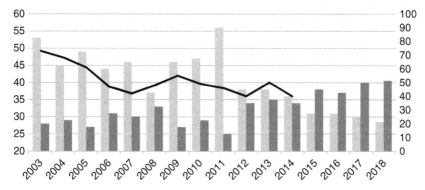

Sources: Macdonalds & Associates Limited (2004–5); Thomson Financial (2006–8); Industry Canada (2008–15); Thomson Reuters (2009–15); CVCA (2015–19).
Notes: Approximate figures. Precise information on investor type for years 2015–18 is unavailable.

upward trajectory after 2007, and the FSTQ and CDPQ were mobilized in 2009 to create Teralys Capital, a $700 million fund of funds combining direct investments and the sponsoring of specialized VCs. This return to direct government involvement after 2007 and the safeguarding of state capacities after 2003 can both be linked to nationalism – perceived needs or preferences for policy asymmetry and public intervention – as much as to institutional path dependency. If a plethora of actors convinced Quebec's government of the persistent necessity of state intervention as early as 2004, the impact of ideological and political variables was also manifest by 2005, notably with the crafting of the PLQ's economic strategy, "L'Avantage québécois" (Québec 2005a).

Quebec therefore maintained its dominant position in Canada's VC industry, attracting between 50% and 70% of all new money raised from 2003 to 2007, and over 48% on average between 2010 and 2015. That was not despite, but by dint of policy initiatives taken *before* the financial crisis, from increased funding of the Centres locaux de développement (CLD) and Fonds locaux d'investissement (FLI) to broadening the investment guidelines for tax-advantaged funds. Important new measures taken *after* 2008 were thus in continuity rather than in break with

Graph 5.2. New VC raised and share (%) of new VC raised, Quebec, 2003–2015 ($ millions)

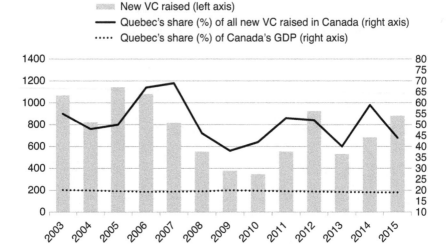

Sources: Macdonalds & Associates Limited (2004–5); Thomson Financial (2006–8); Thomson Reuters (2009–16); CVCA (2015–16); Statistics Canada.

the 2003–7 period. Among these were the sponsoring of the Anges Québec network, the capitalization of various hybrid and private funds, the creation of business succession schemes, and the setting up of many new public funds.

What role did economic nationalism play in this whole process, from the shift toward co-investment funds and specialized VCs to the reaffirmation of state activism? According to Haddow, almost none – given the absence of direct references to ethno-linguistic considerations and the paucity of "interventions that were more 'political' than 'economic,' that is, unlikely to be profitable or to contribute to economic development" (2015, 183). Yet ethno-linguistic and political motivations, such as the mounting concern for local business succession and ownership, can often underpin "economic" ones, as the Relève-PME, Fonds d'investissement pour la relève agricole, and Fonds Relève Québec initiatives would illustrate.

The First Charest Administration (2003–2007)

It was amid growing discontent about significant losses incurred by the CDPQ, IQ, SGF, and FSTQ that the PLQ won the April 2003 election

(Dufour 2003; Sansfaçon 2003; Bérubé 2003, 2004a; Dutrisac 2004; Québec 2005b). Since the late 1990s, this party had been tapping into genuine concerns about the long-term sustainability of public investment activities in the absence of concomitant private investments, concerns which grew with the 2001–2 downturn (Suret 2004). The PLQ denounced the approach of the 1990s as bureaucratic and costly, arguing that Quebec's economic success should not be measured by the number and size of state corporations but by the achievements of entrepreneurs (PLQ 2003, 4).

Despite such severe criticism, transformations made to Quebec's corporate funding ecosystem during the PLQ's first mandate merely amounted to "first order" and "second order" change (Hall 1993, 278–9): the settings of existing policy instruments – i.e., the mandates of public corporations and agencies – as well as the instruments themselves were modified to a certain extent, notably with the shift toward hybrid funds, but the "overall hierarchy of goals behind policy" remained pretty much intact. While there were strategic policy shifts after 2003, no encompassing paradigm shift took place despite the windows of opportunity opened by the 2002–3 capital losses and the election of the PLQ. Policy asymmetry and state intervention continued to be perceived as necessities, with nationalism playing a major role in ensuring continuity.

The "U-curve"

By 2003, private VCs (local and foreign) were still accounting for under 20% of the total value of deals in Quebec, against over 30% for Ontario and over 80% in the US. This dominance of government-backed funds in Quebec's ecosystem, the PLQ and others believed, carried unjustifiable financial risks for the state and distorted markets by (a) subordinating returns on investment to various other objectives, and (b) overcrowding the early-stage niche with capital, thereby leading to smaller deals and a limited capacity for either highly specialized, seed-stage deals or larger, follow-up rounds of investment in expansion-stage businesses (SECOR 2003).

The PLQ's reformist agenda was set out as early as June 2003, in its first budget (Québec 2003c). Among major announcements were the cuts imposed to IQ's FAIRE. The program was phased out in 2004 and replaced by the new Programme d'appui stratégique à l'investissement (PASI), supporting slightly larger projects but endowed with similar objectives: promoting major, strategic, and productivity-enhancing investments from foreign sources, by way of grants, loans, or loan guarantees (Québec 2004a, 14). By 2006–7, interestingly, the PASI was already investing larger amounts ($387 million) than the FAIRE had ($309 million in 2003–4). The year 2002–3 was the exception, as the FAIRE's "governmental mandates" component allocated $625 million before moving down to $95 million in 2005–6 under the PASI, and back up to $165 million in 2006–7 (IQ 2003, 2006, 2007).

This "U-curve" pattern, featuring short-term retrenchment and a subsequent turnaround, also characterized the PLQ's stance toward tax-advantaged funds (Québec 2003d, 70–1, 106–9). Established at $150 million by the PQ, the limit of shares issued in a single fiscal year by CRCD, on which tax credits for subscribers applied, was reduced to $75 million for 2003–4. The FSTQ and FACSN, for which by 2003 no such limit existed, were also imposed respective ceilings of $600 million and $50 million. Yet as much as these restrictions illustrated the PLQ's intention to limit government spending on entrepreneurial finance, they were not overly disruptive: the ceiling imposed on CRCD was temporary and relatively minor given that CRCD's total share capital had already reached $372 million in 2003, only $78 million below the limit of $450 million previously set for 2004 by the PQ (CRCD 2004, 3). As for the FSTQ, the $600 million ceiling was not far removed from what had been levied in previous years: in 2002–3, $725 million in shares had been issued (FSTQ 2007, 1).

These limitations did not represent a long-term trend, moreover. Ceilings on the issuance of FACSN and CRCD shares were quickly brought back up, to $80 million later in 2003 and to $150 million in 2006, respectively. In an effort to support expansion-stage businesses – as part of a strategic objective to increase the average dimension of Quebec's SMBs – the maximum size of companies eligible for these funds' investments was also doubled in 2005, from $50 million in total assets to $100 million (Québec 2005c, 36). FACSN, FSTQ, and CRCD investments therefore all experienced notable growth throughout the PLQ's first mandate: in that order, they soared from $144 to $326, $369 to $668, and $95 to $470 million between 2003 and 2007, a 300% increase on average (FACSN 2004, 2007; FSTQ 2007; CRCD 2007). The government's continued backing *of* and reliance *on* LSIFs and tax-advantaged funds, besides, sharpened policy divergence in Quebec given that Ontario, by contrast, decided to phase out its LSIF tax credits entirely (Cumming and Johan 2010; Johan, Schweizer, and Zhan 2014).

Quebec's VC industry thus actually grew more reliant on the FSTQ, FACSN, and CRCD during the early years of the PLQ administration. A significant portion of the rise in private VC investments in Quebec after 2004 was, for instance, attributable to the sponsoring of specialized VCs by government-backed funds. The FSTQ, FACSN, and CRCD were indeed encouraged, from 2005 onward, to invest some of their capital into hybrid, private, and even foreign VC funds. By 2007, almost 10% of FSTQ investments (by value) were made in specialized VCs like Brightspark (software), Propulsion (software), MSBI (university spin-offs), Novacap (ICT/industrial), Rho (ICT), GeneChem (biotech), and Vimac (ICT) (FSTQ 2007, 24, 62–77).

The "U-curve" pattern that characterized state intervention during this period was also apparent in the case of the CLD and FLI. In December 2003, the PLQ adopted Bill 34, transferring local development responsibilities from the CLD to the Municipalités régionales de comté and filling two-thirds of CLD Boards with local elected officials (Québec 2003e). This represented a shift in management philosophies, from participatory decision-making to political accountability: only the MRC would henceforth coordinate with regional authorities and the provincial government, before effectively outsourcing local development activities – including entrepreneurial finance – to the CLD in accordance with plans devised at the provincial and regional levels (Simard and Leclerc 2008, 620–1). Yet if Bill 34 impacted intergovernmental concertation over economic development, throughout the PLQ's first mandate the CLD budgets were actually increased rather than the opposite. All in all, state intervention in local development thus accelerated between 2004 and 2007,[1] as CLD and FLI budgets rose and funds invested increased significantly (Québec 2009a).

The reform of IQ

Although Bill 34 allowed each MRC to designate a new local entity to act as a CLD, almost none did. There was no logical reason not to continue relying on the existing bodies, which had developed deep ties with local businesses, financial institutions, and other funds from the SOLIDE to the FSTQ, and from credit unions to CRCD (Québec 2009a, 3). Similar path dependency dynamics help uncover why even significant transformations to the ecosystem after 2003 – the shift toward hybrid co-investment funds and the rise of private and foreign investments – in fact concealed overall continuity in public involvement in VC. Policies devised in the wake of large consultations held in 2003–4 by the Quebec National Assembly's Commission des finances publiques attest to that particularly well.

The first consultation was held in September 2003, and dealt with the "orientations, activities, and management" of IQ (Québec 2003g, 2003h, 2003i). Major players who submitted briefs included IQ itself, the FSTQ (2003), FACSN (2003), Association des centres locaux de développement du Québec (ACLDQ 2003), and Canadian Federation of Independent Business (CFIB). The PLQ advocated for two reforms of the IQ model: it should henceforth be self-funding and focus on loans and guarantees, with most grants allocated and managed instead by the Ministère du Développement économique, de l'Innovation et des Exportations (MDEIE). The PQ opposition, as well as the FSTQ, worried that the self-funding requirement would force IQ to neglect economic development objectives. But as Jean Houde, nominated as CEO of IQ in 2003, remarked, the government only required IQ to break even and that could hardly affect its mandates (Québec 2003g). In fact, IQ was even able to reach that objective three years earlier than requested, in 2005–6, precisely as investments reached their second highest point ever at $1.2 billion (IQ 2006, 10).

The demand for an enhanced focus on loans and guarantees, in turn, partly stemmed from a strategic issue of policy autonomy, with the CFIB highlighting that many of Quebec's banks and SMBs were contracting deals through the federal Small Business Loans program rather than through IQ, because of bureaucratic complexities and delays (Québec 2003f). Yet, after having heard the FSTQ, ACLDQ, and IQ argue that since 1998 grants had been one of IQ's major strategic tools for attracting of foreign investments, the government decided not to change the existing model, leaving the prerogative for the allocation of most grants to the MDEIE but their administration to IQ. Aside from the Financière du Québec subsidiary being merged back into the main IQ structure to ensure better coordination between investment prospection and financial aid, not much changed: by 2006–7, as was the case in 2003–4, around 80% of the value of IQ financings consisted of loans, equity loans, and guarantees, against 20% for grants (IQ 2004, 2007).

Further, the nationalist aspects of IQ's prospection activities should not be overlooked. As explained by IQ prospectors,[2] the availability of grants and other types of financial aid allows Quebec to compete for FDI against other jurisdictions. In addition, IQ almost never gets involved in foreign companies' merger or acquisition projects, to avoid supporting setbacks in the ownership structure of Quebec's economy. However, when such mergers or acquisitions are done deals, IQ can get involved to make sure local jobs are safeguarded or even added to. Moreover, before supporting FDI projects in key sectors, IQ consults with major businesses present in those sectors to ensure such projects complete their supply and value chains rather than competing with existing local SMBs. The safeguarding and refinement of much of IQ's mandates after 2003, despite the PLQ's critical stance since 1998, thus had much to do with perceived needs and preferences for state involvement, as voiced notably by the FSTQ, ACLDQ, and IQ itself.

Consistent with such perceived needs and preferences was the introduction of IQ's Relève-PME program in 2005, as part of the government's economic development strategy, L'Avantage québécois. Depicting Quebec's large proportion of SMBs as a comparative advantage because of their local ownership, the government argued that the sponsoring of business succession was warranted to alleviate the effects of demographic aging and avoid closures or foreign takeovers (Québec 2005a, 49). Through Relève-PME, IQ would allocate, yearly, around \$15 million[3] in additional loans and guarantees to finance SMB acquisitions by local interests (IQ 2006, 2007). Overall, the total contributions of IQ remained, throughout the first PLQ mandate, comparable to those of the 1998–2003 period (IQ 2004–7). IQ would moreover be mobilized, from 2004 onward, as a pivotal player in the government's strategic shift toward *faire faire* and *faire avec* approaches.

The "Rapport Brunet"

A second large-scale consultation was launched by the Commission des finances publiques in early 2004, following the report of the Taskforce on the role of the Quebec state in risk capital. The "Rapport Brunet" concluded that public VC funds were too numerous and costly, and were leaving (if not creating) funding gaps at seed and expansion stages in very high-tech sectors because of an excessive focus on early-stage SMBs and a lack of specialized sectoral expertise (Québec 2003b, 5–6). Based on the overarching objective of making state intervention "targeted and complementary" rather than "preponderant," the report made several specific recommendations.

Among those were to (a) privatize the *Innovatechs* and replace them with a hybrid VC fund specializing in high technology; (b) refocus the SGF on large-scale investments of over \$20 million and limit its control of companies to 30% of shares; (c) create a hybrid VC fund for seed and start-up stage ventures, in which one public dollar would be invested for each two from private sources (1:2); and (d) constitute regionally-managed VC funds through which the government would invest on a 2:1 basis with private partners (Québec 2003b, 7–9). The report, in a word, focused on "leverage" (Québec 2003b, 15). Its argument, however, differed from classic ones: stimulating private and foreign investments was presented as a way to fill gaps left open by government-backed funds, instead of the other way around.

This was because the taskforce recognized both the "undeniable relevance" of state intervention and the necessity to "adapt leveraging models to Quebec's institutional context," characterized by a well-developed and coordinated ecosystem heavily reliant on such intervention (Québec 2003b, 15, 51). Reactions to the report were particularly revealing in that regard: while the PQ opposition and some of the press perceived it as advocating massive state retrenchment (Québec 2004b, 2004c, 2004d, 2004e; Dutrisac 2003; Bérubé 2004b; Le Devoir 2004), influential financial experts most critical of the "Quebec model" concluded that it would hardly scale back the government's relative weight in the VC industry (Suret 2004, 17). The very numerous briefs submitted to the Commission, and in particular those of Réseau Capital (2004) and the government's own Conseil de la science et de la technologie (2004), also warned that private and foreign funds were far from ready to substitute themselves for state-backed ones.

Réseau Capital, for instance, whose double mandate is to represent Quebec's ecosystem and make sure its funding chains are complete and efficient,[4] stated that reaching an objective of twelve specialized VCs operating in Quebec by 2010 would require a minimum of $350 million in additional yearly investments by public and tax-advantaged funds (2004, 19). Accordingly, the government's move toward *faire faire*, through the sponsoring of specialized VCs, and *faire avec*, through the establishment of hybrid co-investment funds, hardly rolled back state intervention. This was because of (a) *institutional path dependency*, as state-backed funds were almost the only tools at the government's disposal; (b) *political imperatives*, as most of the major players in Quebec's ecosystem opposed drastic state retrenchment; and (c) *ideological preferences*, as public intervention was considered an efficient way to steer highly specialized VCs toward strategic investment sectors, regions, and deal sizes. As confirmed by an FSTQ official,[5] referring to the coordinated capitalization of private and hybrid funds, *"le rapport Brunet était un point de départ. Brunet disait qu'il y avait un manque de cohésion et de taille. Sans cette concertation, sans cet alignement des intérêts entre les institutionnels et les gens qui étaient prêts à s'investir dans des fonds privés, on ne serait probablement jamais arrivé à quoi que ce soit de tangible."*[6]

One major move toward state retrenchment, however, was the modification of SGF mandates, which resulted in a drop of annual investments but safeguarded existing portfolio assets despite the losses of the 2002–4 period (SGF 2000, 2006, 2008). A second was the privatization of the SIGM in late 2004 and the transformation of the SIRR into a limited partnership fund, Desjardins-Innovatech, in which the government would hold 47% of shares and CRCD the other 53%. Desjardins-Innovatech would keep its focus on Quebec's "régions-ressources" and specialize in seed-to-start-up stage high-technology ventures (CRCD 2006, 6). The formation of such a hybrid fund opened the door for the other Innovatechs: between 2008 and 2012, the SISQ and SIQCA transferred most of their own portfolio to Desjardins-Innovatech in exchange for shares (SISQ 2015; SIQCA 2015).

The second major shift following the Rapport Brunet was toward *faire avec*, with the establishment of the $300 million Fonds d'intervention économique régional (FIER) through a new IQ subsidiary, IQ-FIER, in early 2005 (Québec 2009b). This new program would have three branches, each composed of hybrid co-investment funds: the $42 million FIER-Soutien, the $78 million FIER-Régions, and the $180 million FIER-Partenaires. Via the FIER-Soutien and FIER-Régions, the government would invest on a 2:1 basis alongside private partners through regional funds. The FIER-Régions, aimed at boosting the provision of locally embedded VC, was ambitious: by 2007, its capitalization by the government had reached over $180 million and 28 funds – of $10 million each on average – had been set up, for a total of $274 million under management. Each of these funds had to devote, yearly, at least 50% of investments to its assigned region, and deals were generally limited to $1 million for up to 49% of shares in start-up stage, succession stage, or struggling businesses (Québec 2009b).

FIER-Partenaires, in turn, was designed as a tool combining *faire avec* and *faire faire* approaches. Contributing $90 million, Quebec's government "asked" the FSTQ ($50 million), FACSN (15$ million), and CRCD ($25 million) to chip in and form a $180 million hybrid fund.[7] $100 million would be dedicated to direct investments in strategic, "structuring" projects, and the other $80 million to the sponsoring of foreign and specialized VCs alongside private partners, on a 1:2 basis. By early 2007, FIER-Partenaires had committed $140 million through ten sectoral VCs, including Garage Technology Ventures from Silicon Valley (IQ 2007, 29). IQ and the CDPQ were henceforth also encouraged to invest a part of their capital through specialized VCs, in concordance with the government's sectoral priorities in aerospace, ICT, biotechnologies, and manufacturing. This shift was fairly well received by government-backed investors, given that seed or start-up stage investments in such sectors required increasingly specialized expertise.[8] It would therefore complement, rather than jeopardize, these funds' direct investment strategies.

The CDPQ embraced this approach early on. In 2006, it devoted $100 million to set up the Fonds manufacturier québécois (FMQ), a specialized fund investing, with or without private partners, in Quebec's expansion-stage manufacturing SMBs (CDPQ 2007). By 2007 moreover, the CDPQ (2008, 156–7) had committed close to $250 million in special-ized VCs such as GoCapital (start-ups), iNovia (start-ups), AgeChem (biotech), CTI (life sciences), JLA Ventures (ICT), ProQuest (biotech), and VantagePoint (cleantech). As for tax-advantaged funds, CRCD, FACSN, and FSTQ placements in private VCs would from then on be accounted as part of their 60% annual local investments requirement, provided that those VCs invested 100% of the amounts received in eli-gible Quebec businesses (Québec 2006b, Section 6:26).

The shift toward *faire avec* and *faire faire* should therefore not be con-fused with state retrenchment. The relative importance of private and foreign investments in Quebec's VC ecosystem did increase substan-tially from 2003 to 2007: yearly private investments grew from $49 to $96 million, and foreign ones from $49 to $210 million (Macdonald & Associates 2004; Thomson Financial 2008). Considering, however, the rapid and significant development of indirect investment activi-ties by the CDPQ, FSTQ, FACSN, CRCD, and IQ, this was – just as many had warned it would have to be – an almost entirely state-backed process, promoted for strategic reasons, rather than a market-driven phenomenon.

The Second and Third Charest Administrations (2007–2012)

This shift was, however, challenged by the financial crisis, recession, and long recovery process that marked the second (2007–8) and third (2008–12) mandates of the PLQ. The government notably turned back to a more direct investment strategy during and after the crisis, with "Liberal interventionism reaching its apogee" (Haddow 2015, 179). Counter-cyclical activism would of course be a rational explanation for this development. A closer look at the initiatives taken from 2007 onward, however, reveals that many of the most important justifica-tions originated from other concerns, such as the meteoric rise of the Canadian dollar in 2006–7, or from policy statements and action plans devised *before* the crisis, going back as far as 2005.

Development strategies and the Anges Québec network

The first budget of the second PLQ mandate was published in May 2007, months before the American subprime mortgage crisis began to spread. It gave substance to three national strategies: the Stratégie de développement de l'industrie aéronautique québécoise (July 2006) and the Stratégie québécoise de la recherche et de l'innovation (December 2006), both constitutive of L'Avantage québécois (Québec 2005a), as well

Graph 5.3. Provincial government R&D spending, Quebec vs. Ontario, 2003–2016 ($ millions)

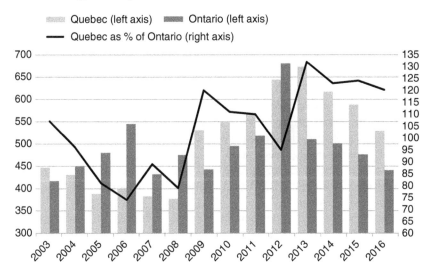

Source: Statistics Canada (n.d.b).

as the Plan d'action en faveur du secteur manufacturier (November 2007). The objectives set out in these strategies remained key motives for the launch of many initiatives after 2008, such as the capitalization of specialized VCs, government support to business "angels," and the establishment of new public and hybrid funds.

L'Avantage québécois was devised to build on Quebec's "comparative advantages," including its "concertation" and "clustering" traditions, its high public R&D spending levels (graph 5.3), and its leadership in sectors such as aerospace, biotechnologies, ICT, and green technologies. Furthering the "competitive position" of Quebec's businesses in these sectors was presented as a key objective, for which "the financial tools of the government and state corporations should be used" (Québec 2005a, 65). Two sectoral strategies were thus published in parallel in the second part of 2006: one for the aerospace industry, involving substantial increases in governmental and SGF equity investments (Québec 2006c, 30–1), and another for R&D spin-offs, which set out various funding initiatives such as the capitalization of two $100 million VC funds – CTI (life sciences) and Go Capital (ICT/greentech) – in partnership with the CDPQ, FSTQ, Desjardins, and FIER-Partenaires.

The capitalization of R&D spin-offs also led the government to deplore the lack of a strong base of angel investors in Quebec, as angels were deemed central to the success of R&D commercialization (Québec 2006a, 51). This justified the subsidization of the centralized Anges Québec network in 2008, as part of a new manufacturing action plan (2007c, 24). This was a patent case of policy divergence: not only would Anges Québec receive millions in public subsidies between 2008 and 2015 but, in contrast with Ontario where more than a dozen regional angel groups operate in parallel, it was set up as a peak organization, centralizing and coordinating angel investment in Quebec. Government support thus had a clear economic purpose: unlike most VCs, angels typically invest in high-risk, seed or start-up stage ventures, adopting a "hands-on" approach and providing mentoring services to investees. According to Quebec's R&D and manufacturing strategies, this was exactly what was needed.

This support also had nationalist strategic purposes. Promoting angel investment is a good way to ensure private VC benefits local businesses, because angels are known to engage in "proximity capital," investing in businesses located relatively close to their workplace (Crevoisier 1997; Mason and Botelho 2014; Mason and Harrison 1995, 2002a; Paul, Whittam, and Johnston 2003; Paul and Whittam 2010). As corroborated by Anges Québec's President François Gilbert, the establishment of a centralized organization also made it easier for Quebec's government to ensure the coordination of angel activities with its own economic strategies.[9] That is because business angels are also known to be good co-investment partners for VCs and institutional funds, given their specialized expertise but limited financial capabilities. This was to be demonstrated by the government capitalizing, in 2008 and 2009, many seed-stage co-investment funds to work alongside Quebec's angels.

Specialized funds, Teralys, CCPME, and the FIRA

If, on the one hand, the 2007 manufacturing strategy presented state support to angels as a good way to help small exporters cope with a rapidly rising Canadian dollar (Québec 2007, 20–4), it also made clear that Quebec had to take advantage of a strong dollar by boosting investment in capital-intensive sectors, such as green technologies. It was therefore announced that IQ would invest $25 million in a limited partnership fund specializing in clean technologies, "to establish Quebec's position within the new low carbon economy emerging in Europe, northeastern US, and California" (Québec 2007, 42). Administered by Cycle Capital Management, this new fund – Fonds Cycle

Capital I – reached a capitalization of $80 million by early 2009 with contributions from the FSTQ, FACSN, and CDPQ. The establishment of such a specialized fund also became one of the centerpieces of yet another national strategy, the Stratégie de développement de l'industrie québécoise de l'environnement et des technologies vertes.

Cycle Capital I would indeed be part of a "vision" for a new, greener Quebec: "*Que le Québec devienne le leader canadien de l'industrie de l'environnement et des technologies vertes et que cette industrie contribue à l'image de marque du Québec sur la scène internationale*" (Québec 2008, 13).[10] This could have been relegated to the proverbial policy "back burner" with the financial crisis quickly erupting in September 2008, but in fact the counter-cyclical budgets tabled from 2009 onward introduced new tools to secure the implementation of the strategies adopted since 2005. In its pre-budget submission to the government in February 2009, Réseau Capital recommended the adoption of "structuring" measures in addition to counter-cyclical ones, so that the efforts made to refine Quebec's VC industry and, especially, to reinforce seed and start-up stages' financing ecosystems would not have been in vain:

> *Au-delà des problèmes immédiats, la crise actuelle risque donc d'annihiler le cadre mis en place par le gouvernement et les efforts consentis par l'ensemble des joueurs pour créer une industrie locale de fonds de démarrage d'entreprises technologiques … L'étranglement financier actuel menace (i) la survie des entreprises technologiques et celle des fonds de capital de risque technologique qui les financent, (ii) l'ancrage au Québec de l'expertise et de la richesse technologique générées par les générations successives d'entreprises technologiques financées depuis une quinzaine d'années, (iii) la capacité de valoriser au Québec les montants investis en R&D depuis des années … Si la chaîne s'interrompt, les talents vont se replacer, éventuellement hors du Québec.*[11] (Réseau Capital 2009, 4–5)

Many counter-cyclical measures were also launched as part of the 2009–10 budget: a billion dollars in additional investment funds were allocated to the SGF; $1.2 billion was injected in IQ's new Renfort program of subsidies, loans, and guarantees; a $500 million "emergency fund" for large businesses was capitalized by the FSTQ and SGF; and close to $100 million was added to the FIER-Régions and FACSN (Québec 2009c, Section F). Yet even in the midst of the recession, this budget also introduced four major initiatives directly informed by strategic national objectives established *before* the crisis.

Three new specialized VC funds were first set up as limited partnerships between IQ, FIER-Partenaires, the FSTQ, and private investors. Each was capitalized with around $42 million, with the "exclusive mission" to fund seed-stage companies "based in Quebec" and operating in "strategic" sectors: FounderFuel Ventures would concentrate on ICT, AmorChem on life sciences, and Cycle-C3E Capital on green technologies (Québec 2009c, F91). The fourth initiative, closely related to these funds, was the creation of Canada's largest hybrid "fund of funds," Teralys Capital, with the objective of capitalizing up to twenty new specialized VCs in the three abovementioned sectors. Teralys brought Quebec's *faire faire* approach to a new level: no less than $700 million were put into that fund of funds by IQ ($200 million), the CDPQ ($250 million), and FSTQ ($250 million), and its managers were specifically mandated to establish formal links with FounderFuel, AmorChem, and Cycle-C3E "to ensure consistency and coherence within Quebec's high tech funding chain" (Québec 2009c, F95).

The scale of such public sponsorship allowed Quebec's government to impose clear conditions on Teralys: "It will invest 75% of its capitalization in Québec and Canadian sector-based venture capital funds, where the latter undertake to invest in Québec. The fund's investments will target existing and emerging niches of excellence in technology in Québec" (Québec 2009c, F92). Interestingly, Teralys was launched only months after the establishment of the Ontario Venture Capital Fund (OVCF), a $205 million fund of funds notably capitalized by OMERS, the Business Development Bank of Canada (BDC), and the Ontario government. Policy emulation and nationalist competition was thus also part of the rationale behind the establishment of Teralys. The original intention was for Teralys to reach a capitalization of $825 million, with an additional $125 million coming from private partners. But even without this supplementary contribution, the government decided to go forward with a $700 million fund because of its strategic advantages. As confirmed by FSTQ and IQ officials, an important underlying motive was to promote concertation and complementarity between the indirect investment activities of the FSTQ, CDPQ, and IQ:[12]

> *Pré-création de Teralys, tout le monde faisait à peu près n'importe quoi. Il n'y avait pas de concertation, de complémentarité. C'était chacun pour soi, puis de temps en temps on pouvait s'allier mais c'était pour des raisons plus personnelles. Ce n'était pas concerté. C'est ce manque, justement, de concertation qui a mené à la création de Teralys. On s'est dit: si on veut que le Québec se distingue, créons un regroupement qui aura les compétences pour faire les bons choix et mettons en place une stratégie qui pourrait être pérenne.[13]*

Such concertation and complementarity became a key aim of the government coming out of the recession. The first recovery budget, in March 2010, announced a "concertation table" regrouping major actors from the financial sector, dedicated to Quebec's "financial specializations" such as VC and investment capital. This initiative gave birth to Finance Montréal, a concertational and promotional body of which IQ, FSTQ, CRCD, FACSN, and CDPQ representatives became prominent members. The perceived need for such enhanced concertation (and policy asymmetry) emerged from two further comparisons with Ontario.

First, the Toronto Financial Services Alliance, a similar body, had just launched a strategy to expand Toronto's leading role in the Canadian financial sector (Québec 2010a, 194). Second, it was realized that Quebec's annual "business birth rate" had been declining relative to Ontario's since the early 1990s. As a result, the proportion of Ontario citizens self-employed or owning a business (14.1%) was now double that of Quebec (Québec 2010a, 183–4). After Teralys in 2009, two state-sponsored initiatives thus sprung from the 2010–11 budget that were prime examples of concertation. One was a $600 million investment fund capitalized equally by the CDPQ and CRCD: Capital Croissance PME (CCPME). CCPME would issue loans and make equity investments from $100,000 to over $5 million in early-to-expansion and even succession stage SMBs (Québec 2010a, 179–80). While CRCD needed additional resources to expand its activities, the CDPQ needed Desjardins's deep regional roots to maximize the impacts of its investments,[14] and Quebec's government needed this sort of involvement from institutional players to complement its own initiatives.

The second major announcement was the creation of the FIRA (Québec 2010a, 185–7). This $75 million fund, sponsored by the FA, CRCD, and FSTQ ($25 million each), was put in place at the demand of the government to offset population aging in the farming industry and land grabbing by foreign speculators.[15] FIRA investments were thus restricted to young applicants (18–39 years old) seeking either to start, expand, or buy into agricultural businesses. The FIRA would issue loans, buy equity, or even lease land to farmers and entrepreneurs, thereby extending the activities of the FA. Like CCPME, the FIRA was a concrete example of the strategic concertation and complementarity Quebec's government was calling for. It was also the sign of a renewed interest for business succession in Quebec, a recurrent concern for a government seeking to safeguard the province's corporate ownership structure.

The new IQ, the FRQ, and Anges Québec Capital

The economic recovery process set in motion in 2010 provided the background for an important institutional change. In late October of that year, the PLQ introduced Bill 123, merging IQ and the SGF (Québec 2010b). The arguments used to justify the SGF-IQ "amalgamation" once again referred to the perceived need for enhanced synergy within Quebec's entrepreneurial finance ecosystem. Potential economies of scale deriving from the merger were also part of the picture, but such was not the main motivation. The crucial motives of the government were, instead, fivefold and closely mirrored the arguments of key economic organizations having submitted briefs as part of the consultations (Québec 2010c).

First, the new IQ would provide a "one-stop-shop" for Quebec businesses, an important step applauded by the Fédération des chambres de commerce du Québec (FCCQ 2010). This would not only be advantageous for investees, but also for IQ itself: as per André Petit-clerc, previously responsible for the ICT division at the SGF and now head of "small capitalizations and investments" at IQ, the integration of a body specialized in equity to IQ's structure allowed for a much better coordination and streamlining of banking (loans & guarantees) and investment (VC & equity) activities (personal interview). A second justification for the new IQ rested on the fact that it would constitute a provincial counterpart to the BDC and its subsidiary BDC Capital, established in 2006. The third major argument was therefore that the new IQ would allow for improved complementarity between public, private, and institutional financial products, something the Conseil du patronat du Québec considered essential (CPQ 2010).

Through IQ's many branches outside of Montreal, besides, regional SMBs would now have a more direct access to equity, a very important improvement according to the Canadian Federation of Independent Business (FCEI 2010). Finally, the government, FSTQ, and Manufacturiers et Exportateurs du Québec all argued the new IQ would allow for a much-improved alignment between business capitalization and the state's economic development strategies (MEQ 2010; FSTQ 2010). Following the merger, IQ would no longer function on the basis of particular funding programs, but adopt a sectoral approach directly informed by governmental strategies and priorities. As stated in IQ's 2011–13 strategic plan (IQ 2011, 4),

> *l'intervention de la Société au niveau du capital de risque sera concertée et tiendra compte des orientations des ministères à vocation économique … de manière à cibler les secteurs définis comme prioritaires par le gouvernement et à y intervenir. L'action concertée des ministères et de la Société constituera une force de frappe peu commune et bénéficiera à l'économie du Québec.*[16]

Graph 5.4. Contributions of the SGF, 2003–2010 ($ millions)

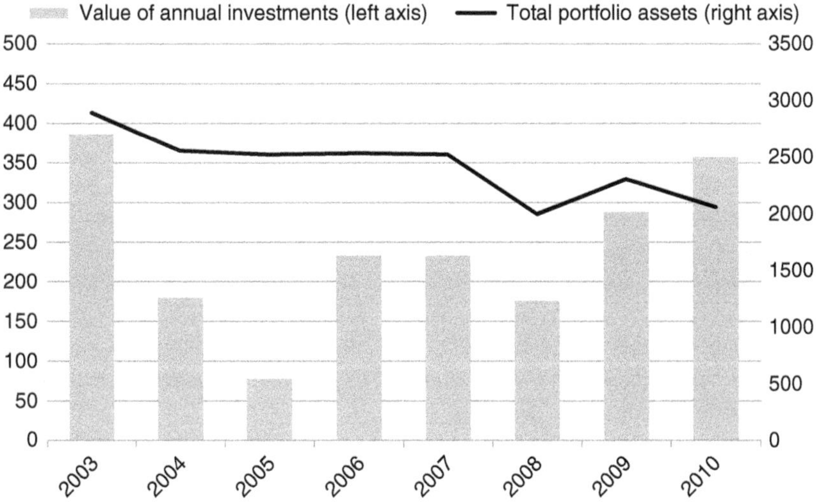

Sources: SGF (2000–11).

The SGF-IQ merger should not, therefore, be interpreted as motivated by disdain for the SGF. In fact, this initiative took place after years of increasing SGF investments (graph 5.4). By 2010, at over $350 million, SGF investments had attained some of their pre-2003 levels. It should not be interpreted, either, as a willingness to "depoliticize" the investment activities of public bodies. Instead, Bill 123 clarified the fact that IQ's mission was not merely to act on market opportunities, but to help carry out state-defined strategies:

> The mission of the Company is to contribute to the economic development of Quebec in accordance with the economic policy of the government ... In order to carry out its mission, the Company supports the creation and development of enterprises of all sizes through adapted f nancial solutions and investments, in a complementary fashion with its partners. In accordance with the mandate it is given by the government, the company conducts foreign investment prospecting and carries out strategic interventions. (Québec 2010b, 5–6)

The allusion to "strategic interventions" notably referred to the establishment of the Fonds du développement économique (FDÉ), a

MDEIE-IQ jointly managed fund dedicated to "political calls," i.e., to funding decisions taken by the government itself:[17]

> *Avec la mise en place du Fonds, le gouvernement affirme son leadership en mat-*
> *ière de développement économique, d'accompagnement des entreprises, ainsi que*
> *dans la coordination des intervenants en matière de prospection d'investissements*
> *étrangers … Les interventions réalisées à travers les programmes d'aide financière*
> *et autres mandats gérés dans le Fonds seront structurantes et devront générer*
> *des retombées économiques importantes pour le Québec. Toutefois le risque asso-*
> *cié à ces interventions, généralement plus élevé que celui encouru dans le cadre*
> *des activités régulières d'IQ, sera endossé par le gouvernement. Le gouvernement*
> *assume ce risque compte tenu des impacts associés à ces projets, en termes de*
> *création d'emploi, de développement local, de création de niches d'excellence,*
> *de restructuration d'entreprise et de développement de nouveaux marchés*
> *d'exportation.*[18] (Québec 2011a, 17–18)

Not only did the government establish, with this new IQ, a more complete public financing tool, aligned with its sectoral priorities and benefiting from a reinforced expertise in equity, but it also gave itself, with the FDÉ, a vehicle allowing for the extensive funding of politically-defined economic development initiatives (see graph 5.5). The FDÉ received renewed attention after the 2015–16 investment in Bombardier Aéronautique's "CSeries" venture, but it was actually very active from its inception. In 2011–12, $365 million was invested through the FDÉ on the sole basis of "government mandates." Two examples of such investments are worth mentioning here: the creation of the Fonds Relève Québec (FRQ) in 2011, and that of Anges Québec Capital (AQC) in early 2012.

A study on the "renewal of entrepreneurship" released by the MDEIE in October 2010 (Québec 2010d), as well as subsequent consultations on a new "entrepreneurial strategy" (Québec 2011b) gave way to an "entrepreneurial forum" in the spring of 2011 and, finally, to the publication of the "Stratégie québécoise de l'entrepreneuriat" in November (Québec 2011c). Throughout this process, key concerns were raised about Quebec's "entrepreneurial culture," seen to be fading. This conclusion rested on a comparison with Ontario and the RoC, which showed that Quebec still had significantly lower rates of business birth and survival, as well as a lower potential for entrepreneurial renewal because of demographic aging (Québec 2011c, 9). To catch up with Ontario and the RoC, two main targets were set for 2020 (Québec 2011c, 15): (a) to increase the number of business owners in Quebec by 20,000 and the number of Québécois having "entrepreneurial intentions" by 140,000;

Graph 5.5. Contributions of IQ/FDE, 2007–2019 ($ millions)

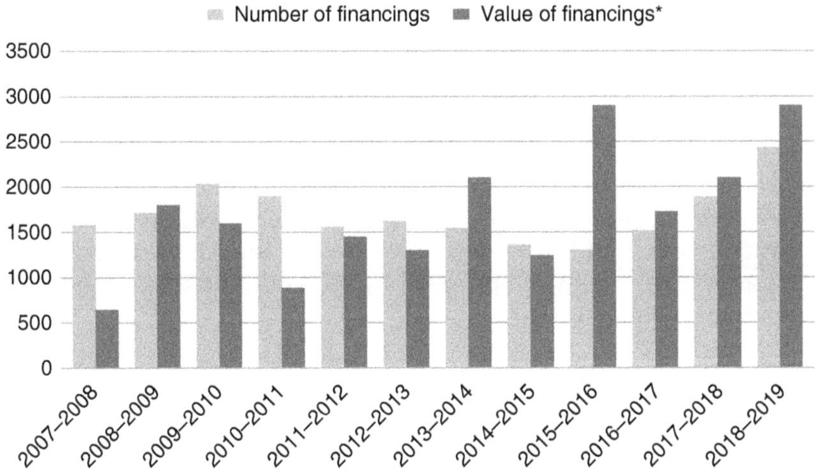

Sources: IQ (2008–19), annual reports.
* These figures include occasional overlaps between IQ and FDE investments but exclude all FIER investments.

and (b) to drive up the one-year survival rate of SMBs by 7.5% and to reach a success rate of 75% for business transfers, measured by the three-year survival rate of transferred businesses.

The first major initiative launched for these purposes was the $50 million FRQ, a partnership between the FDÉ ($20 million), CRCD, FSTQ, and FACSN ($10 million each). Managed by IQ, the FRQ's interventions would take the form of preferential loans, loan guarantees, or equity investments and would hopefully lead to between 330 and 500 successful business transfers over the next twelve years (Québec 2011d, E85–E87). Apart from the nationalist underpinnings of this concern for local business succession, which mainly rested on a fear of closures and foreign acquisitions, the partnership with the three tax-advantaged funds was strategic, banking on their expertise in the cooperative sector and, in the case of CRCD, in business transfers as well. Besides, not only would all FRQ investees have to be wholly based in Quebec, but the advent of the FRQ itself reinforced policy divergence with Ontario, where no such public or even government-backed support is offered except through the federal BDC.

The second major policy launched in the wake of Quebec's entrepreneurial strategy was the capitalization of the $30 million AQC in

April 2012, a partnership between the FDÉ ($20 million) and Anges Québec ($10 million). This new fund, first, would maximize the angels' capacity to provide larger investments, follow-up investments, patient capital, and mentoring.[19] Secondly, such a hybrid fund would "contribute to a better structuration of angel investors' activities in Quebec" (Québec 2011d, E80). This meant the contribution of the FDÉ would help ensure enhanced compatibility between angels' investments and the government's economic priorities. That is why it was established that AQC would specialize in seed-to-early-stage financing of ICT, industrial technologies, and life sciences, with each investment having to be approved by a board where two IQ representatives would sit.

The Marois (2012–2014), Couillard (2014–2018), and Legault (2018–2019) Governments

From 2003 to 2012, economic nationalism thus continued to play key ideational and institutional roles by (a) producing path dependency dynamics favouring continuity; (b) establishing state involvement and sponsoring as the best ways to steer the private sector toward strategic directions; and (c) highlighting the necessity of policy asymmetry in view of national interests. The PLQ's last budget confirmed this with the creation of three new government-backed funds: the $750 million Capital Mines Hydrocarbures (CMH), through which IQ would acquire shares in mining and energy companies; the $170 million Fonds Valorisation Bois, a partnership between IQ ($95 million) and the FSTQ ($75 million) to promote local timber processing; and the $30 million Coop-Essor, a partnership with CRCD aiming to provide "a tool by which workers can obtain an interest in the capital of their business and contribute to its enrichment, but also a succession planning tool for entrepreneurs concerned about preserving their business' autonomy after their retirement" (Québec 2012, 23).

The years 2012–18 were, in turn, particularly interesting. First, the nationalist PQ regained power as a minority government, which, although short-lived, introduced many important *faire* initiatives such as the Banque de développement économique du Québec (BDÉQ) project and the Gazelles program. Most revealingly, this period offered a mirror image of the 2003 shift between the PQ and PLQ. The latter was reinstated as a majority government in 2014, elected on an austerity platform somewhat hostile to state intervention and yet giving way to an overall continuity and even to a refinement of the Quebec model through numerous new partnerships with state-backed investors.

The BDÉQ

Even if most of the PQ's policies were not fully implemented, it is useful to discuss some of the most important. Its pledge to establish a BDÉQ, for instance, was clearly underpinned by perceived imperatives for policy asymmetry fueled by nationalism. As initially devised, the BDÉQ was to regroup provincial and federal economic development tools, to provide a "one-stop-shop" for Quebec businesses. Although references to federal programs were dropped when the process to create the BDÉQ was launched in late 2012, part of the original intention was indeed to counterbalance the BDC's influence: by 2012, over 33% of BDC loans and around 50% of the BDC's debentures portfolio were still Quebec-based, against 28% and 27% for Ontario (BDC 2012, 96–7). Moreover, the federal government was about to launch its $400 million Venture Capital Action Plan as part of the 2012 budget, which promised to increase BDC Capital's presence in Quebec.

The BDÉQ initiative was set in motion in November 2012, as part of the economic plan introduced alongside the 2013–14 budget. This plan unveiled the other key rationale behind the proposed development bank: by 2011, Quebec was still lagging far behind Canada as a whole and slightly behind Ontario in terms of private investments, both as a percentage of GDP and per worker. If Canada's figures were boosted by the oil and gas sector, Ontario's lead was particularly concerning: "Per capita GDP in Québec is approximately 15% lower than in Canada and Ontario. The relative weakness of GDP in Québec thus masks an under-investment in absolute terms" (Québec 2013, 4). The BDÉQ was to provide Quebec's government with a powerful leveraging tool, built on the merger of IQ and the MDEIE's[20] "front-line" financing and mentoring programs. Its financing activities – including loans, loan guarantees, debentures, VC, and equity – were to be closely "coordinated" and "synchronized" with those of existing financial institutions, from the Centres locaux de développement to commercial banks (Québec 2013, 41).

The BDÉQ was also devised to centralize and streamline the government's *sponsoring* activities: it would provide "permanent consulting," business development counselling, market research, and financial planning services (Québec 2013b, 6). Bill 36 summarized the BDÉQ's projected mission:

> To support, in particular through f nancial interventions, the economic development of Québec in accordance with the government's economic policy. The Bank will offer f nancial services, ensure that enterprises are

provided with assistance services, coordinate the interventions of Government departments and bodies regarding any project the Government considers strategic, and draw up economic development strategies. (Québec 2013c, 2)

Clearly, the BDÉQ was to be much more than just another leveraging tool. It would have refined Quebec's "state-influenced" model by establishing ubiquitous governmental presence in the realm of entrepreneurial finance and accompaniment. The BDÉQ would have had several subsidiaries, including Capital Émergence Québec, a branch specialized in VC formed of the entire IQ portfolio plus an additional $50 million for new investments, and Développement économique Québec, to manage the FDÉ and act on governmental mandates (Québec 2013c, 12).

The proposed BDÉQ had a mixed reception. On the one hand, groups like Réseau Capital applauded the initiative on the basis that it would establish an *"investisseur d'envergure"* that, in collaboration with the FSTQ and CDPQ, would be able to counter foreign acquisitions of Quebec's expansion-stage businesses, thus favouring the local growth of strategic SMBs into medium businesses: *"La BDÉQ [pourra] jouer un rôle prépondérant pour permettre à des entreprises performantes de se développer, permettant ainsi le passage de la PME à la ME, facilitant le transfert d'entreprises et le maintien de sièges sociaux au Québec"* (Réseau Capital 2013, 4).[21]

On the other hand, it was denounced by players like the Canadian Federation of Independent Business as a political initiative ill-suited to the real needs of expansion-stage SMBs, a clear majority of which had never received or even sought financial aid from the state and would prefer fiscal incentives over the provision of entrepreneurial finance (FCEI 2013, 7–9). Both perspectives showed the BDÉQ project was not underpinned by market imperatives or the pressing financial needs of Quebec's businesses so much as by strategic, nationalist objectives. The context in which this initiative was promoted also favours this interpretation. Indeed, following the American company Lowe's hostile takeover bid on Quebec's RONA hardware stores in 2012, a heated debate on the vulnerability of Quebec's flagship companies arose. The PQ thus set up, in June 2013, a Groupe de travail sur la protection des entreprises québécoises to elaborate strategies to protect the province's headquarters.

A study published as part of this taskforce's consultations established that Quebec had, since 2001, developed a $36 billion deficit in terms of the differential between foreign takeovers of Quebec businesses and foreign acquisitions by the latter (SECOR-KPMG 2013, 10). In Ontario, this deficit stood at only $4 billion. Moreover, the proportion of business headquarters located in Quebec was, at 20% of the Canadian total, down from 24% in 2001 while Ontario's share, at 40%, was up from 36% (SECOR-KPMG 2013, 22–3). Three months later, the taskforce would highlight that foreign takeovers of Quebec's businesses were responsible for significant job losses as well as for the relocation of subcontracting, production, and part of the financial services industry outside of Quebec (Québec 2014b, 14). Among the recommendations figured an increased recourse to cooperatives, as well as the recapitalization of investment funds specialized in business transfer and succession (Québec 2014b, 39–44).

In parallel to the BDÉQ, the PQ thus launched new industrial policies in October 2013, pointing to the small size of Quebec's manufacturing businesses as an advantage in terms of local ownership, but as an impediment with regards to productivity and exports. A key objective was to favour the advent of new, medium-sized flagship companies – *"fleurons québécois"* – in seven priority sectors: aerospace, biotechnologies, biofood, renewables, creative industries, health services, and ICT (Québec 2013d, 52). Over $100 million were to be invested, notably through the FDÉ, to help at least twenty companies in each administrative region reach a "critical mass" of over 100 employees and $200 million in annual revenues by 2017. To this end, the new Gazelles program was devised in partnership with the Centres locaux de développement (Québec 2013e, 30–1), to offer sponsoring and financing services – *"Accompagnement-conseil stratégique"* – to 300 "high-growth" and 200 "promising" SMBs over the next three years. The aim would have been to help each gazelle reach an average annual growth of 20% to build the new "fleurons," which were to attract, help retain, or replace Quebec-based headquarters by expanding supply-chains and "revitalizing the [local] industrial fabric" (Québec 2014c).

The recapitalization of AQC and Teralys Capital Innovation

After the Liberals regained power in early 2014, part of this concern for Quebec's leading role in entrepreneurial finance and the stabilization of its corporate ownership structure remained. The PLQ's platform contained a pledge to use public resources to help businesses facing hostile foreign takeover threats[22]:

> Our approach benef ts from having access to the use of public funds to meet society's objectives within the framework of maximizing performance. It is a practical and effective way to protect our head off ces. The

holdings in the capital stocks acquired in the f ght against a hostile takeover bid will contribute to forming a strong core of Quebec institutional shareholdings. (PLQ 2014, 31)

The investment in Bombardier's CSeries, realized through the FDÉ, reflected this strategic commitment to safeguard vulnerable "fleurons." This investment was thus underpinned by political imperatives, but it was also essential in that both Bombardier and the CSeries were to become centerpieces of the next Stratégie québécoise de l'aérospatiale (Québec 2016b).

Weeks after the election, furthermore, the new head of the Ministère de l'Économie, de l'Innovation et des Exportations and ex-President of IQ, Jacques Daoust, argued that Quebec's public funds had to refocus their interventions on equity.[23] This positioning had a direct impact on IQ, which after discussions between senior management and the government set up a new "small capitalizations" division specializing in equity transactions of $2 to $5 million, supporting SMBs with $5 to $30 million in shares. This renewed *faire* approach had two key objectives: to avoid foreign takeovers of high-tech companies and to fund – in collaboration with CRCD and the FSTQ – strategic mergers and acquisitions to foster the advent of medium-to-large businesses, especially outside of Montreal.[24]

As for early-stage VC, *faire avec* and *faire faire* tools were to be further developed. First, AQC benefited from a major recapitalization led by the government and supported by new partners: $65 million in new funds were injected in early 2015 – $25 million from IQ, $25 million from the CDPQ, and $15 million from the FSTQ – bringing AQC's total capitalization to $85 million. According to François Gilbert, CEO of Anges Québec and AQC, the CDPQ and FSTQ were interested in becoming co-investment partners for two related reasons: they recognized that AQC had built a portfolio large enough to maximize profitability ratios, and most importantly they realized that AQC's specialized expertise in seed and start-up financing could provide follow-on investment opportunities for bigger funds. This account was further confirmed by representatives from the CRCD and FSTQ. As CRCD's Gérald St-Aubin also explained (personal interview):

> On va dire à l'ange financier qui a moins de capacités: "mets le montant que tu es prêt à risquer dans cette société, puis on peut le doubler ou le tripler." On va évidemment le faire en collaboration ... Il faut les motiver à faire grandir cette société. Plus tard, lorsqu'un investisseur américain arrive et veut injecter 15 millions $ dans cette société en échange de telle valorisation et de l'élimination des

Graph 5.6. Evolution of Quebec's VC industry IV, 2007–2018

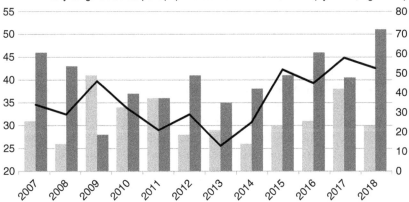

Sources: Thomson Financial (2008); Industry Canada (2008–15); Thomson Reuters (2009–15); CVCA (2015–19); Thomson Reuters (2015).
Note: Approximate figures. 2018 figure for early-stage deals in Quebec only include investments for the first semester of 2018.

avantages de tous les autres actionnaires, la dilution est très forte … Alors ce qu'on dit aux anges, c'est que quand ces étapes arrivent, on va les protéger. On a le capital pour le faire, et on va se substituer à l'offre de l'étranger.[25]

Another major announcement made for early-stage VC in the 2014–15 budget was the setting up of Teralys Capital Fonds d'innovation (TCFI), a partnership between the FSTQ ($50 million), CDPQ ($50 million), IQ ($62.5 million), and other players ($162.5 million) such as the BDC, FACSN, Desjardins, and Banque Nationale (Québec 2014a, B36). This new hybrid fund, managed by Teralys, would invest both directly in early-stage ventures, and indirectly through VCs. It was to specialize in ICT, green technologies, and most importantly life sciences, to which it would have to dedicate between 25% and 35% of its portfolio.[26] This initiative was strategic for many reasons. First, a $375 million fund of funds would have a significant impact on Quebec's VC ecosystem: most importantly, it contributed in reinforcing the upward trend in early-stage deals, which had declined since the 2008 financial crisis (graph 5.6).

The second strategy behind TCFI was sectoral. It would serve as a specialized financial arm of the government for the pursuit of new priorities. In the case of ICT, it would invest (alongside IQ and the CDPQ) in sector-specific VCs such as Montreal-based iNovia and White Star Capital, thereby underwriting Quebec's Plan d'action en économie numérique, whose central objective is to increase local SMBs' use of productivity-enhancing technologies (Québec 2016a, 14, 39). In the case of life sciences, TCFI would become part of a larger strategy announced in the 2016–17 budget. Quebec's government was to invest more than $100 million in this sector over the next five years, in order to maintain Montreal's North American "leadership status" and favour the commercialization of "Quebec discoveries" (Québec 2016b, B128–B131). To that end, an additional $96 million was injected into TCFI so that it could sponsor VCs acting as follow-on investors for biotech and health sciences start-ups already financed, at R&D and seed stages, by the new hybrid fund AmorChem II (Québec 2016b, B213–B222).[27]

Finally, but perhaps most importantly, nationalism and perceived imperatives for policy autonomy played a major role since TCFI was set up precisely as Ontario's Northleaf Venture Catalyst Fund, a hybrid fund of funds also specializing in ICT, green technologies, and life sciences, reached its full capitalization of $300 million.[28] Like the initial Teralys, TCFI was thus established in part to safeguard Quebec's competitive position vis-à-vis Ontario. As Quebec's Finance minister Carlos Leitao argued, "le Québec est un leader au pays en matière de capital de risque et de capital de développement. Avec l'annonce d'aujourd'hui, nous posons les gestes nécessaires pour maintenir cette position."[29] As well, TCFI represented another occasion for Quebec's government to establish large-scale partnerships with the province's most powerful institutional investors.

Strategic partnerships and the expansion of IQ

The 2015–16 budget, it should be remembered, was published as the federal government was phasing out its tax credits to LSIFs (Québec 2015a, B78–B82). The Quebec government's decisions to (a) eliminate ceilings for the annual issuance of FSTQ and FACSN shares; (b) increase this ceiling by $150 million for CRCD in 2015; and (c) expand its tax credits applicable to FACSN shares from 15% to 20% were all informed by a dedication to policy asymmetry, underpinned by pressures from Quebec's VC industry. The government's choice to impose, in addition, a 5% hike on all three funds' annual investment quotas in local SMBs tells the other side of this story.

Along with the budget, the government had tabled the final report of the Commission d'examen sur la fiscalité québécoise established a year earlier. This commission recommended that the three funds be imposed a 10% hike on their annual investment requirement, in order to "augment their contribution to Quebec's economic development" (Québec 2015b, 132). This further legitimized the government's decision, aside from other strategic considerations. Three governmental strategies were indeed launched in 2015–16 that would mobilize Quebec's tax-advantaged funds. The first was PerforME – the Stratégie d'accélération des projets d'entreprises performantes – in essence a rebranding of the Gazelles program. One major difference, however, was that while Gazelles would mostly have given investees access to IQ or the BDÉQ, PerforME established a $50 million partnership fund between IQ, the CDPQ, FSTQ, FACSN, and CRCD.

PerforME offered "high-potential" expansion-stage SMBs (less than 250 employees, at least $25 million in turnover) personalized sponsoring in the form of managerial mentoring, market intelligence, and financial support (Québec 2015c, 10–12). The objective was to "accelerate" innovation and export projects in various sectors, in conjunction with the government's economic priorities. Also in 2015, the Stratégie québécoise de développement de l'aluminium was launched with the objective to double the volume of aluminum processing in Quebec by 2025, notably by fostering the development of local SMBs in this sector (Québec 2015d, 9, 44–8). To reach this objective, PerforME services were made available to the most promising businesses, and state-backed funds like IQ and Desjardins-Innovatech were also involved.

In addition, PerforME was to support two other development strategies: one for the digital economy (along with TCFI), and one for aerospace. The 2016–26 aerospace strategy was of particular importance given the FDÉ's historic investment in the CSeries. This strategy underlined the national objectives pursued by the government through this investment: "The Government of Québec's support in developing Bombardier's C-Series demonstrates its willingness to back major investment projects, on which the sector's future growth will depend … This assistance is directly in line with the government strategy to support major Québec aerospace investment projects" (Québec 2016b, 31). The CSeries investment was to become part of a program mobilizing an additional $265 million from the FDÉ over five years for this sector (Québec 2016b, 43).

The government's partnerships with state-backed investors, either in the case of TCFI or PerforME, were thus based in part on strategic considerations, aiming not only to leverage but to *steer* institutional and

private investment toward priority sectors and projects. Close relationships between the government and tax-advantaged funds were thus
of key strategic concern, as the Liberals knew they would need these
partners for some of the major policy initiatives they were planning
(Québec 2016c, B232). As a matter of fact, the ministers and deputy ministers of finance and the economy meet with senior officials from the
FSTQ and CRCD many times every year to discuss priorities, investment opportunities, and avenues for collaboration. As CRCD's Gérald
St-Aubin explains (personal interview):

> *Nous, on a un pouls économique incroyable, et souvent les gouvernements*
> *vont venir nous consulter en disant: "on a pensé faire telle chose, comment cela*
> *s'appliquerait-il chez vous?" C'est beaucoup de consultation et, à l'inverse, cela*
> *nous amène aussi souvent des opportunités car le gouvernement va dire: "je veux*
> *développer tel créneau." Alors un coup qu'on sait qu'il s'oriente vers tel ou tel*
> *aspect de l'économie du Québec, on va aussi orienter nos stratégies en fonction*
> *d'un renforcement mutuel de ces actions.*[30]

Another good example of that was the Stratégie maritime announced
as part of the 2015–16 budget and necessitating $400 million in investments over five years, including $100 million from the FSTQ (Québec
2015e, 34). As the FSTQ's Alain Denis confirms, "*le gouvernement nous*
indique de façon régulière ses priorités. Là, par exemple, il impose une stra
tégie maritime, alors c'est certain qu'il s'attend à ce que des fonds comme le
FSTQ aient des initiatives pour collaborer à ses plans. Ce n'est pas le gou
vernement qui nous dit d'y aller, mais on n'est pas fous, on s'aligne sur les
priorités gouvernementales" (personal interview).[31] In September 2016,
finally, the government launched the Fonds Innovexport, a hybrid
VC fund specialized in seed and start-up stage exporting businesses.
Capitalized with over $30 million from the FDÉ, FSTQ, FACSN,
CDPQ, Quebec City, and private investors, this was yet another prime
example of state-led collaboration, mobilizing multiple government-
backed funds.

This approach paid real dividends: since the financial crisis, the two
largest state-backed funds steadily increased their presence in Quebec,
with $2 billion in development capital investments on average each
year (graph 5.7). These funds' capacity and willingness to support
structuring economic development initiatives should therefore not be
overlooked. In early 2016, for instance, after it was confirmed that the
federal tax credits for LSIFs would be safeguarded after all, the FSTQ
announced it would double its investments in Quebec and put aside
a $500 million reserve to send the signal of "economic patriotism": it

Graph 5.7. Contributions of the FSTQ and CDPQ in Quebec, 2007–2018 (development capital, $ millions)

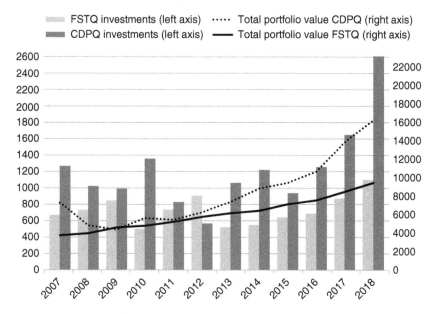

Sources: CDPQ and FSTQ (2010–19), annual reports.

would henceforth be ready to counter foreign takeovers of "flagship" Quebec businesses.[32]

This very transparent appeal to economic nationalism and the rentention of business headquarters has been a central aspect of Quebec's political discourse and debates since then, particularly as the provincial elections of 2018 approached. Running on a platform notably advocating for a renewed resort to state intervention in entrepreneurial finance, innovation, and economic development more generally (Carbasse 2018), the nationalist Coalition Avenir Québec (CAQ), headed by the current Prime Minister François Legault, won over 37% of the vote in these elections and formed a majority government with 74 seats out of 125. In accordance with its program and electoral pledges, one of the new government's very first initiatives was to launch a further reform and expansion of IQ through Bill 27, "An Act respecting mainly government organization as regards the economy and innovation" (Québec 2019). Among other measures, this Bill seeks to broaden IQ's mandates while specifying and accentuating its economic development mission.

Most notably, the wording of IQ's mission is modified to emphasize the new, more proactive approach the Quebec government wants it to adopt as well as its added responsibilities (Québec 2019, 16):

> The *priority mission* of the Company, as regards its own activities and the administration of f nancial assistance programs or the carrying out of other mandates, is to *actively* participate in Québec's economic development in accordance with the Government's objectives in that area. The goal of the Company is to *stimulate innovation* in enterprises and the growth of investments *and exports*, and to promote *high-value added* jobs in all regions of Québec.[33]

Among other measures put forward by this proposed expansion and reform of IQ, and aside from the merger with existing governmental units dedicated to export promotion – most notably "Export Québec", from the Ministère de l'Économie et de l'Innovation (MEI) – three stand out and highlight the interventionist and nationalist approach of the Legault government. First of all, a billion dollars was added to IQ's share capital (bringing it to a total of 5 billion), allowing for a more aggressive investment style and the for the further growth of IQ's private equity and VC portfolios, which had already been catching up to its portfolio of loans over the past few years (Rioux 2019a). This additional billion dollars was accompanied, moreover, by the creation of a new one-billion-dollar fund managed by IQ – the *Fonds pour la croissance des entreprises québécoises* (figure 1.2) – specialized in equity investments of $5 million or more and dedicated to the growth of Quebec's "strategic" SMBs, their protection against foreign takeover threats, and the retention of business headquarters in the province (Québec 2019, 24–5). The new fund will, moreover, be accompanied by a dedicated task-force mandated to develop specific market intelligence on headquarter retention and the acquisition of blocking minorities in such "strategic" companies.

Secondly, all of IQ's regional offices in Quebec – by which most of IQ's financings are attributed to investee businesses – will henceforth be merged with the regional offices of the MEI, offering managerial advice and various corporate financing programs (Rioux 2019b). The intention, here, is to offer entrepreneurs and businesses a "one-stop-shop" for all their financial and/or organizational needs, as well as to favor the regionalization of VC and development capital financing (Québec 2019, 16–17). Finally, and perhaps most importantly given the recent efforts and resources dedicated by IQ for the technological modernization and re-shoring of Quebec's manufacturing processes (Rioux

2019a), the preexisting "Centre de recherche industrielle du Québec" (CRIQ), specialized in R&D integration, commercialization, and technological transfers will be incorporated into IQ in order to streamline the financing and implementation of productivity-enhancing industrial innovations (Québec 2019, 27–8). At the time of writing, the ultimate fate of Bill 27 was unknown, but given the majority status of the Legault government and considering the enthusiastic support the Bill received from peak-level business organizations – such as the Conseil du Patronat or the Fédération des chambres de commerce du Québec – it is likely to be adopted and implemented.

Concluding Remarks

With regards to state activism in entrepreneurial finance and VC, the past decade and a half was equally dynamic as the 1990s and early 2000s. Not only has Quebec continued, since 2003, to reap a highly disproportionate share of all new VC raised in Canada (over 50% on average), but its businesses also continued to be involved, on average, in over 40% of all VC deals made in Canada. The persistence of the government's sponsoring activities was partly responsible for this dominant position. IQ and FDÉ financings, for instance, as well as the value of investments leveraged by those, have been steadily increasing since 2003. FSTQ and CDPQ local investment portfolios, similarly, more than doubled in size since the financial crisis. As a result, Quebec maintained a dominant position in Canada's private equity industry, consistently attracting a larger share of deals than Ontario.

Furthermore, the persistence and renewal of government intervention after 2003 cannot simply be attributed to institutional path dependency, or to the fact that "Quebec interventionism was now well established as the appropriate, perhaps necessary, way to promote growth there" (Haddow 2015, 196). Even initiatives taken in the wake of the Rapport Brunet had as much to do with *new* government priorities and strategies as with institutional legacies. The launch of various hybrid funds had leveraging objectives but was also a way, for the government, to steer increasingly influential institutional investors toward politically defined priority sectors.

If various market rationales indeed became recurrent justifications for state intervention, the establishment of many business succession funds clearly demonstrated that economic imperatives can also be underpinned by nationalist ones, and more precisely in these cases by apprehensions about foreign takeovers, land grabbing or speculation, and business survival rates. The persistence and deepening of policy asymmetries since 2003 therefore highlighted the influence of economic nationalism. Through institutional but also ideological and political mechanisms, nationalism continued to impact policymaking in very significant ways.

The capitalization of Anges Québec as well as that of hybrid funds such as Teralys, Capital-croissance PME, or Teralys Capital Fonds d'innovation clearly derived from perceived imperatives and preferences for policy asymmetry. Many governmental decisions, finally, proceeded from political motivations as much as from economic ones. Modifications to tax-advantaged funds' capitalization and investment guidelines, in 2015, were a message sent to the federal government and to Quebec's entrepreneurial finance ecosystem, just as the historic investment in the CSeries venture was part of larger concerns regarding Quebec's "fleurons" as much as it was of strategic necessity. The proposed expansion of IQ, which would for the most part take effect in 2020, also clearly reflects the nationalist and interventionist inclinations of the Legault government.

Chapter Six

Scotland, 2003–2019

The last fifteen years in Scotland were also characterized by a shift toward *faire faire* and *faire avec*, although the Scottish government and SE/HIE continued to engage in significant direct investment activities. By the turn of the century, the need to leverage private sector investments and to bridge funding gaps for seed- and early-stage ventures already transpired in a number of limited partnerships and co-investment funds. From 2003 onward, the second SLP-SLD coalition government moved further down that path with the launch of several new hybrid initiatives. It would be a mistake, however, to reduce the strategic motivations behind this shift to leveraging and/or market failure issues. Instead, perceived imperatives and ideological preferences for policy asymmetry and state intervention – i.e., economic nationalism – permeated most of those initiatives.

The new hybrids established after 2003 were geared as much toward policy autonomy and divergence as toward funding gaps (Hayton Consulting 2008; Mason and Harrison 2010; PACEC 2012, 2013; Sunley et al. 2005). They were also clearly designed to facilitate the implementation of government strategies (Scotland 2004a, 2004b, 2004c), and to complement each other as well as private actors. This was well illustrated when the SNP government, in the wake of the 2008 financial crisis, regrouped public and hybrid funds to build what became a hallmark of the Scottish VC ecosystem: the Scottish Investment Bank (SIB).

As in Quebec, the shift to *faire faire* and *faire avec* proved compatible with the active state involvement that already characterized the "Scottish model" and Scotland's economic strategies. Such continuity transpired in the establishment of many new direct investment tools during this period. A good example was the Intermediate Technology Institutes (ITIs), a £450 million public investment program created alongside the Scottish Co-Investment Fund (SCIF) to increase linkages between local

Graph 6.1. Public spending on economic development and technology,* Scotland vs. UK, 2003–2018 (£ millions)

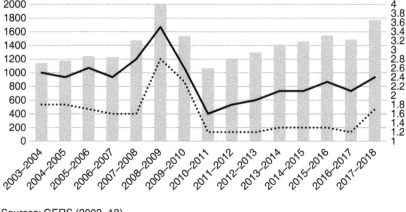

Sources: GERS (2003–18).
* "Enterprise & Economic Development" and "Science & Technology" categories as % of total public spending (including debt servicing).

businesses and university R&D, a strength of the "Scottish innovation system" (Adamek 2007; Roper et al. 2006). Another was the £70 million National Renewables Infrastructure Fund (NRIF) later set up to foster the advent of a Scottish cluster in offshore wind power, as part of the SNP government's Low Carbon Economic Strategy (Scotland 2010c) and Economic Recovery Plan (Scotland 2011b).

Consequently, high levels of public spending for economic development and technology were maintained since 2003 and kept increasing both in absolute terms and relative to overall public spending in Scotland or the UK (graph 6.1). Except for the crisis and recession years from 2008–11, the asymmetry between Scottish and UK levels of spending on economic development widened considerably. While in 2003–4, Scotland devoted 38% more public resources to economic development, as a proportion of total public spending, then the UK, this discrepancy had doubled by 2016–17, at 75%, before coming back down to 42% in 2017–18 (graph 6.1). If the 2003–18 period in Scotland was thus characterized, as in Quebec, by some degree of "first order" and "second order" change (Hall 1993) in the way policy instruments were designed, such changes did not amount to paradigmatic transformations and, in fact, increased government influence rather than the opposite. Economic nationalism played a significant role in this overall continuity and the broadening asymmetry distinguishing the Scottish ecosystem. This became especially evident as the SNP government systematically underlined the necessity of autonomy and divergence, devising policy accordingly.

Yet the policy impacts of Scottish nationalism were also clearly felt before the SNP era. In the aftermath of the dot.com bust, the SLP-SLD coalition also focused on the preservation and improvement of the Scottish corporate ownership structure. As Dr. Geoffrey Whittam explains, the launch of new state-backed investment tools revealed a widespread "recognition that Scotland's biggest problem in terms of business [was] not really a shortage of new, potentially high-growth businesses more than businesses getting to a certain size and selling out, in particular in the computer gaming sector. It was an attempt to provide funding for those who wanted to continue as Scottish-based companies" (personal interview).

The Second SLP-SLD Administration (2003–2007)

The second mandate of the SLP-SLD coalition was characterized by a shift toward a co-investment model bringing together the public sector, business angels, and VCs. Between 2003 and 2006, three hybrid funds were established and formed what became known as SE's "funding escalator" (Gordon 2013; PACEC 2013, 15–16). The SCIF, first, was devised with a particular focus on early-growth ventures, providing equity investments in the £250,000–£2,000,000 range. The Scottish Seed Fund (SSF) and Scottish Venture Fund (SVF), in turn, were respectively crafted to cover the seed and expansion stages, offering investments of £20,000 to £250,000 in the first case and £2 to £10 million in the latter.

The "official" story about these funds is that they were mainly intended to fill funding gaps following the dot.com bust (Pierrakis and Mason 2008; Mason and Pierrakis 2013). Yet, there was much more to this than gap filling, leveraging, or counter-cyclical motives. The advent of the co-investment model in Scotland widened policy divergence with the RoUK by favouring the growth of state-sponsored VC deals and co-investment alongside angel syndicates. By 2008, state presence in Scottish early-stage VC deals reached almost 100%, more than triple that in South East England/London (Mason and Pierrakis 2013). Most importantly, the advent of such public activism and asymmetry was in itself, as I will show, a key policy objective.

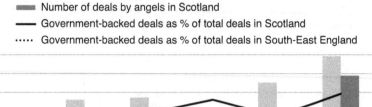

Graph 6.2. Government-backed VC deals as % of total early-stage VC deals,*
Scotland, 2003–2008 (by number of investments)

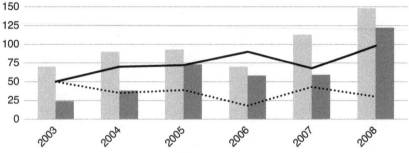

Sources: The Risk Capital Market in Scotland (2008–16); Pierrakis & Mason (2008);
Mason & Pierrakis (2013); Mason & Harrison (2010).
* Figures for angel investments in 2003 and 2004 only include LINC members. I classify
angel investments as "government-backed" because most of those investments were
made alongside public sector investors. Approximate numbers.

The Scottish Co-Investment Fund

The SCIF was the fruit of consultations launched in 2002 and was set up
by the end of that year, although operations really began in the spring of
2003 (GEM Scotland 2002; Kemp, Lironi, and Shakeshaft 2017). As Scottish businesses faced dwindling private sector investments – dropping
from £440 million in 2001 to £109 million in 2003 – the Scottish Executive and SE (in consultation with LINC and its first two member syndicates, Archangels and Braveheart) conceived this fund as a response to
the downturn, but also as an alternative to projects aborted in the wake
of the dot.com bust. As LINC's David Grahame recalls, the SCIF was
first capitalized[1] with money that had been earmarked to support FDI
projects in 2001–2, many of which were canceled following the closure
of high-tech branch plants in "Silicon Glen." Thus, "the Minister found
himself with a grant which had already been set aside and was able to
build a political announcement around it by establishing a co-investment fund. Then, they opened negotiations with partners" (personal
interview).

Scotland was by then losing ground as a private VC destination, with a smaller proportion of Scottish businesses receiving investments each year (BVCA 2007). In addition, it was indeed witnessing the closure and/or flight of foreign-owned high-tech companies, after decades of efforts in building this sector and its pool of indigenous suppliers. In such a context, the perceived necessity of a renewed intervention model, geared toward the transition of "high growth potential" ventures into Scottish-owned, medium-sized businesses – or "indigenous global companies" (Hood and Paterson 2002, 245) – capable of sustaining local supply chains was sharpened (Brown 2002). From then on, "the most explicit policy objective was the need to focus on high-growth new starts on the grounds that they would eventually become larger, more established-size 'companies of scale'" (Brown and Mason 2012, 23).

As Dr. Whittam explains, the SCIF was intended to provide such SMBs the necessary capital to grow, instead of selling out: "The idea behind promoting co-investment and syndication was to try and support the potentially high-growth businesses. It was partly risk reduction and partly this idea of overcoming the perennial problem of firms getting to a certain size and selling" (personal interview). This was confirmed by the plethora of business support tools developed after 2002, of which the SCIF became part. One example was the creation of Business Gateway (BG) in July 2003, an extension of the Small Business Gateway. As a subsidiary of SE, BG was to continue as a network of local "one-stop-shops," but its remit was extended beyond start-ups and small businesses, to companies of all sizes and especially to high-growth firms (O'Hare 2004). BG was to be a conveyor belt between local and national levels, referring growing SMBs and gazelles to SE/HIE.

This emphasis on growing businesses was complemented, at SE, by the development of the High-Growth Start-Up Unit in 2003, given the objective of supporting, through funding and managerial assistance, at least thirty young high-tech businesses in reaching a valuation of over £5 million within three years (GEM Scotland 2003, 32). The SCIF was thus part of a shift in state support, away from business birth rates and toward the development of "high-growth starts" into medium-sized businesses capable of replacing foreign companies as contractors and job creators (Brown and Mason 2012, 19, 23–5). It was also part of government-devised economic plans, such as the refreshed Framework for Economic Development in Scotland, which underlined that "many of the overseas-owned operations that had prospered during the 1990s came under great pressure, with a significant number being forced to cut back their operations and, indeed, close in some cases" (Scotland

2004a, 14). For the Scottish Executive, closures and foreign takeovers stressed the need for a more balanced corporate ownership structure. The new economic strategy, "A Smart, Successful Scotland" (Scotland 2004c), confirmed this emphasis on Scottish businesses' productivity and growth levels (Scotland 2004a, 10) and aimed at generating new "national champions":

> Increasing new business starts are not enough to impact signif cantly on overall productivity. There remains signif cant scope to increase productivity levels in established businesses and, while Scotland has successful, innovative businesses, we lack a critical mass of larger businesses. A key challenge is *growing and sustaining businesses of scale – both nationally and relative to others in their local area.* (Scotland 2004c, 15)

One way to achieve this was to ensure a better connection between existing businesses and R&D activities conducted by universities (Roper et al. 2006), as "research had highlighted the potential for greater commercialisation of academic research in Scotland" (Brown and Mason 2012, 23). This led to the launch of three ITIs for the biotechnology (Dundee), ICT (Glasgow), and energy (Aberdeen) clusters in 2003 (Scotland 2004a, 72–3; Brown et al. 2016).

ITIs were to act as intermediaries between university R&D and Scottish SMBs, identifying innovations likely to enhance productivity and assisting in their implementation in coordination with SE's instruments such as the High Growth Start-Up Unit, Proof of Concept Fund, and SCIF (SE 2005, 12; Roper et al. 2006, 60; Adamek 2007; Brown et al. 2016, 1265). Each ITI was endowed with £150 million over ten years, for a total of £450 million. As such, they contributed to widening the divergence between Scotland and the RoUK with regards to government-backed R&D (graph 6.3). They were also an important complement to the second strategic approach privileged to increase productivity and growth: improved access to VC (Scotland 2004c, 15–16).

Such improved access entailed both a surge in the quantity of capital available to SMBs and a more selective approach to investment. As Joan Gordon,[2] head of Development and Market Intelligence at SE, explains:

> The people who developed the SCIF did so in a way that was collaborative: they talked to the private sector and understood what would work in Scotland. There was a recognition that equity investment is not something that's appropriate or suitable for a large number of companies; but the small number of companies where it was suitable were also the companies that could make a material difference for the Scottish economy.

Graph 6.3. Government-backed R&D as % of GDP, Scotland vs. RoUK, 2000–2017

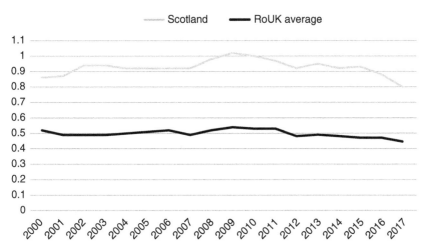

Source: Scottish Government, *Gross Expenditures on Research and Development* (GERD). Note: R&D financed/performed by governmental and higher-education institutions.

The SCIF was to form part of SE's "equity investment package" (Scotland 2004a, 76), alongside the Business Growth Fund and High-Growth Unit's "Investment Readiness Programme." It was to be highly selective, only investing in "eligible sectors" and in businesses identified as having high-growth and high-impact potentials. Over its first four years in operation, two-thirds of SCIF investments (graph 6.4) were made in electronics / ICT and biotechnology / life sciences (Hayton Consulting 2008, 105, 111).

The SCIF was to partner mainly with LINC members and angel syndicates: close to 85% of deals were made with angel syndicates during the first five years (graph 6.5) and, in fact, the SCIF was specifically designed to act as a catalyst for angel syndication (Mason and Harrison 2010; Paul and Whittam 2010). This was for two related reasons. First, the SCIF was launched in part as a reaction to the establishment, between 2000 and 2003, of the smaller Regional Venture Capital Funds in England, which mainly partnered with VCs and were criticized for investing in companies neither owned nor even based in their respective region (Sunley et al. 2005, 264–6; Webster 2009). For the SCIF, which had to invest in Scottish-owned or Scottish-based companies

Graphs 6.4 & 6.5. Contributions of the Scottish Co-Investment Fund, 2003–2007

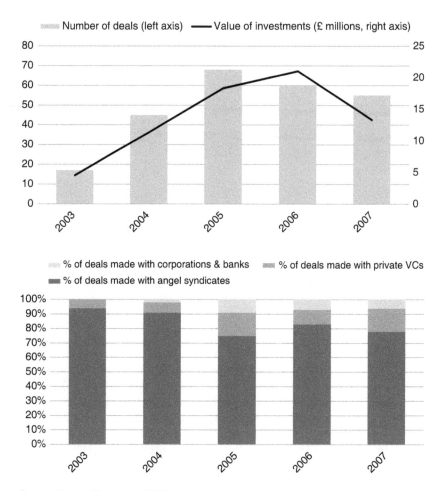

Source: Hayton Consulting (2008).
Note: Approximate figures, including leverage ratio of 2.43.

(Hayton Consulting 2008, 105), the government thus favoured the "home-biased," hands-on, and patient approach of angels.

The justifications for the SCIF favouring angel *syndicates* were in turn twofold. On the one hand, this would allow for more numerous deals, larger investments, and the provision of a higher number of funding rounds for investees (Hayton Consulting 2008; Mason et al. 2016, 329).

Relatedly, angel syndication was to provide a "Scottish solution to a Scottish problem," as Scottish angels were "poorer," less experienced, and less numerous than their counterparts in England (Harrison et al. 2010, 231).

Through both syndication and co-investment with SE/HIE, Scottish angels were able to invest larger amounts of capital in a higher number of businesses, and to adopt an even more hands-on approach to their investments, providing significant follow-on funding for investees:

> Angel investors organized in the form of syndicates and with access to co-investment fund monies are adopting a different approach to their investment portfolio. They appear to be following more of a "cradle-to-grave" funding model in which they provide the follow-on f nance necessary, rather than the "relay-race" model in which angel investors pass deals on to other investors, typically VCs, for follow-on funding. (Mason and Harrison 2010, 29)

A divergence thus widened at the time between the Scottish and English angel markets (Mason and Botelho 2013; Mason et al. 2016; Gregson, Mann, and Harrison 2013): "The Scottish [angel] market is distinctive – deals are larger, there is more co-investment activity, more follow-on investing and larger investee companies. This is attributable to the different institutional structure and organisation of the market in Scotland – notably the greater prominence of angel groups and presence of the SCIF" (Mason and Harrison 2010, ix). In 2002, only two angel syndicates existed in Scotland, accounting for around seventy angels; by 2008, there were nineteen regrouping over 400 angels, most of whom were by then LINC members.

The Scottish Seed Fund (SSF) and the Scottish Venture Fund (SVF)

After 2002, governments across the UK became increasingly worried about the stagnating levels of private sector investment for early-stage businesses, therefore compensating with public sector initiatives (Mason and Pierrakis 2013; NESTA 2009; Pierrakis 2010). Between 2000 and 2008, VC deals comprising some degree of public sector involvement climbed from around 10% of annual deals to over 40% in the UK (Mason and Pierrakis 2013, 1161). Although public sector presence in the Scottish VC sector was also growing rapidly, in the specific context of the early 2000s Scotland was not an outlier or anomaly of the British VC ecosystem.

Yet what distinguished Scottish as opposed to English or UK-wide public sector initiatives, which mostly had supply-side, counter-cyclical, and/or leveraging purposes (NESTA 2009; Pierrakis 2010; UK 2012; Baldock and North 2012), was that state involvement in Scotland almost always had clear strategic underpinnings and regional-level national objectives. Most notably, there was an overarching nationalist concern for Scotland's corporate ownership structure. In biotechnology, for instance, over one-third of businesses and a majority of the largest employers were still foreign-owned by the early 2000s (Peters and Hood 2002, 96), while the ten largest employers and contractors of the "Silicon Glen" ICT cluster were in turn American-owned, with Scottish SMBs concentrated in the "lower value segments of the supply chain" (Brown 2002, 132, 134).

As the SCIF was launched, SE thus ordered a study of the status of corporate headquarters in Scotland. As in the early 1990s, South East England was used as a comparator case because it was home to a disproportionate number of headquarters (Botham and Clelland 2005, 22). Most significantly, since the mid-1990s Scotland had been seeing many locally-owned businesses "drift" toward London (2005, vi–vii). Although the report did not include specific policy prescriptions, it left no doubt as to whether the loss of corporate ownership to foreign interests, in high-value-added sectors most specifically, should be cause for concern. Studying "the impact of acquisition on five small Scottish high-tech companies" in the 1990s and 2000s, the report concluded:

> The entrepreneur generally sold out for good business reasons and the new parent provided resources (e.g., capital, distribution channels) which enabled the business to grow. However, in the longer term, the outcome has been fairly or completely negative for both the company and the Scottish economy. While all the founders recycled[3] some of their assets resulting from the sale (e.g., as business angels, business advisors, etc.), the possibility of growing a new, independent company with its corporate HQ in Scotland was closed off by the acquisition. (2005, 84)

Noting that, from 1994–2004, over 75% of Scottish-owned businesses that joined Scotland's 500 largest companies did so through growth or mergers and acquisitions (Botham and Clelland 2005, 32), the report also underlined that

> the "case for HQs" is little different from the case for indigenous development ... The question is not about HQs, but rather whether suff cient and appropriate support is provided for Scotland's indigenous businesses ...

As indigenous companies grow, their HQ functions can drift away from Scotland. In some cases, it may be possible to work with individual companies to offer assistance which prevents such relocation. (2005, 91)

The impact such a concern for Scotland's corporate ownership structure had on policymakers could not be overstated. In February 2005, an inquiry on business growth in Scotland was launched by the Scottish Parliament's Enterprise and Culture Committee, to "identify why Scotland's rate of business growth continues, in many respects, to lag behind its competitors and what needs to be done to change this" (Scotland 2006, n.p.). The report, published in March 2006, notably identified a "disincentive to grow" created by the British taxation system:

Current tax differentials encourage the sale of a company before it reaches a size and level of prof t that would begin to turn it into a mature, expanding company from its original start-up period. In essence, the money a business owner takes out of a company's prof ts as income is taxed at over 50%, whereas the windfall (capital gains) that could be earned from selling the business would be taxed at only 10%. This reality means that there is a very strong incentive to sell on a nascent Scottish business and, therefore, the desire to develop the company into a successful medium-sized Scottish business is weakened. It reinforces the problem of Scotland's "wine glass syndrome": lots of small companies, a healthy number of very large companies but few medium-sized companies with the potential to grow into larger, world leaders. (Scotland 2006, n.p.)

In such a context, refined state intervention *and* policy asymmetry seemed necessary, and the Committee therefore recommended that the Executive and SE/HIE sharpen their focus on "increasing the proportion of Scottish SMEs that develop into bigger and more profitable firms and eventually become, perhaps, world-leading, larger companies" (Scotland 2006, n.p.). A massive reinjection of capital into Scottish businesses was advocated to this end, notably through the creation of new hybrid funds "providing investment capital at *all levels* of the young and expanding company market."

In its Operating Plan for 2006–9, published weeks after the Committee's report, SE identified five "national priority industries" in which high-potential businesses would be targeted: life sciences, energy, electronics, food and drink, and tourism (SE 2006, 5). By November 2006, two new co-investment funds had been established to complete the existing suite of financing tools (R&D funds, ITIs, SCIF, BGF). The £14 million SSF, for one, was to have three main functions (PACEC 2013,

7–9). First, as confirmed by SE's Joan Gordon (personal interview), it was to act as a screen and "pipeline," identifying and funding promising start-ups which could then be taken to development and expansion stages by the SCIF and SE. Pat McHugh,[4] who helped set up the SSF, explains that it was also devised to replace pre-existing local, seed-stage funding schemes:

> Both SE and HIE had agreed with the Scottish government that it made a lot of sense for a small country like Scotland that its investment funds should be national instead of having a plethora of "me too" schemes. Most LECs provided investment support, so we looked at those that were the best, and that was the starting point to the national scheme that we introduced in 2006, the SSF. It was meant to be an improvement on the best.

As LINC's David Grahame also remarked, "the SSF was then simply an adjustment, recognizing that the very bottom end was being ignored" (personal interview). By fostering angel syndication, the SCIF had indeed contributed to a concentration of angel investment in larger deals, above £100,000. The SSF was intended to fill the gap opened by the SCIF in the seed-stage, £20,000–£100,000 niche. It was thus crafted to both complement *and* feed the SCIF, with the same objective of supporting the local growth of Scottish-owned, high-potential companies in key sectors. Accordingly, close to 70% of investments made by the SSF up to 2010 (graph 6.6) were in electronics/ICT and life sciences (PACEC 2013, 30).

The second co-investment fund launched in late 2006, the £20 million SVF, was even more clearly geared toward the sponsoring of Scottish-owned "national champions," investing in the £2 to £10 million range and in expanding businesses most vulnerable to delocalization or takeover: "SVF is to provide capital and expertise that will enable more Scottish companies to develop and grow from a Scottish base, retaining high-value services in Scotland, and with the aspiration that more Scottish companies can become internationally competitive companies of scale" (PACEC 2012, 19).

Like the SSF, the SVF was thus partly intended to complement the SCIF: around one-third of SVF investments, according to SE's Joan Gordon, were provided as follow-on funding for SCIF investees (personal interview). Most importantly, the SVF was crafted to steer its partner VCs, of which 25% were then overseas-based (PACEC 2012, 62), toward priority sectors and key Scottish businesses. No less than 80% of SVF investments (graph 6.7), consequently, were also made from the onset in electronics/ICT and life sciences (PACEC 2012, 30): "The partners

Graphs 6.6 & 6.7. Contributions of the Scottish Seed Fund (6.6) and Scottish Venture Fund (6.7), 2006–2010

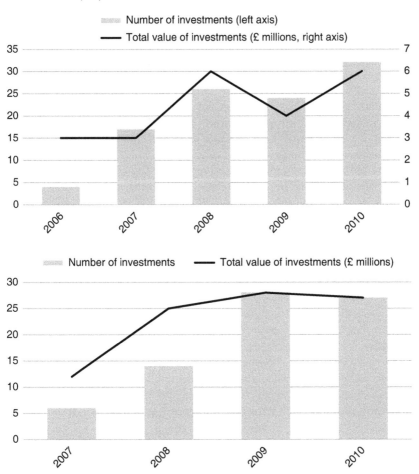

Source: PACEC (2012, 2013).
Note: Approximate figures, including leverage ratios of 2.3 for the SVF and 2.2 for the SSF.

know our investment criteria, they know the sectors we will invest in" (Joan Gordon, personal interview). That, in a nutshell, is the core character of a "sponsor state": public resources, in such a model, are not only used to leverage private investments but also to give them a national purpose and direction.

The First SNP Government (2007–2011)

In May 2007, the secessionist SNP won a parliamentary minority in Scotland (47 out of 129 seats) and formed an alliance with the (also secessionist) Scottish Greens. This was significant in that the Greens would support the SNP's ministerial appointments and the latter, in return, pledged to "pursue a progressive programme which places addressing climate change at the heart of its agenda."[5] In the wake of the 2008 financial crisis, the SNP government accordingly launched a countercyclical investment strategy geared toward the establishment of Scotland as a world leader in renewable energy. This strategy reflected the ambitions set for the Scottish economy by the SNP, clearly rooted in a nationalist perspective on Scotland's place in the UK and Europe.

Higher ambitions, better targeted investments, and a much greater degree of policy asymmetry were still needed, according to the SNP, to match the growth rates of other autonomous regions such as Bavaria, Catalonia, and Lombardy, but also that of "small European nations" like Ireland and the Nordic/Scandinavian countries:

> Scotland's challenge is to compete with London, as well as Dublin, Frankfurt and other hubs across Europe ... If we are to compete with the world we must f rst compete at home which is why we are setting a goal to be the most competitive of the present UK nations ... Countries and regions within nations are competing with each other whether they acknowledge it or not. The question is whether they succeed. Labour is fond of comparing the UK's economic performance with France, Germany, America and Japan. What the Government doesn't mention is that within the UK, Scotland is underperforming due largely to its London-centric policies. (SNP 2005, 9–11)

In the party platform for the 2007 election, the SNP advocated a refocusing of business support as well as "increased access to venture capital" for Scottish companies, all in order to emulate the economic success of the "Arc of Prosperity" countries: Iceland, Ireland, Denmark, Norway, Sweden, and Finland (SNP 2007, 18). Although the first term of the SNP government was deeply marked by the financial crisis and recession, this commitment to enhanced policy asymmetry and state intervention was maintained and clearly influenced policy choices.

The "statecraft phase," part II (2007–2009)

During the autumn of 2007, the SNP launched a new Government Economic Strategy and announced two initiatives reflecting this nationalist perspective. The rhetoric was unmistakable: "One hundred years ago, Scotland was an economic giant which left the rest of the world in its shadow. Today, we have everything it takes to be a Celtic Lion economy, matching, and then overtaking, the Irish Tiger" (Scotland 2007a, v). The objectives were to catch up to the UK's productivity and "entrepreneurial activity levels" by 2011, and to "Arc of Prosperity" countries' by 2017 (2007a, 11–14).

Weeks after the election, the SNP also imposed its first major reform: the dissolution of the LECs and the withdrawal of professional training responsibilities from SE/HIE to form the separate public agency Skills Development Scotland. This aimed at "the de-cluttering and refocusing of public sector business support in Scotland, allowing the enterprise agencies to focus more strategically on maximizing their impact" (Scotland 2007a, 28). It was also an endorsement of the selective approach implemented since 2003, steering investment toward "companies of scale": "The enterprise networks will now be focused on supporting investment and innovation by companies and sectors which have growth potential and are of national or regional significance" (2007a, 27). By April 2008, the LECs were dissolved and training responsibilities spun out of SE.

Merely a decade after devolution, the changes imposed in 1990 were thus completely reversed, with SE/HIE activities recentralized and refocused (Scotland 2008d). The activities of the LECs would henceforth be performed by local authorities in collaboration with BG, with the specific purpose of building a "pipeline" of high-potential Scottish businesses. As Scotland's Cabinet Secretary for Finance, John Swinney, remarked, "if an emerging start-up company does well and begins to grow, the key point about the business gateway process is that it should identify where the growth potential is and how the range of added-value services that SE can deliver can apply to that company" (Scotland 2007b, n.p.).

To this end, "prospecting managers" were hired to work as intermediaries between BG and SE/HIE: "They will go out prospecting among the companies served by BG for companies that have the potential to grow to £1 million turnover within three years, and those companies will transfer to account management at SE" (Scotland 2008d, n.p.). On top of that, the ITIs were integrated to SE as subsidiaries in January 2009, to streamline R&D commercialization and give SE-backed companies priority (Scotland 2007b, n.p.).[6] The SNP, in sum, put SE/HIE and the economic development apparatus as a whole through significant recentralization as soon as it took power. As a result, business financing and sponsoring became the sole focuses of SE/HIE, and after a peak in

Graph 6.8. Contributions of SE and HIE, 2002–2011 (£ millions)

Business financing/sponsoring (left axis)

Business financing/sponsoring as % of total expenditure budget (right axis)

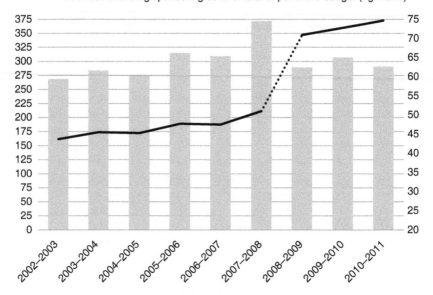

Sources: SE & HIE (2004–12), annual reports and accounts.
Note:. Dashes represent the reform of 2007–8, when professional training activities were spun out of SE/HIE and into Skills Development Scotland.

2007–8, their spending levels were maintained at around £300 million per year, despite the financial crisis and budget cuts imposed by Westminster (graph 6.8).

The importance of the strategic and ideological underpinnings of these reforms could hardly be overstated. Recentralization was justified on the grounds of enhanced "alignment with the Government's purposes: the complex landscape of public bodies has, in the past, resulted in different organisations having priorities that are not always compatible with each other and do not assist consistent approaches to the delivery of Government's overall policy objectives" (Scotland 2009a, 6). For one anonymous high-level SE official, "the shift in the relationship with the SNP administration that came in 2007 was highly significant ... SE was given a clear mandate, to focus on the growth of companies and of sectors. We've been able to use that sharper focus to develop our activities better and we've been on a lot better trajectory because of that" (personal interview).

This perceived imperative for centralization and coordination was also rooted in ideological preferences for the kind of government leadership the SNP (and SE) were observing in Nordic/Scandinavian countries. During a parliamentary inquiry on the reforms of 2007–9, SE's Chairman Crawford Gillies argued that the Nordic countries' economic success rested on such leadership: "The real enablers of their growth have been the political will of, and support from, their national governments and the collaboration between all public agencies behind a single strategy and approach" (Scotland 2011a, n.p.). SE even started to send taskforces to Scandinavia after 2007, with Finland drawing particular attention: "What's of interest for us in Finland is how they organize in relation to innovation, because that's been an area of underperformance for Scotland. One thing they seem particularly good at is collaboration and integration across different parts of the public sector" (Brian McVey, personal interview). The "Arc of Prosperity" and nationalist rhetoric used to promote policy asymmetry and state intervention thus wasn't only symbolic: behind the SNP's "statecraft phase" was a true preference for economic development models very different from the UK's.

Asymmetry and government activism gained further prominence during the second part of the SNP's term. The financial crisis of 2008 and the following recession provided opportunities for strategic recovery initiatives not merely geared toward economic takeover but also devised to counterbalance the central government's austerity measures and to build on Scotland's own comparative advantages. From 2009 onward, Scotland entered an "investment phase" during which new public sector funds were created for strategic objectives. The first initiative of that phase consisted in a major increase in government support for Scotland's "third sector" businesses (Scotland 2007c, 10), starting with the launch of the Scottish Investment Fund (SIF) in late 2008 (Scotland 2008e).

The crisis and the investment phase (2009–2011)

By 2007 the crisis was looming, and Scotland's economy was stagnating. The recession took hold in 2008, with six negative quarters from mid-2008 to 2010 for a total GDP drop of around 3% (Scotland 2015b). With tightening budget transfers from the UK Treasury (Scotland 2007c, 1) and an unsteady market, it made sense for the Scottish government to invest in stable social enterprises and co-ops. Almost £100 million was thus earmarked for this sector in the 2008–9 budget (Scotland 2007c, 10), along with the Enterprising Third Sector Action Plan

Graph 6.9. Budget spending on Third Sector and Social Economy, Scotland, 2002–2011 (£ millions)

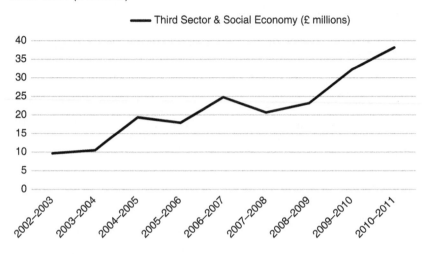

Source: Scotland (2008f, 119).

(Scotland 2008e). The core initiative of this plan was the £30 million SIF, offering a mix of grants, loans, and VC to social enterprises and co-ops. The SIF quickly proved successful in generating new job opportunities in a challenging economic context (Scotland 2010a; Social Investment Scotland 2014), therefore becoming part of the Scottish government's wider recovery strategy, with similar initiatives such as the Third Sector Enterprise Fund and Third Sector Resilience Fund (Scotland 2009b, 14, 2009c, 19, 2010a).

The SIF, however, was far from being a mere counter-cyclical tool. It formed part of an overarching and long-standing effort to build on the higher survival rates of third-sector businesses. Budgets dedicated to this sector had more than doubled between 2002 and 2007 (graph 6.9), as the sustainability of social enterprises and co-ops had been at the centre of nationalist efforts to strengthen Scotland's corporate ownership structure. The "autonomy and independence" of co-ops, which "cannot easily be bought up or closed arbitrarily," were presented as a key advantage of this business model (Scotland 2004d, 6, 11). This mounting interest had led to the establishment of the SE subsidiary Co-Operative Development Scotland in late 2006. Its responsibilities included managerial support, market intelligence, and the "conversion of other business structures to the co-operative model" (Ekos Limited 2008, 6; Scotland 2004d, 19), but not corporate funding per se. This is where the SIF was to fit in.

This intermingling of recovery and strategic objectives characterized other SNP initiatives. One was the creation of the National Renewables Infrastructure Fund (NRIF) in 2010, which merged the counter-cyclical strategy (Scotland 2009b, 2009c) with an objective established as soon as 2007: "For Scotland to take the lead and become the green energy capital of Europe" (Scotland 2007c, 13). Hence the publication of the *Renewables Action Plan* in July 2009, which, as the minister for enterprise then put it, was "more than a set of measures to cope with short-term challenges [but sought] to drive low carbon energy production, in a way which capitalises on Scotland's unique resources" (Scotland 2009d, 4). Among such resources was offshore wind, for which this plan established as an objective to "champion and coordinate the delivery of appropriate Scottish regions as clusters for integrated innovation, manufacturing, port and grid infrastructure" (2009d, 7). In early 2010, as the UK Treasury was cutting back on stimulus packages (Scotland 2010b, 10), the Scottish government thus embarked on its own program of "large scale infrastructure investment in the offshore wind, wave and tidal sectors" (2010b, 20).

In November 2010, the Scottish government and SE/HIE capitalized the £70 million NRIF, offering grants and equity "to support the development of port and near-port manufacturing locations for offshore wind turbines and related developments including test and demonstration activity, with the overall aim of stimulating an offshore wind supply chain in Scotland."[7] This fund was clearly part of a reinforced nationalist drive for policy asymmetry, as it was launched at the exact same time as the announcement of a UK-wide Green Investment Bank with similar purposes, to be headquartered in Edinburgh (Edinburgh Green Investment Bank Group 2012). The NRIF thus wasn't designed merely to boost capital investment, but also to give Scotland a competitive edge over other UK regions. This is why the SNP government and SE/HIE added another £35 million initiative only months later, the Prototype Offshore Wind Energy Renewables Support (POWERS) Fund, launched in September 2011, specifically aimed at supporting the development of turbine prototypes in NRIF-backed facilities.

Moreover, this drive for a sustained public expenditure effort rooted in asymmetry was reinforced by another study on high-growth firms that had been commissioned as the Scottish government and SE/HIE were shifting their policy focus away from high-growth starts and toward high-growth firms, that is, toward businesses with a proven record of performance (Brown and Mason 2012, 25–7). Published in late 2010, this study notably emphasized that, in economic downturns, businesses financed by private sector investors are more vulnerable to foreign takeovers: "Companies that have raised finance from private equity funds, either to grow the business or to finance a management buyout, are vulnerable to being sold because of the short-term investment horizon of such investors" (Mason and Brown 2010, 48). The first reaction of the SNP was the refinancing of the SCIF and SVF with support from the European Regional Development Fund: the SCIF then attained £67 million in capitalization, and the SVF £50 million (SE Investments 2009, 3).

The second was the establishment of the Scottish Investment Bank (SIB) in September 2009, notably regrouping the SCIF, SSF, and SVF under a single, rebranded "investment arm" of SE/HIE. This reorganization was primarily symbolic and aimed at increasing the three funds' visibility, as SE's Joan Gordon explains: "It was quite political because you had an economic downturn, and a reduction in available finance for SMEs. So politically, there was probably a need to enhance and widen our profile. The rebranding was part of that" (personal interview). This "reduction in available finance for SMEs," indeed, also applied to public sector investors (see graphs 6.10 and 6.12) and thus contributed to the shift in policy focus[8] toward high-growth firms by forcing a more selective investment strategy (Brown and Mason 2012, 26). The creation of the SIB addressed this issue to a certain extent. As SE's Brian McVey remarks, "it also created a vehicle where returns could be recirculated, reinvested into companies. Rather than the money getting back to SE's main account, it would get recirculated back into investments and companies" (personal interview).

The launch of the SIB was accompanied, besides, by the addition of another link to the SSF-SCIF-SVF funding "escalator." First announced in late 2009 as the market for bank lending to SMBs was drying out, the £95 million[9] Scottish Loan Fund (SLF), a limited partnership with the private sector Maven Capital Partners, started operations in early 2011 (Scotland 2011a). The SLF was first designed to operate as a bridge connecting the lending market and the VC market, between which the relative "lack of linkages" was a persistent problem (North, Baldock, and Ekanem 2010, 182). Second, it was to provide "mezzanine finance" in the form of £250,000–£5 million loans for businesses too established for VC, but too young and risky for bank lending.

At the time that the NRIF, SIB, and SLF were established, SE listed as its first priority to "maximise [its] contribution to the goals of the Government Economic Strategy" (SE 2011, 7). This was done through the supply of additional VC and debt finance (2011, 12) and through enhanced focus on renewables (2011, 14). Unsurprisingly, the contributions of SIB funds thus really took off from 2010 onward (graph 6.10). The SNP's economic nationalism played key roles in that regard, with the drive for policy asymmetry and strategic state involvement underlying counter-cyclical and recovery initiatives.

Graph 6.10. Contributions of the Scottish Investment Bank, 2009–2018

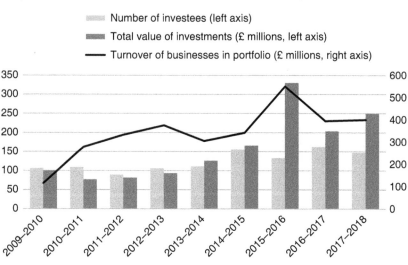

Sources: Scottish Investment Bank (2010–18), annual reviews.
Note: Including the SCIF, SSF, SVF, SLF, Portfolio Fund, REIF, and other direct investments. Value of investments include leverage.

The Second and Third SNP Governments (2011–2019)

In the Scottish election of May 2011, the SNP gained a majority of seats with a platform criticizing Westminster's "one-size-fits-all" economic policies (SNP 2011, 5, 8). Through enhanced asymmetry and ultimately secession, the SNP pledged to "reindustrialise Scotland" and turn it into "Europe's green energy powerhouse." Two initiatives, the Renewable Energy Investment Fund (REIF) and the Scottish Business Development Bank (SBDB), were evoked, and in both cases the drive for policy asymmetry would prove crucial. The creation of REIF would require a deal with the British Treasury in order to use capital earmarked for the UK-wide Green Investment Bank (SNP 2011, 35), while the idea of the SBDB emerged out of concerns with the local banking sector: "We want to see greater competition in the Scottish banking market and wider access to capital for businesses … We believe banking must be more closely aligned with the real economy" (2011, 10).

From 2011 onward, public spending on renewable energy increased almost fivefold (graph 6.11) in a context of stagnating expenditure on business sponsoring at SE/HIE (graph 6.12). This surge was driven by a government-led repositioning of SIB investments toward renewables

Graph 6.11. Public spending on renewable energy, Scotland, 2002–2015 (£ millions)

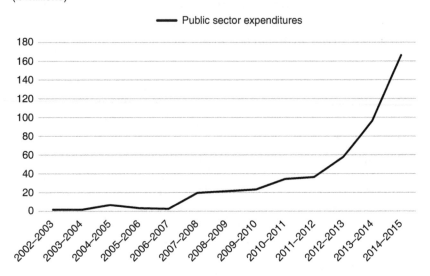

Source: Audit Scotland (2013).
Note: Figures include Scottish Government and SE/HIE/SIB spending.

Graph 6.12. Contributions of SE and HIE, 2010–2018 (£ millions)

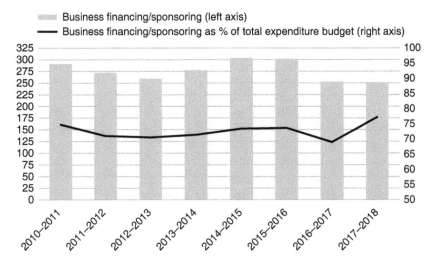

Sources: SE & HIE (2011–18), annual reports and accounts.

following the establishment of REIF and was accompanied by a general intensification of state sponsoring in this sector, with the introduction of a number of new co-investment funds and limited partnerships. In each case, key motives of the Scottish government included underlying nationalist rationales, for which the long journey to the 2014 referendum on independence and, later, Scotland's opposition to Brexit set the stage.

REIF and the Scottish Life Sciences Fund

In July 2011, the SNP published its *2020 Routemap for Renewable Energy in Scotland*, establishing very ambitious targets that would not only require that SE/HIE intensify efforts to promote "indigenous supply chains" in the green-tech sector, but also that fiscal resources levied in Scotland for environmental purposes be reinvested locally (Scotland 2011d). When the SNP learned that Westminster intended to use money from the Fossil Fuel Levy – a UK-wide tax imposed on non-renewable electricity suppliers – for its Green Investment Bank, negotiations on asymmetry were engaged:

> The UK Government has proposed that Scottish Ministers agree to waive our right to the Fossil Fuel Levy, now standing at over £200 million, in return for a guaranteed investment of £250 million by the Green Investment Bank in Scotland. This does not meet the clear wish in Scotland to see early investment of the Fossil Fuel money in Scotland by Scottish Ministers, and discussions are continuing with Treasury. (Scotland 2011d, 34)

Given how central the "transition to a low carbon economy" and Scotland's comparative advantages in renewable energy were to the new Government Economic Strategy (Scotland 2011c), maximum discretion over investment was perceived as necessary: "Targeted investment in renewable energy in partnership with our enterprise bodies will act as a key motor of the Scottish economy. Scotland is blessed with abundant energy resources and we are committed to taking full advantage of the opportunities that exist in transforming to a low carbon economy" (Scotland 2011e, 94).

By November 2011, "the UK Treasury agreed to a Scottish Government proposal to release half of the £206 million Fossil Fuel Levy surpluses generated from Scotland's energy industry to invest in renewable projects, with the remainder being made available to capitalise the UK Green Investment Bank."[10] Almost immediately, as SE's Pat McHugh confirms (personal interview), SE and the SIB were asked to sharpen their focus on renewables as well as to set up, with the £103 million from the Fossil Fuel Levy agreement, a targeted investment fund. SE accordingly identified renewables as its very first "strategic priority" and vouched to spend at least £120 million in this sector through the NRIF and other initiatives (SE 2012a, 16). The SIB also announced that the £103 million would be used to capitalize the new REIF, to "complement" the Green Investment Bank by investing in the sub-sectors of marine energy (wave and tidal), community renewables (wind and hydro), and district heating systems (SIB 2012, 26–7).

This agreement was an important asymmetry gain not only because it allowed Scotland to invest according to its priorities, but also because REIF would relieve other SIB funds from the financial pressures associated with renewables (SIB 2012, 16): "Before the REIF was set up, the Scottish Venture Fund was doing renewables deals. But these were putting pressure on the SVF budget because renewables don't really fit its model. Renewables take much greater sums of money then classic technology" (Pat McHugh, personal interview). REIF was thus devised without a specific deal size range: "In marine renewable energy investments, deal sizes are expected to be in the order of several millions whereas for community-owned renewable investments, these could be more variable and as small as £100k or less" (SE 2012b, n.p.).

At REIF's launch in October 2012, SE's Chief Executive Dr. Lena Wilson and Scottish Renewables' chief executive Niall Stuart recognized its favourable timing, with Scotland entering a new and more expensive phase in the development of renewable energy:

> This new fund is key to providing an economic, community benef t and environmental legacy based on our natural competitive advantage in renewable energy and comes at a critical time in the development of the sector ... Scotland is already at the forefront of developing and testing emerging wave and tidal technologies and, with the correct level of government support, we can become a global centre of excellence in both the deployment of these technologies and their accompanying supply chains.[11]

Unlike the Green Investment Bank, REIF was thus set up to "offer long-term investment support" and to "focus explicitly on Scottish opportunities." Moreover, REIF's remit was to be flexible: "The fund will also consider projects which do not fall into the priority sub-sectors but ... accelerate Scotland's transition to a low carbon economy" (SE 2012b). Along with the NRIF and POWERS, REIF clearly accelerated the SIB's shift toward renewables (graphs 6.13 & 6.14). By 2014, energy and renewables had become the prime investment sector, way ahead of

Graphs 6.13 & 6.14. Scottish Investment Bank investments by sector, 2010–2018 (% and £ millions)

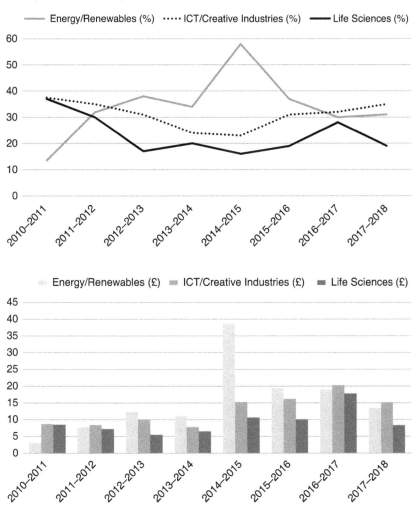

Sources: Scottish Investment Bank (2011–18), annual reviews.
Note: Annual value of investments (excluding leverage).

ICT and life sciences, thanks to a tenfold increase in annual investments between 2010 and 2015.

In fact, SIB contributions as a whole kept progressing at a rapid pace after 2011 (graph 6.10). Investments in life sciences, for instance, doubled following the launch of the £50 million Scottish Life Sciences Fund (SLSF) in January 2013, to which the SIB contributed £5 million. In this case as well, national objectives were key: in its economic strategy, the SNP government identified life sciences, alongside renewables, as one of the priority "growth sectors" in which "Scotland typically has distinctive capabilities and businesses with the potential to be internationally successful" (Scotland 2011c, 45).

The new *Scottish Life Sciences Strategy* aimed to double the entire sector's turnover by 2020, notably by "anchoring" existing businesses in Scotland and "building" new national champions out of successful SMBs (Life Sciences Scotland 2011, 3–7). Capital requirements in health technologies and pharmaceuticals were so important that many start-ups had been, until then, funded by the SVF rather than the SSF or SCIF. In this context, a £5 million contribution might seem small, but it still allowed the SIB to play a significant role in the SLSF, which was managed by the private sector Rock Spring Ventures[12] but capitalized in good part by other public sector partners such as the European Investment Fund, Strathclyde Pension Fund, and many Scottish universities. As SE's Joan Gordon explains, public sector presence imposed a *national* investment focus (personal interview):

> Because we would invest alongside Scottish universities and the EIF, it gave us comfort and we were able to ensure that 60% of funds would be invested into Scottish companies. For our £5 million, that was particularly good value for money. Life sciences were identif ed as a sector where having a specif cally targeted fund in Scotland would be benef cial. That's the reason why we invested: we recognized it would really benef t the sector, and that was the only fund that wished to locate in Scotland and do this.

To be sure, REIF and the SLSF were devised with gap filling, leveraging, and spillover purposes in mind. What these two cases demonstrate, however, is that limiting the explanation for state intervention to these motives without accounting for the impact of the SNP's drive for policy asymmetry and the development of Scottish-owned medium-sized businesses – i.e., for economic nationalism – would be a mistake. In the months preceding Scotland's 2014 referendum on secession, the SNP made it clear its efforts were intended to counterbalance the "one-size-fits-all" policies favouring London's financial sector, and that such interventions were aimed at the development of an alternative economic model, closer to small European and Scandinavian countries' (Scotland 2013a, 2013c, 2014).

The Scottish Business Development Bank (SBDB)

In 2013, the SNP government started publishing policy statements on the economic development model of an independent Scotland. In its "Scotland's Economy: the Case for Independence," the SNP's perspective was unambiguous:

> Since devolution our economic performance has improved because of our ability to use even limited levers in the interests of Scotland … There are also numerous examples in particular areas of economic development – such as in our renewables ambitions – where a distinct approach in Scotland has provided real economic benef ts. However, the paradox we face is that despite all of these strengths, we are not as successful as we should be … The evidence for the proposition that Westminster isn't working for Scotland lies in current Westminster policy, in our long-term economic performance relative to other small nations, in the growing gap between rich and poor, and in a system which has clearly benef tted London and the South East to what is now a quite startling degree. (Scotland 2013a, 26)

The SNP government considered the lack of policy asymmetry constitutive of the British system as the prime cause of Scotland's unbalanced corporate ownership structure and lack of medium-sized businesses, notably as compared to Germany:

> Firstly, merger and acquisition strategies have led to Scottish companies being taken-over by larger UK or international rivals (despite the consequences for market concentration or economic activity in Scotland) … Secondly, the existence of "one-size-f ts-all" economic and business policies that ref ect Scotland's increasing emergence as an economy within the UK have acted as a barrier to local business growth. Thirdly, the lack of autonomy to prioritise policies to help business invest, secure appropriate f nance, tackle local challenges (such as distance from markets) and take advantage of local opportunities, has put Scotland at a disadvantage. (Scotland 2013c, 88–9)

In "Reindustrialising Scotland for the 21st Century," the SNP continued to advocate for an "alternative model" inspired by countries like Germany, Austria, Finland, and Sweden, where economic development depends on "close cooperation and coordination across partners," "innovation and investment in R&D," "the importance of strategic planning" (Scotland 2014, 38–9), and even a degree of import substitution: "strengthened, and competitive domestic supply chains can also make an important contribution to rebalancing the economy through import substitution. For example, more competitive domestic suppliers can capture a larger share of input markets from producers; whilst stronger domestic suppliers for emerging industries should prevent the need for large elements of the production chain to be imported" (Scotland 2014, 47).

The idea of the SBDB then emerged out of a perceived need to provide growing Scottish businesses with enhanced access to debt finance. This idea was first expressed in the SNP's "Sustainable, Responsible Banking: A Strategy for Scotland," published in 2013 (Scotland 2013b). The plan was to expand the SIB's remit to include the provision of long-term loans and guarantees for growing and exporting SMBs, to ensure a more efficient coordination between public sector players and Scotland's banking sector (Scotland 2013b, 28). There were also strictly nationalist motives behind the SBDB project, relating to the establishment of the British Business Bank (BBB) in 2012–13, a state-owned holding integrating all UK-wide public funding schemes (Baldock and North 2012). An anonymous, influential player in the Scottish VC ecosystem indeed remarked (personal interview):

> It is completely political. Party-political. There was no lobbying for it from any part, although the small business organizations were concerned about the lack of bank borrowing and expressed themselves about that. But it was a complete political reaction to the launch of the BBB, because we have a separatist government. No one is opposing it, because it is completely political, and it will happen.

Although devised in response to a British policy however, financial issues specific to Scotland also justified the idea. As early as 2011, the SNP expressed concern with the banking sector's response to the financial crisis, denouncing a lack of alignment with the "real economy" and a drought in corporate lending (SNP 2011, 10). This was reiterated in the aforementioned banking strategy, as the SNP argued that the Scottish lending market was still much too focused on short-term considerations, risk averse, and "concentrated," with 70% of loans issued to SMBs coming from only two banks (Scotland 2013b, 16). This was confirmed by many governmental, state-ordered, and independent studies (North et al. 2010; Royal Society of Edinburgh 2014; Scotland 2015c).

The SBDB was presented as a good way to link the public sector's existing equity tools with new lending tools, in order to inject competition in Scotland's banking sector, forcing it to be more responsive to SMBs' needs and thus leveraging debt finance at lower interest rates.

The SBDB's close relationships with the Scottish government and SE/ HIE, moreover, would distinguish it from the BBB. A well-informed, anonymous source explains (personal interview):

> The SIB does not offer the money on its own, without companies being able to also look at SE's wider support. The BBB just does money, it does not give advice and support and that's another key difference. Ministers here also have a wider approach, one they call the "National Outcomes Approach:" this is largely about access to f nance, but they set out a much bigger agenda on the drivers around company growth, employment, exports, internationalization, and innovation. It's not just about how much money we put into the system or the return on investment; it is a much wider "social return" on investments, the impacts those investments have on us as well. So, there is a philosophical difference, that's about outcomes as well as inputs; and there's a service difference, in the advice being part of the Scottish model and having to be integrated into a SBDB.

The SBDB initiative was thus also about policy *divergence*, aiming to provide "Scottish solutions to Scottish problems." This explains why the Scottish government looked well beyond the BBB for blueprints, gathering information on business development banks such as the German Kreditanstalt Für Wiederaufbau (KfW), Finland's Finnvera, and Sweden's Industrifunden (Michie and Wishlade 2014). From 2014 to 2016, with the Scottish government's focus shifting to the independence referendum and its aftermath (Rioux 2016), the SBDB initiative progressed slowly. In its new "Scotland's Economic Strategy," however, the SNP reiterated its intention to go forward:

> Building on the work of the SIB, we are establishing a SBDB, to work directly with small and medium-sized enterprises and the f nancial markets to support businesses with high growth potential in Scotland. Scotland has a lower proportion of medium-sized enterprises than other European countries such as Germany, Austria, Finland and Sweden. The SBDB will therefore, in particular, help to build more medium-sized enterprises, and is an important addition to the institutional landscape in Scotland. (Scotland 2015a, 44)

Major steps toward the establishment of the SBDB were taken in late 2016, first with a £21.5 million grant from the Scottish government to the SIB for expansion purposes, then with the launch of two new measures, the Scottish Growth Scheme (SGS) and SME Holding Fund. The SGS was announced in September, after the SNP was re-elected and 62% of the Scottish electorate rejected Brexit. It was directly motivated by the Brexit vote – and thus by perceived imperatives for policy asymmetry and state involvement – and was presented by Scotland's PM Nicola Sturgeon as "an exceptional response to an exceptional economic challenge ... a half-billion-pound vote of confidence in Scottish business, Scottish workers and the Scottish economy."[13]

The SGS was also the first concrete step towards the SBDB: its £500 million budget would essentially be used to provide loans and guarantees of up to £5 million for growing, early-stage businesses in technology-intensive sectors, thereby complementing SIB funds and boosting Scotland's lending market. Besides, this scheme was accompanied by the £40 million SME Holding Fund announced in December, capitalized by the ERDF and managed by the Scottish Government as a fund of funds (Scotland 2016b, 74). In its 2017–18 Programme for Government, the SNP announced the elaboration of a "full implementation plan" for the SBDB (by then rebranded as the Scottish National Investment Bank, or SNIB) and presented it as "a key cornerstone of the future Scottish economic development policy landscape."[14] It also announced the launch of a first fund capitalized through the SGS, the £100 million Scottish-European Growth Co-Investment Programme specialized in later-stage equity financing (Scotland 2017, 49–50).[15]

Finally, in February 2018, after months of consultations and studies (Scotland 2018c), the "Scottish National Investment Bank Implementation Plan" was released by the Scottish Government (Scotland 2018b). This plan, which sets out the missions, primary financing tools, and structures of the SNIB clearly reflects the nationalist underpinnings of this project and the government's preference for policy asymmetry and the further development of a Scottish "sponsor state." Ultimately to be self-funding, the SNIB is to remain within the public sector realm "perpetually," and to collaborate closely with both the Scottish government and its agencies, such as SE and HIE. Capitalized with over £2 billion from the Scottish government for the first ten years, the SNIB will be fully operational by 2020 and will notably offer micro-loans (up to £100,000), regular loans and mezzanine finance (up to £2 million), early-stage venture capital (up to £2 million), development and expansion-stage – "scale-up" – equity capital and loans (up to £10 million), as well as "mission-based finance focused on the transformative change agenda set by the Programme for Government" (Scotland 2018b, viii; see also Mazzucato and Penna 2016; Mazzucato and Macfarlane 2019).

This last aspect of the SNIB's projected responsibilities highlights the interventionist perspective from which it emerged. Not only, indeed, will it contribute to the implementation of the Scottish Government's economic development strategies, but in doing so the SNIB will adopt a patient and targeted investment approach aimed at "market leadership:" in other words, "this new, mission-oriented institution will actively create and shape markets, … providing finance to support the projects and initiatives aimed at realising opportunities to transform the economy" (Scotland 2018b, xii). The SNIB will therefore not be merely geared toward leveraging private capital or filling market gaps, but most importantly toward the *steering* of private investment and the generation of new, strategic market opportunities for Scottish entrepreneurs and investors. Moreover, and this is certainly significant from a nationalist perspective, the SNIB is expected to expand Scottish participation in foreign investment transactions: "Many large deals involve foreign investors and our participation by share of deals – both by number and by value of investment – is low in comparison with other regions of the UK. The Bank should be capable of amplifying the voice of Scotland in this important regard" (Scotland 2018b, iii).

These "mission-oriented" and "market-creating" mandates imparted to the future SNIB, besides, reflect the consensus which emerged from the consultation process and calls for "a more ethical, socially-just and environmentally-aware investment strategy" as well as for a "focus on Scotland's regions" (Scotland 2018c, 1–3). This kind of social, environmental, and regional awareness – also central, it should be noted, to the imminent launch of the new South of Scotland Enterprise agency (Scottish Parliament 2019) – is indeed at the root of the different investment approach the SNIB will adopt: "mission-oriented policies focus not on sectors but on societal challenges, that require different sectors to invest and innovate. This involves picking the problems and helping any organization (across the public sector, private sector, third sector, and across all manufacturing and services) that are willing to engage with the investments and activities that such challenges require" (Mazzucato and Macfarlane 2019, 9). As of 2019, twenty years after devolution, the Scottish government was thus already present, either directly or indirectly, at all VC stages and deal sizes in Scotland. With such a public, national investment bank, it now clearly aims to extend its influence over the Scottish lending and equity markets in order to safeguard the ownership and increase the size of Scotland's promising businesses in strategic sectors.

Concluding Remarks

The policy impacts of economic nationalism, which led to the deepening of asymmetries between Scotland and the RoUK throughout the 1990s and early 2000s, have clearly persisted since devolution.

Graph 6.15. Total number and value of early-stage VC deals, Scotland, 2003–2017 (£ millions)

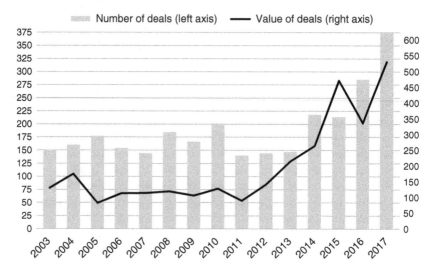

Sources: Young Company Finance (2006–18).

Despite an uninterrupted decline in the provision of private sector VC and equity to Scottish businesses from 2004 onward, the number and value of early-stage VC deals made in Scotland actually followed an upward trend (graph 6.15). The explanation for such a paradox is that government presence in Scotland's entrepreneurial finance ecosystem, through either direct investment (*faire*) or hybrid co-investment schemes (*faire faire / faire avec*), was not only maintained since 2003 but enhanced (graph 6.16).

The very core of what is known today as the "Scottish model" was put in place since then, with the launch of co-investment funds that established the foundations for the SIB and for a national investment bank. Initiatives introduced during this period refined the Scottish approach to entrepreneurial finance, grounded in an influential public sector and a mix of *faire*, *faire avec*, and *faire faire*. Economic nationalism thus continued to play key roles and to exert a strong influence on the elaboration and implementation of such initiatives. Even during the financial crisis and recession, classic market rationales for state intervention were always complemented if not subordinated by political imperatives and ideological preferences for policy asymmetry and strategic government involvement.

Graph 6.16. Public and angel VC investments, Scotland, 2009–2017

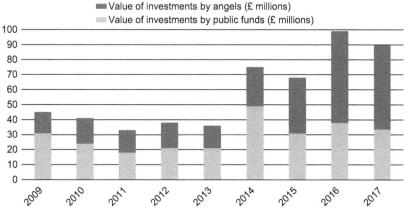

Sources: Young Company Finance (2008–18).

From the promotion of angel syndication (SSF, SCIF, SVF) to the inexorable recentralization of the economic development apparatus (SE/HIE and LECs); from the strengthening of Scotland's corporate ownership structure (SVF, SIF, SLF, SBDB/SNIB, SGS) to the maximization of its comparative advantages in renewables (NRIF, POWERS, REIF); and from the denunciation of Westminster's "one-size-fits-all" policies to the promotion of secession as the best way to safeguard and perfect the "Scottish model," the drive for policy autonomy and divergence always remained central.

Chapter Seven

Discussion and Conclusions

With this book, I was determined to go "from *whether* to *how*" with regards to the effects of minority nationalism on economic policymaking. The main challenge was to demonstrate if and how nationalism in Quebec and Scotland constitutes a crucial explanatory factor for high levels of government intervention, as well as for the persistence of policy asymmetry with the RoC and RoUK. The demonstration required an in-depth, long-term process tracing effort aimed at uncovering the mechanisms through which nationalism affects concrete policy choices in the sector of entrepreneurial finance and VC. By now, it should be clear that Quebec and Scotland did converge toward the state-influenced market economy (SME) model, through a plethora of sponsoring initiatives requiring active state involvement. The two regions converged as well in their increasing reliance since 2003 on hybrid co-investment funds (*faire faire* / *faire avec*).

Such convergence could not be adequately explained without reference to nationalism, which produces ideological, political, and institutional pressures in favour of policy asymmetry and state intervention. Early on, I paraphrased sociologist Ernest Gellner (1983) by stating that if nationalism's core principle is that political and national "units" should be congruent, then at the heart of *economic nationalism* is the idea that economic and national "units" should be as well. The major contribution of this book is thus to demonstrate that, consistent with this classic definition, Québécois and Scottish nationalisms have concrete impacts on economic policymaking, and thereby to show that the various policy asymmetries that minority nationalism generally leads to within multinational states also apply to the field of economic development, and specifically the VC sector.

General Overview

This book's objective, accordingly, was not solely to explain state intervention in VC, but also the development, preservation, and deepening of policy asymmetries between Quebec and the RoC/Ontario, and Scotland and the RoUK/South East England. Therefore, even if they all played key roles in specific contexts, classic market justifications for state involvement in VC – funding gaps, economic downturns, geographic concentration of investments, leveraging, positive externalities, etc. – could not provide complete and satisfying answers to our questions.

Instead, I argued that the explanation for the development and persistence of state intervention and policy asymmetry had to lie in the influence of *minority nationalism*, defined as explained in chapter 1 by a set of "collective commitments *to* and demands *for* significant policy self-determination, carried by national communities forming demographic minorities within sovereign nation-states." The major challenge was to demonstrate *how* nationalism was linked, in the particular cases of Quebec and Scotland, to major policy initiatives having marked the development of regional VC ecosystems. From my perspective, it should be reiterated, *economic nationalism* was not to be reduced to protectionism or ethno-linguistic considerations.

Adapting my definition of economic nationalism to the *subnational* contexts within which Quebec and Scotland evolve as well as to a focus on *policy*, I expected it to take the following forms: (1) perceived needs and ideological preferences for policy asymmetry and strategic planning; (2) political and institutional imperatives to uphold such asymmetries; and (3) a concomitant tendency for governments – secessionist or not – to intervene based on those needs, preferences, and imperatives. Although the focus was on the last thirty years, it would have been difficult to ignore the thirty previous ones, which saw the creation of the major organizations and funds that established the bases of regional VC ecosystems in Quebec and Scotland.

Despite the different institutional contexts within which Quebec and Scotland were evolving, the first as an autonomous province in a decentralizing federation and the second as part of a unitary state, both regions dedicated significant amounts of public resources from the 1960s onward to the establishment of state-backed funds devoted to regional-level, national interests. Although such strategic interventions were more directly informed by ethno-linguistic considerations in Quebec, with organizations such as the Société générale de financement (1962), the CDPQ (1965), and the SDI (1971) favouring Francophone-owned businesses, the agencies launched in Scotland during the 1960s (HIDB) and 1970s (SDA) were also dedicated to the enhancement of Scottish ownership in key industrial sectors.

The advent of such organizations reflected ideological preferences and perceived needs for higher levels of policy asymmetry. Their primary objectives were to contribute to building and sustaining *regional* investment ecosystems, in order to transform and diversify industrial structures by fostering the development of locally-owned SMBs in high-value-added sectors. By the early 1990s, thanks to such efforts, Quebec and Scotland had both become important VC markets. This was in good part due to the upsurge in public sector activism. Quebec's government was by this time present in all deal sizes, deal stages, and industry sectors, already accounting for over 40% of the total value of annual VC investments in the province. In Scotland, most UK-wide initiatives (Loan Guarantee Scheme, Enterprise Allowance Scheme, Business Expansion Scheme) aimed at boosting entrepreneurship levels in the 1980s failed, while both the SDA and HIDB were investing and leveraging, each year, tens of millions in equity investments.

Quebec's VC market then literally skyrocketed from 1990 to 2003, with the launch of major government-backed initiatives from the SRIs and FDT in the late 1980s to the Innovatechs, CLDs, IQ, and tax-advantaged funds (SOLIDE, FACSN, FRS, CRCD) during the 1990s and early 2000s. In Scotland, public spending per head on economic development remained around 50% greater than the UK average throughout the 1990s and was sustained by the increasing amounts – a 115% growth between 1991 and 2001 – dedicated to business sponsoring and financing at SE/HIE. Public sector-led or backed initiatives such as the BBRS, LINC, SEP, STF, and BGF, moreover, contributed to efficiently mitigating the VC downturn of the early 2000s.

Most of the major initiatives launched in Scotland during this period were crafted either as parts *of* or as complements *to* the BBRS, whose objectives were to help Scotland catch up to South East England's entrepreneurial levels. In Quebec, similarly, the 1990s were characterized by a further push toward policy divergence from the RoC, with the establishment of new LSIFs and tax-advantaged funds and the extension of such models to the regional and local levels. Initiatives such as Objectif emploi (1998) and CRCD (2001) were specifically geared toward the enhanced channelling of Québécois' savings into local businesses and the strengthening of Quebec's corporate ownership structure. Throughout this period, in this sense, economic nationalism continued to complement, if not to supersede, market rationales for state involvement in both regions.

Although Scotland and Quebec progressively turned to more indirect investment approaches over the last fifteen years, launching hybrid co-investment funds and limited partnerships with specialized VCs, this did not result in less state influence or policy asymmetry, but quite the opposite. Quebec's hybrid initiatives (Relève-PME, Desjardins-Innovatech, FIER-Partenaires, Capital-croissance PME, Cycle Capital, AQC, Teralys) most often involved other state-backed or public partners (FSTQ, FACSN, CRCD, CDPQ, IQ) and stabilized state presence in Quebec's VC industry. The upsurge in "private" and foreign VC investments in the province, therefore, had a lot to do with steadily intensifying sponsorship by government-backed funds such as IQ and the FDÉ, the FSTQ, or the CDPQ.[1]

The Scottish VC ecosystem evolved along similar lines. Mostly until but also after the financial crisis, it was marked by the creation of limited partnerships (SLF, SLSF) and hybrid co-investment funds (SCIF, SSF, SVF, REIF[2]) investing alongside private partners and angel syndicates, whose formation was supported and to an extent subsidized by the Scottish government and LINC. Such initiatives were complemented by direct investment tools (ITIs, SIF, NRIF, POWERS, SGS) and as a result, overall government presence in Scotland's VC industry increased rather than receding. The establishment of the SIB (2009), finally, contributed to institutionalizing public involvement in the VC ecosystem, facilitating coordination with the government's industrial strategies and establishing bases for the SNIB project.

Beyond leveraging and counter-cyclical motives, nationalist rationales continued to have significant impacts on this evolution. In Scotland, major initiatives up to 2008 were aimed to nurture Scottish-owned medium-sized businesses and "national champions." After 2008, policy asymmetry and the promotion of Scotland's "competitive advantages," notably in renewables, became key focuses of the SNP. In Quebec, even hybrid schemes launched after the Rapport Brunet (2003) had as an objective to steer private investors in strategic directions, while many of the post-2008 measures were crafted in reaction to Ontarian initiatives, to support local entrepreneurial succession and avoid foreign takeovers, or both. Perceived imperatives for state involvement and for policy asymmetry thus remained central in Quebec as in Scotland.

Evaluation of Findings

The specific case of VC offers a good illustration of the magnitude and type of influence the Quebec and Scottish states exert on market actors. Namely, the strategic role of Quebec and Scottish governments since the 1990s consisted in "sponsoring" domestic firms in priority sectors. Such sponsorship consists in (a) allocating significant amounts of public resources to the development of SMBs; (b) assisting such businesses in securing appropriate funding throughout their growth stages; and (c) supporting the establishment of organizations promoting coordination in the sector of entrepreneurial finance.

This book's major argument is that Québécois and Scottish nationalisms provide a crucial explanation for the development of such state sponsorship. In order to adequately identify the policy effects of nationalism, I approached economic nationalism as a set of "nationalizing mechanisms" (Pickel 2006) taking *ideological, political*, and *institutional* forms. From this perspective,

> It is the nationalizing mechanisms that we need to take into account in order to make sense of the relationships between national identity and political economy. These nationalizing mechanisms include the political legitimation of states; the reproduction of a repertory of common epistemic and moral orders fundamental for the coordination of political and economic action; a constantly evolving national discourse; and national identities as processes of shared social representations, social practices, and forms of collective action (Helleiner and Pickel 2005, 13).

More precisely, I contend that in Quebec and Scotland economic nationalism generally takes the form of *ideological preferences, perceived political imperatives*, and *institutionalized (path dependent) sets of ideas favouring state intervention and policy asymmetry*. This approach allowed me to elaborate four main hypotheses:

> *Hypothesis 1:* The causal inf uence of nationalism on economic development is mediated through ideological, political, and institutional mechanisms.

> *Hypothesis 2:* In Quebec and Scotland since the 1990s, nationalism favoured policy asymmetry (involving autonomy or divergence) and greater government intervention (compared with neighbouring regions in Canada and the UK) in economic development, thereby fostering the emergence of autonomous "sponsor states" in these two regions.

> *Hypothesis 3:* The effects of nationalism on the sponsoring activities of Quebec and Scottish governments are manifest in the sector of entrepreneurial f nance and subsector of venture capital, where they offer crucial explanatory complements to classic economic justif cations for state intervention.

> *Hypothesis 4:* Given the mixed ideational-institutional nature of economic nationalism, I expect its effects to be constant since 1990, giving way to both ideational and institutional

path-dependency. Therefore, the development of regional "sponsor states" in Quebec and Scotland – through policy asymmetry and state activism – will have persisted regardless of the alternation between secessionist (PQ, SNP) and non-secessionist (SLP-SLD, PLQ, CAQ) governments.

The policy effects of economic nationalism, as was demonstrated, were indeed manifest in the VC sector, in which both Quebec's government and Scotland's maintained a very important presence (graphs 7.1 and 7.2). In Scotland, a steadily increasing proportion of the value of early-stage VC investments made since devolution is represented by government-backed deals. Whereas this proportion was approximately 35% at the turn of the century, it increased sharply after the financial crisis of 2008 to reach an annual average of almost 65% since 2009. In Quebec, the trend was somewhat different although the end result was the same: after having reached very high levels – between 55% and 70% – during the 1990s and early 2000s, government-backed deals stabilized between 45% and 55% of the annual value of VC investments since 2006. A review of Quebec's and Scotland's flagship policy initiatives of the 1990s and 2000s, for all three sponsoring styles (*faire, faire avec, faire faire*), is offered below and distinguishes the "nationalizing mechanisms" that impacted their elaboration (table 7.1).

Graph 7.1. Government-backed VC investments as % of Quebec's, 1990–2014

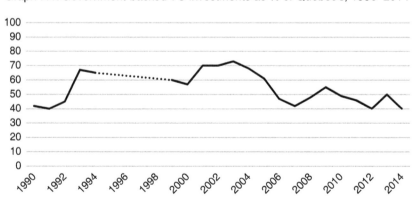

Sources: Macdonalds & Associates Limited (1990–2004); Thomson Financial (2008); Industry Canada (2008–15); Thomson Reuters (2009–15); CVCA (2015a, 2016a). Notes: Approximate figures. By value. Information on investor type for the years 1995 to 1998 unavailable.

Graph 7.2. Government-backed VC investments as % of Scotland's, 2000–2015

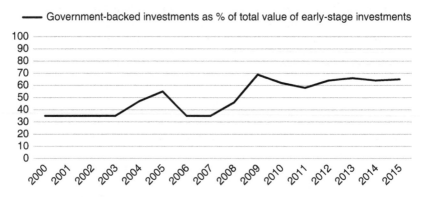

Sources: Don and Harrison (2006); Mason and Harrison (2002a); Harrison et al. (2010);
Mason and Pierrakis (2013); Young Company Finance (2016, 2015, 2014, 2009).
Note: Approximate figures (including public, hybrid, and angel investments).
I classify angel investments as "government-backed" because most of those
investments were made alongside public sector investors, such as SIB funds. I
also added a conservative 5% portion of "institutional investments" to government-
backed investments, to reflect the presence of hybrid co-investments and limited
partnerships with VCs. "Government-backed investments as % of total value of
investments" refers to investments in the Scottish VC market's "middle band" range
(£100,000–£2,000,000).

As these flagship initiatives demonstrate, state intervention and policy asymmetry in Quebec and Scotland indeed mostly persisted since
1990, regardless of the alternation between non-secessionist and secessionist governments, confirming my fourth hypothesis. Even though,
for instance, the PLQ government presided over a drop in the proportion of government-backed VC investments in Quebec between 2003
and 2007, this was compensated for by a sharp increase in the public
sponsorship of specialized VCs, through initiatives such as Teralys.
In Scotland, similarly, the co-investment model (SCIF, SSF, SVF) was
mainly developed by the SLP-SLD coalition before 2007, and the SNP
government actually built on these policy efforts to establish the SIB,
REIF, and SNIB project.

Part of the explanation for this continuity lies in the institutional and
ideational path dependency dynamics economic nationalism induces.
The most telling example in Scotland probably was the recentralization of the SE/HIE networks. This was first done through internal reorganization, but after devolution it was conducted politically, with the

Table 7.1. Flagship policies, sponsoring styles, and nationalizing mechanisms, Quebec and Scotland, 1990s–2000s

Sponsoring style	Quebec's policies	Nationalizing mechanisms	Scotland's policies	Nationalizing mechanisms
Faire & Faire avec	**1990s:** Objectif Emploi / Investissement Québec (1998) *PQ government*	**Ideological**: surpassing Ontario's job creation rates **Political**: Action Nationale's reports **Institutional**: PLQ's amendment to IQ's initial mandate * * *	**1990s:** Business Birth Rate Strategy (1993) *Pre-devolution / Tory government*	**Ideological**: catching up to South East England's business birth rates **Political**: first national strategy following UK-led reforms of HIDB/SDA (LECs) **Institutional**: BBRS as a national "coordination" effort * * *
	2000s: Relève-PME, FIRA & FRQ (2005–11) *PLQ government*	**Ideological**: SMBs as "comparative advantage" (local ownership) **Political**: comparisons with Ontario & RoC (business creation & survival rates); land grabbing/foreign speculation **Institutional**: ecosystem coordination (CDPQ, FSTQ, CRCD, FACSN)	**2000s:** Scottish Co-investment Fund (2002–3) *SLP-SLD coalition*	**Ideological**: sponsoring of medium-sized, national champions ("companies of scale") **Political**: reaction to canceled FDI projects & launch of RVCFs **Institutional**: promotion of angel syndication; SSF-SVF complements
Faire faire	**1990s:** FACSN (1995) *PQ government*	**Ideological**: LSIF model promoting "sense of belonging" among workers **Political**: mustering CSN support for secession (1995 referendum) **Institutional**: complement to FSTQ; coordination with Desjardins * * *	**1990s:** LINC Scotland (1993) *Pre-devolution / Tory government*	**Ideological**: preference for angels' "home bias" and early-stage focus **Political**: reaction to closure/relocation of multinational corporations (Maastricht) **Institutional**: recentralization of LEC's services (national coordination); integral part of BBRS * * *
	2000s: Teralys Capital / Teralys Capital Fonds d'Innovation (2009–15) *PLQ government*	**Ideological**: steering specialized VCs (proportion of investments in Quebec, sectoral focuses) **Political**: reactions to Ontario's funds of funds (OVCF & NVCF) **Institutional**: ecosystem coordination (IQ, CDPQ, FSTQ, FACSN)	**2000s:** Scottish Business Development Bank / SNIB *SNP government*	**Ideological**: intensifying economic nationalism; preference for "coordinative" models **Political**: reaction to the launch of the BBB **Institutional**: need to mitigate Scottish banking sector's "concentration;" refining the "Scottish model" (expanding the SIB)

SLP-SLD coalition and the SNP government reintegrating the LECs to SE/HIE structures before abolishing them. Both governments justified such reforms exactly as the early 1990s' SE/HIE officials justified their efforts to ensure continuity: by stating a preference for the long-standing "Scottish model," allowing for close coordination between development agencies and the government as well as for the efficient implementation of national strategies.

A good example of such dynamics in Quebec, in turn, was that of the creation of Investissement Québec in 1998. When the initial IQ Bill was introduced, it was planned that the new organization would be formed out of the previous Société de développement industriel (SDI). The Bill, however, did not at first explicitly mention that IQ would perpetuate the economic development and job creation missions of the SDI. To ensure continuity, thus, the Liberal opposition introduced an amendment reformulating IQ's mandate to include a responsibility to "contribute to the economic development of Quebec and the creation of employment opportunities" (Québec 1998e). This, as explained in chapter 3, had important consequences on IQ's subsequent roles.

In addition to ideational and institutional path dependency dynamics, economic nationalism also impacted many policy initiatives through ideological and political mechanisms. IQ for instance, was created in the wake of the PQ's Objectif emploi strategy (1998), which first revealed an ideological preference for government involvement and asymmetry in order to surpass Ontario's average annual rate of job creation by 2002. Most importantly, this strategy was a political reaction to L'Action Nationale's 1996–7 reports on Canadian mutual funds, which showed how peripheral Quebec – and Francophone businesses in particular – still were as destinations for private sector investments. Both to meet employment objectives and to mitigate this persisting weakness, the Action Plan to Promote the Development of the Financial Sector was launched as part of the strategy and led to the establishment of many new state-backed investment funds, such as the FAIRE, Services financiers CDPQ, SIRR, and IQ.

The same can be said of Scotland's 1993 Business Birth Rate Strategy (BBRS), which stemmed from a political imperative for intervention in that it represented the first national-level economic strategy following the UK-led reforms imposed in the early 1990s. SE and HIE officials wanted to retain an institutional capacity for nationally coordinated, autonomous interventions. Such perceived imperatives for public intervention and policy asymmetry clearly had ideological underpinnings, in that the objective of the BBRS wasn't simply economic development, but to have Scotland catch up to the UK's leading entrepreneurial region, South East England, by sponsoring the birth of tens of thousands of businesses by 2000.

Comparable arguments can be made with regards to Local Investment Network Company (LINC) Scotland. Launched in 1993, this publicly-subsidized organization was an integral part of the BBRS and, as such, of the *institutional* effort to recentralize economic development policy. First established as a national "introductory service" linking angel investors with Scottish businesses, LINC was crafted out of a perceived need for the national coordination of such services, to maximize Scotland's comparative advantages as a small nation and small VC market. LINC was also part of perceived political imperatives for public involvement in the wake of the Maastricht Treaty and the ensuing relocation of multinational corporations. In that context, LINC came to represent ideological preferences for policy asymmetry in that it was specifically crafted to offer a "Scottish solution to Scottish problems" by sponsoring the home-biased, hands-on investment approach of business angels.

From a *political* standpoint, the FACSN (1995) was in turn established in part to muster CSN support for Quebec's secession referendum, in October 1995. The sponsoring of a second LSIF, however, also reflected genuine *ideological* support for this model. Not only was PM Jacques Parizeau a long-time proponent of the provision of "patient capital" to local SMBs, but Quebec nationalists always saw this model as promoting a "sense of national belonging" among workers and business owners. On the one hand, thus, the FACSN represented *institutional continuity* and the extension of a successful model; on the other, it represented *institutional complementarity* in that it was notably devised, as opposed to the FSTQ, to specialize in the financial support of cooperatives and to supplement, as such, the work of Investissement Desjardins.

The *faire faire* approach developed after 2003 in Quebec was not devoid of nationalist motivations either. The Teralys fund of funds (2009) and its adjoining Teralys Capital Fonds d'innovation (TCFI) were for example driven by an ideological preference for the steering of specialized VCs toward strategic sectors. Capitalized by state-backed investors (IQ, CDPQ, FSTQ), the $700 million Teralys was to dedicate at least 75% of its resources to Quebec VCs or Canadian VCs investing in Quebec. The result was to promote institutional coordination between state-backed funds with regards to indirect investment activities. Both Teralys and the TCFI, indeed, were to focus on the ICT, green-tech, and life sciences sectors. As such, they were also political reactions to the launch of similar funds of funds in Ontario, also focused on these three sectors.

In Scotland, similarly, policy asymmetry with the RoUK and England was furthered in the early 2000s by the development of the co-investment (*faire avec*) approach. The SCIF and, later, the SSF and SVF were crafted to promote angel syndication, and thus to perpetuate and refine the process of institutional divergence initiated with LINC. This allowed the Scottish angel ecosystem to become the most dynamic in the country. Beyond syndication, furthermore, the SCIF was launched as a political response to canceled FDI projects in the wake of the dot.com bust, and to the creation of Regional Venture Capital Funds in England. Most importantly, it responded to an ideological commitment to the public sponsoring of growing SMBs and their transformation, through appropriate funding, into locally-owned, medium-sized national champions or "companies of scale."

This approach paved the way for the SNIB project, initiated by the SNP. Its establishment would represent institutional continuity in that it would aim to boost Scotland's corporate lending market through an expansion of the SIB. That said, this initiative is also informed by nationalist motives. The project was launched as a political riposte to the creation of the BBB in 2012, and it was introduced in a context of intensifying economic nationalism, in the months preceding the September 2014 referendum on Scotland's independence. This ideological preference for policy autonomy and state intervention, stemming from Scottish nationalism, was also made evident by the investment bank models closely studied by the SNP government, which revealed its inclination for "coordinative" models mixing investment *and* management support.

Quebec's Liberals also created a number of direct investment funds, from 2005 onward, representative of *faire* and *faire avec*. Such were the "business succession" funds created between 2005 and 2011, aimed at the preservation of indigenous SMBs. As part of the L'Avantage québécois economic strategy, which presented Quebec's reliance on locally-owned SMBs as a "comparative advantage" (ideological preference), IQ's Relève-PME (2005) was to complement the CDPQ's existing Accès-Relève fund. Such institutional coordination between public and other state-backed funds also distinguished the creation of the FIRA and FRQ in 2011, capitalized alongside partners such as the FSTQ, CRCD, and FACSN. As with Relève-PME, the FIRA and FRQ were underpinned by perceived political imperatives: in the first case, to offset land grabbing by foreign speculators and safeguard locally-owned farms; in the latter, to catch up to Ontario's business survival rates.

These flagship policy initiatives are representative of the way in which, through *faire*, *faire avec*, and *faire faire*, Quebec and Scotland developed regional "sponsor states." The mechanisms through which each of these initiatives was influenced by Québécois and Scottish nationalisms are good illustrations of this book's general findings. Such mechanisms were present, in one form or another, behind most of the policy measures, strategies, and funds studied. My hypotheses 1, 2, and 3, accordingly, have been confirmed: nationalism did play key roles and continues to have crucial impacts on the elaboration of sponsoring schemes and, consequently, on the deepening of asymmetries between the Quebec/Scottish and Canadian/British VC ecosystems. Quebec and Scotland moved away and remained distinct from Canadian and British liberal market economies in the sector of entrepreneurial finance. In both cases, this would not have happened – at least not in the same way or to the same extent – without economic nationalism.

**Final Remarks: Contributions and Avenues
for Further Research**

Two questions remain to be answered at this point: *so what*, and *now what*? In chapter 1, I remarked that this book would mostly be useful in "generating hypotheses *about* and methods to assess *for* the effects of minority nationalism on economic policymaking." Given its scope, it primarily served the purpose of demonstrating *how* the policy impacts of economic nationalism can be studied. In this contribution lie opportunities for further research: if minority nationalism *does* affect economic policymaking, could its effects be uncovered in other cases, by focusing on similar "nationalizing mechanisms?" Quebec and Scotland demonstrate how nationalism can exert similar policy influences – notably with regards to state involvement and policy asymmetry – across institutional contexts. This book shows that such influences are best uncovered through deep knowledge of policy intent, and of the roles played by specific initiatives as part of evolving "ecosystems." Apart from the obvious possibility of a focus on alternative policy sectors, two major doors are thus left open: the comparative evaluation of the impacts of nationalism and policy asymmetry on economic and entrepreneurial performance, and the study of other regions and states where (minority) nationalism is politically salient.

So what?

The first major contribution this book makes has to do with the study of ideas and public policy. As observed by Béland and Cox (2011b, 13), "an epistemological tension arises when we ponder whether ideas are central to political processes if no one utters them. This is an important concern when the ideas under investigation are part of a broad political ideology or public philosophy." Anyone studying economic development policy today will indeed rarely find policymakers openly justifying programs or investments in plain political, let alone ethnolinguistic terms. Yet, this book demonstrates that economic rationales behind policy choices can in fact be underpinned by such a "broad political ideology" as nationalism.

For sociologist Jal Mehta (2011, 27), "a public philosophy is an idea about how to understand the purpose of government or public policy in light of a certain set of assumptions about the society and the market. That the local government is more attuned to the needs of the people than the federal government is one such public philosophy." Minority nationalism also consists in such a "set of assumptions" in that it notably favours – or produces perceived imperatives for – policy asymmetry and strategic state intervention. The challenge was to illustrate *how* this is so. Only through an in-depth process tracing effort was I able to uncover the ideological, political, and institutional mechanisms through which economic nationalism affected policy choices. The lesson, therefore, is that deep knowledge of a limited number of cases and policy sectors probably is necessary to understand the precise impacts of minority nationalism on economic development strategies and policies.

From a political economy perspective, this book also establishes the relevance of a study of "regional" and "sectoral" cases to refine the classic "Varieties of Capitalism (VoC)" perspective (Hall and Soskice 2001). It demonstrates that distinct regional and sectoral models can develop within liberal market economies. This is not an entirely novel contribution, but what is original about it is that it revealed how *nationalism* can impact degrees of regional divergence not merely with regards to particular industrial sectors, but with respect to key determinants of the VoC typology itself: corporate financing and, to a lesser extent, R&D. To illustrate how Quebec and Scotland have been moving toward the state-influenced market economy model (Schmidt 2009) in these domains, I also developed a new concept, that of the "sponsor state."

This concept illustrates the conjunction between state influence and economic nationalism. In the VC sector most particularly, the "sponsor state" is indeed one in which policymakers take it as their responsibility to ensure not only that indigenous businesses have access to capital, but also that the investment activities of market actors become or remain congruent with both the needs of businesses *and* government strategies or objectives. Most of the VC literature has so far explained and/or justified state involvement – and its design – through economic lenses, focusing on market failures or "spillover" effects present, to various degrees, in any given market (Lerner 2009). This book studies it instead through a *political* lens, thus explaining variations in state involvement and the formation of regional ecosystems by looking *beyond* market imperatives.

Doing so, it most importantly contributes to the advancement of knowledge on economic nationalism in general, and minority nationalism in particular. This book confirms that economic nationalism should not be conflated with protectionism or perceived as an "outdated" lens, through which policy choices can no longer be understood (Helleiner and Pickel 2005). Instead, economic nationalism should be approached based on its "nationalist content," which can take protectionist forms but also more liberal ones. The study of our cases thus led to three major observations with regards to economic nationalism. First, it entails policies which, although not "protectionist" in the restrictive sense of the word, will tend to favour the needs of locally-owned businesses, thereby aiming at the preservation or strengthening of national corporate ownership. Second, policies influenced by nationalism will tend to be crafted to complement government-devised strategies, through the coordination of public and private sector players.

Thirdly, and this is where *minority* nationalism comes to the fore, economic nationalism will tend to push policymakers to react to initiatives of neighbouring governments and/or economic competitors. In the context of a region or province, therefore, economic nationalism will tend to produce, in addition to state involvement, varying degrees of policy asymmetry. Such an argument had rarely been applied, and certainly not with such detail, to the sector of economic development or the subsector of VC. This book is thus the first of its kind, the only work to have established a clear causal relationship between minority nationalism and the development trajectories of regional VC ecosystems.

A legitimate question to ask at this point would be whether the VC models developed in Quebec and Scotland under this impulsion of nationalism have led to an improvement in these regions' entrepreneurship levels and corporate ownership structures since the 1990s. Although, as mentioned in chapter 1, policy evaluation was not the focus of this research and would necessitate a book in and of itself, it is still worth pointing out that the evidence in that regard is mixed. Neither Quebec nor Scotland, indeed, were able to catch up to Canadian or British average business creation levels since the 1990s. Perhaps most importantly, however, evidence shows that both Quebec and Scotland have maintained lower business death rates, lower levels of inward foreign acquisitions, and higher post-takeover business survival rates than

Graph 7.3. Business Birth Rate, Scotland vs. South East England/UK, 1994–2017

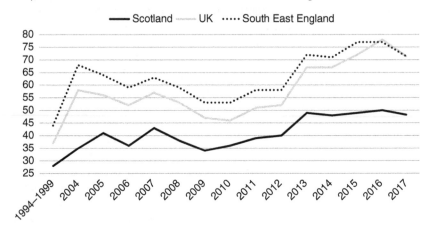

Sources: Dow and Kirk (2000); Scottish Government, https://www2.gov.scot/Topics/
Statistics/Browse/Business/TrendData.
Note: As measured by the ratio of new business registrations per 10,000 adults.

Canadian and British averages, which suggests that public sector efforts in securing local companies' funding chains throughout their growth stages – notably via the injection of "patient" and follow-on capital – did bear fruit and help maintain or in some cases improve levels of domestic corporate ownership.

The Scottish case is particularly interesting in that sense. As noted in chapter 4, during the 1990s Scotland ranked second-to-last among UK regions – only Wales ranked lower – with regards to entrepreneurial levels as measured by the annual proportion of new business registrations (graph 7.3). The fact that this lag could not be mitigated by the Business Birth Rate Strategy before 2000, given that the objective of this strategy was precisely to catch up to the average UK level and ideally, to South East England's, was presented as proof of policy failure (Dow and Kirk 2000). Yet, as pointed out by others, one positive effect of this strategy was certainly to improve institutional support for Scottish entrepreneurs and thereby to establish bases for subsequent, post-devolution policy initiatives such as the SCIF and many others (McVey 2000; Hood and Paterson 2002). This could help explain why the situation clearly improved since the early 2000s, as evidenced below. Indeed, even though Scotland did not catch up to British or South East English entrepreneurial levels, it did achieve one of the country's most rapid rates of growth in annual new business registrations – a 37% positive change between 2004 and 2017, against 4% for South East England and 22% for the UK as a whole (graph 7.3).

As a result of this progression, Scotland has been consistently out-performing not only Wales, but also Northern Ireland and North East England since the financial crisis of 2008. Besides, data shows that Scotland has also been outperforming both South East England and the UK in the wake of this financial crisis and during the subsequent economic downturn: not only did Scotland's annual business birth rate rebound more rapidly than the UK's or South East England's after 2009, but it also improved by almost 18% as a whole between 2008 and 2012, against 11% and 9% in the latter two cases, respectively. It is not unreasonable to think, based on such evidence, that this resilience of Scottish entrepreneurship might be correlated to the counter-cyclical functions of Scotland's public and hybrid investment schemes. The most interesting hints about the possible impacts of the Scottish model, however, are perhaps to be found elsewhere: notably, between 2003 and 2017 Scotland faced one of the lowest levels of foreign corporate acquisitions not only among UK regions but also among Western European countries, considerably inferior to the UK's and closer to that of the "Arc of Prosperity" nations (Hopkins 2018).

As compared with most other UK regions, therefore, and measured as a percentage of the total business population, Scotland's companies have been acquired by foreign investors at a lower rate since the early 2000s – 0.12% on average, against 0.18% in South East England for instance (Hopkins 2018, 16–17). Two further facts, besides, are even more revealing of the roles played in this regard by the Scottish "sponsor state." First, Scotland has maintained by far the highest "post-acquisition activity rate" of all UK regions, and ranks first on that indicator among comparator European countries (Hopkins 2018, 28–9). This means that, of all the Scottish businesses acquired from outside of Scotland since 2003, almost 60% remained active in Scotland after the foreign takeover, against less than 50% in the case of RoUK businesses. The most common and straightforward interpretation that can be made of this is that Scottish businesses are, generally, more deeply rooted in their local market and "customer base" then their British or even European counterparts, and therefore that "current policies designed to support, nurture and ultimately embed companies within Scotland are proving successful in yielding benefits for companies and the wider economy" (Hopkins 2018, 34).

A second revealing fact, which speaks to this policy aspect, is that the highest rates of foreign acquisition in Scotland have been found, since

2003, in the industrial sectors lying *outside* of the priority areas identified by the Scottish Government and SE. These rates indeed remained very low in most priority "growth sectors," such as energy / renewables, food and drink, life sciences, tourism, or the creative industries. The only exception to this rule is that of the financial and corporate services sector, where levels of foreign acquisition have been noticeably greater (Hopkins 2018, 9). Partly as a result, the stock of Scottish-owned businesses among these priority industrial sectors has been growing more than twice as fast as the stock of Scottish-owned businesses in Scotland more generally over the last ten years. Between 2008 and 2017 for instance, the number of Scottish-owned companies in priority sectors has grown by over 28%, against a mere 14% growth across all sectors. This trend was particularly acute for the creative industries (54% growth) and especially for the energy / renewables sector (263% growth), to which significant policy attention has been granted during this period, as discussed in chapter 6.[3]

In short, thus, while it is true that Scotland failed to reach the same levels of business creation as South East England or the UK since the 1990s, much progress has been made since the early 2000s which can be attributed in part to the Scottish "sponsor state" and its nationalist objectives. Similar conclusions can be drawn from the Quebec case, moreover. As can be observed in graph 7.4, Quebec was already lagging behind Ontario and Canada as a whole in terms of business creation during the late 1990s, and that was still the case in recent years. However, just as in Scotland, interesting trends were observable for most of the 2000s that highlight some of the effects of Quebec's distinctive policy model. First, it should be noted that if Quebec's business birth rate indeed remained substantially inferior to Ontario's or Canada's, this can be explained in part by the fact that since the 1990s Quebec's demographic aging has surpassed theirs and that as a result its "active" population (15–64 years old) has also been getting smaller – and will continue to decrease – relative to theirs and relative to Quebec's total population (Institut du Québec 2017).

It is therefore particularly interesting to note that, despite this trend, Quebec's business death rates have in turn been among Canada's lowest since the 1990s. For 2000–14 for instance, Quebec's average business death rate (10.8%) has been significantly lower than Ontario's (12%) or British Columbia's (13.8%),[4] a gap that could be attributed in part to the various, well-funded initiatives sponsoring business expansion and succession in Quebec since the early 2000s. Moreover, and relatedly, it clearly appears that Quebec's business birth rate was much less affected by the financial crisis and following economic downturn than

Graph 7.4. Business Birth Rate (%), Quebec vs. Ontario/Canada, 1996–2015

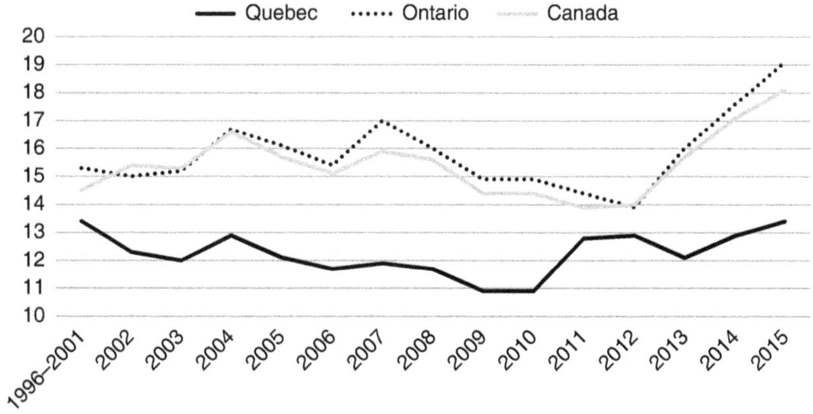

Sources: Institut de la Statistique du Québec, www.stat.gouv.qc.ca/statistiques/science
-technologie-innovation/entrepreneuriat/mesure-entrepreneuriat.pdf; www.stat.gouv
.qc.ca/statistiques/science-technologie-innovation/bulletins/sti-bref-201501.pdf; www.stat
.gouv.qc.ca/statistiques/science-technologie-innovation/bulletins/savoir-stat-vol18-no3
.pdf); Statistics Canada (n.d.a).
Note: As measured by the number of new businesses as a proportion of the existing
stock of businesses.

Ontario's or Canada's. Indeed, as graph 7.4 illustrates, Quebec's business birth rate actually grew by a factor of 10% between 2008 and 2012,
whereas the same rates dropped by almost 15% in the case of Ontario,
and by over 10% in Canada as a whole. Although Quebec's entrepreneurial rates remained inferior to other provinces', therefore, it seems
that Quebec's entrepreneurs fared better than their Ontarian or Canadian counterparts in difficult economic times, a resilience that could be
correlated, as in the case of Scotland, to the counter-cyclical functions of
Quebec's public and hybrid investment schemes.

As a result of this good performance during and immediately after the
financial crisis, Quebec's business birth rate almost caught up to those
of Ontario and Canada in 2012, even though it was lagging between
four and six percentage points behind those two only five years earlier, in 2007. There certainly were, thus, some positive developments
with regards to Quebec's entrepreneurial levels during the 2000s and
recent statistics tend to show that, in some regards, Quebec is even now
outperforming the RoC on some crucial indicators. Between 2014 and
2016 for instance, Quebec's new entrepreneurs have been much more

inclined toward product innovation and the development of new markets than the RoC's, and so have its "established entrepreneurs," active for over three years and a half. Similarly, Quebec's new entrepreneurs have been slightly more oriented toward technology-intensive activities than their Canadian counterparts, and significantly more ambitious on international (export) markets. Perhaps most importantly, furthermore, between 2014 and 2016 Quebec's entrepreneurial levels were superior to the RoC's among 18–35 year-olds and in particular among 18–24 year-olds (St-Jean and Duhamel 2016, 2017).

Finally, it is important to note that if Quebec still trails behind the RoC on many indicators of entrepreneurial activity, Canada itself is a world leader among the thirty or so "innovation-driven economies," of which the UK is also part along with the US, most Western and Central European nations, and Asian counties such as Taiwan, Japan, and South Korea (Schwab and Sala-i-Martin 2013). Therefore, if Quebec's entrepreneurial rates, with the exceptions mentioned above, remain slightly inferior to the RoC's they are in turn among the highest within this group of innovation-driven economies, ahead of the rates of the UK and even of the US (St-Jean and Duhamel 2017, 20–2). By 2015, moreover, Quebec ranked fifth among innovation-driven economies – behind the UK but ahead of the RoC – with regards to "intrapreneurship" levels, as measured by the intensity of entrepreneurial activities initiated from *within* existing businesses and organizations and leading to marketable innovations, the creation of corporate subsidiaries, or the launch of spin-off ventures (St-Jean and Duhamel 2016, 29). As a matter of fact, when merging business creation rates with intrapreneurship levels to measure "total" entrepreneurial activity, Quebec thus ranked fourth among innovation-driven economies in 2016, slightly trailing the RoC but leading the US and UK (St-Jean and Duhamel 2017, 30).

In sum, there is clearly some evidence that improvements did take place since the 1990s, both in Quebec and Scotland, in terms of entrepreneurial activity and business survival. The broad picture, however, remains mixed: on the one hand, both Quebec and Scotland outperformed other provinces and regions on some important indicators during this period, and most especially, it seems, in the wake of the financial crisis and economic downturn; on the other hand, Quebec and Scottish business birth rates still lag, for a number of reasons, behind the Canadian and British averages by a wide margin. Although the identification and measurement of precise relationships between public sector interventions and economic performance are beyond the scope of this book, the argument can thus be made in conclusion that the impacts of the development of distinct VC and entrepreneurial finance models in Quebec and Scotland are most likely to be found at the "meso" and "micro" levels: while policy asymmetry and state involvement might not, on their own, have transformed industrial structures or entrepreneurship levels as a whole, they could well have exerted significant sectoral, conjunctural, organizational, regional/local, and firm-specific effects.

Now what?

Aside from this issue of policy evaluation, which certainly opens avenues for future research, is the issue of generalizability. Given that a major contribution of this book was to test hypotheses about the policy effects of minority nationalism and to provide process tracing methods to assess for such effects, it is only natural to ask whether its arguments and findings could apply to other potential cases. One such interesting case could be that of Catalonia, an "autonomous community" of Spain where minority nationalism has been politically influential for decades and even more so in recent years (Paquin 2001; Gagnon and Requejo 2011; Boylan 2015; Gagnon and Sanjaume-Calvet 2016). Similar to that of Quebec and Scotland, Catalonia's economy, accounting for around 20% of Spain's GDP, is highly reliant on SMBs, with over 98% of its registered businesses having fifty employees or less.[5]

In addition, since 2010 and increasingly so lately, Catalonia has been reaping a disproportionate share of Spain's annual VC investments, both in terms of their number and value (graph 7.5). Accounting for a fifth of Spain's GDP, Catalonia has been receiving, on average, around a third of VC deals made in Spain each year, and between 25% and 37% of their total value up to 2017. Although the peaks of 2014 and 2015 were due to unusually large investments in expansion-stage businesses, the general trend remains interesting: Catalonia systematically receives a greater proportion of VC investments than its economic weight would justify.

Moreover, the relative strength of Catalonia as part of Spain's VC market seems to be partly related to the involvement of its public sector. This involvement notably takes the form of VC investments – both direct and indirect – by the Institut Català de Finances (ICF), a public agency owned by the Generalitat de Catalunya. This agency, founded in 1985 in the wake of the adoption of Catalonia's "statute of autonomy" in 1979, is to "promote and facilitate access to financing for the business community of Catalonia, so as to contribute to the growth of the Catalan economy" (ICF 2016, 7). Through its VC subsidiaries such as ICF Capital, but also through a plethora of sponsored hybrid and private

Graph 7.5. Evolution of Catalonia's VC industry, 2010–2017

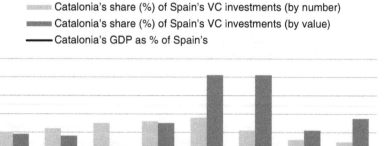

Sources: Asociación Española de Entidades de Capital – Riesgo (2011–18), *Survey: Venture Capital and Private Equity in Spain.*

VC funds, the ICF accumulated over €167 million in VC investment commitments by the end of 2018 (graph 7.6), for a total value of over €1,850 million including leverage (ICF 2019, 34), a significant part of the region's VC market.

Not only is Catalonia the most important VC market among Spanish autonomous communities, on par with the Community of Madrid, but the Catalan government plays key roles in the region's ecosystem through public and state-sponsored funds. Those roles extend far beyond VC, moreover, as the ICF itself engages in massive business lending initiatives through the issuance of loans, equity loans, and guarantees. Between 2011 and 2018, the ICF sponsored close to 17,000 companies in Catalonia, issuing over 21,900 loans and guarantees for a total value close to €5.5 billion, the equivalent of over €690 million in financial aid every year (ICF 2017, 33; ICF 2018, 2019). The Catalan case thus raises interesting questions, similar to those this book sought to answer: What were the main strategic imperatives behind the establishment of the ICF in 1985 and what roles, if any, did Catalan nationalism play in it? How influential, notably as compared to other autonomous communities in Spain, is the Catalan government in the region's economic development in general and in the sector of entrepreneurial finance in particular?

Graph 7.6. Institut Català de Finances' total venture capital commitments, 2005–2018 (€ millions)

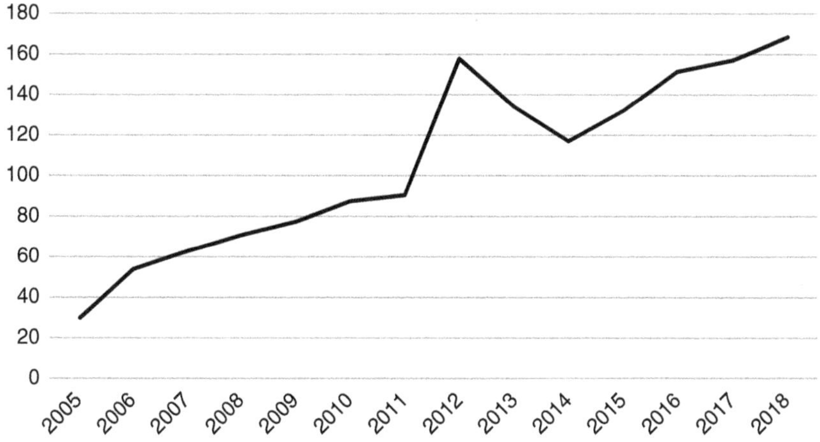

Source: Institut Català de Finances (2012–19).

One of the most important contributions of this book might thus be to provide a framework and a set of approaches allowing future researchers to answer such questions. Reconciling the study of economic policymaking and that of minority nationalism remains an important challenge for political scientists. If anything, this book will have demonstrated *why it should*, as well as *how it can* be done. It will also have served as a theoretical and empirical reminder: while its elaboration took place in the historic context of a resurgence of populist and protectionist nationalism across the globe, the Quebec and Scottish cases clearly demonstrate that nationalism in general and *economic* nationalism in particular are not by definition illiberal ideologies. Underlying Quebec's and Scotland's "sponsor state" model is, above all, a long-standing and continuing commitment to the "general interest" (Bernier, Bouchard, and Lévesque 2003; Simard, Dupuis, and Bernier 2006), rooted in self-determination principles.

What this book adds to the discussion is thus perhaps a richer sense of the ways in which national identity and minority nationalism, without challenging the liberal economic order within which Western democracies evolve, can contribute to making sure that order remains compatible with a diversity and a variety of economic models, where the "entrepreneurial state" (Mazzucato 2014) can be geared toward community empowerment, technological progress, and environmental preservation – i.e., toward the "common good" – as much as toward "competition" and profit for their own sake. From this perspective, "small nations with high ambitions" such as Quebec and Scotland can play a key role: that of demonstrating how the "rescaling of political economy" still ongoing can benefit *peoples* and not only corporations. "Sponsor states" can be a means to an end.

List of Interviews

Quebec

David Brulotte, Directeur au développement des affaires – Europe, Investissement Québec, Paris, May 18th 2015.

Jack Chadirdjian, Président-directeur général, Réseau Capital, Montreal, March 1st 2015.

Alain Denis, Vice-Président principal Nouvelle Économie, Fonds de solidarité des travailleurs du Québec, Montreal, April 9th 2015.

François Gilbert, Président-directeur général, Anges Québec & Anges Québec Capital, Phone interview, February 10th 2015.

Hugo T. Lacroix, Directeur au développement des affaires – Europe, Investissement Québec, Paris, May 18th 2015.

André Petitclerc, Directeur principal de l'investissement Petites Capitalisations, Investissement Québec, Phone interview, April 13th 2015.

Gérald St-Aubin, Vice-Président Investissements stratégiques et Partenariats, Capital Régional et Coopératif Desjardins, Montreal, March 1st 2015.

Scotland

Joan Gordon, Head of Development & Market Intelligence, Scottish Investment Bank, Glasgow, August 14th 2015.

David Grahame, Executive Director, LINC Scotland, Glasgow, August 17th 2015.

Lisa Hamilton, Business Advisor, Glasgow City Council (Business Gateway), Glasgow, August 11th 2015.

Pat McHugh, Investment Director, Scottish Investment Bank, Glasgow, August 11th 2015.

Brian McVey, Director of Strategy, Scottish Enterprise, Edinburgh, September 5th 2014.

Dr. Geoffrey Whittam, Reader in Entrepreneurship, School for Business & Society, Glasgow Caledonian University, Glasgow, August 17th, 2015.

Anonymous interviewee # 1.

Anonymous interviewee # 2.

Notes

Introduction

1 Web: https://www.sba.gov/sites/default/f les/articles/SBIC_Program
  _Deck_general_2017.pdf (12/18/2017).

1. Minority Nationalism and Economic Policymaking

1 See, among others: Alesina and Spolaore (1997); Amin and Tomaney (1995);
  Krugman (1995); MacLeod (2001); Porter (1994, 1998); Trigilia (1991).
2 For this literature and for notable exceptions, see: Hobson and Ramesh
  (2002); Garrett (1998b); Giddens (2000); Gilpin (2001); Mann (1997);
  McBride and Williams (2001); Rodrik (1998); Skogstad (2000); Swank
  (1998); Vogel (1996); Woods (2000).
3 For Quebec, see Graefe (2000, 2003, 2005); Quebec (1993a). For Scotland,
  see Taylor and Raines (2001); Learmonth, Munro, and Swales (2003);
  Scottish Enterprise (1992).
4 See Herman (2016).
5 Federal funds and institutions in Quebec as well as UK funds and
  institutions in Scotland have been deliberately excluded in order to
  provide a better perspective on the specif cally "regional" ecosystems.
6 "Hybrids" typically refer to public-private, public-angel, and/or public-
  institutional co-investment funds but also, more generally, to "any investor
  which (or sometimes who) has an agenda that combines f nancial returns
  with policy objectives or returns" (Don and Harrison 2006, 37–8). See also
  Murray (2007, 130).
7 Later rebranded as the Fonds de transfert d'entreprise du Québec.
8 Another of our activities which a private fund would rarely do is to acquire
  businesses. I'll give you an example, from Thetford Mines: Industry X. has
  300 employees, and is a good company with growth potential. The owner,

Mister X., is now seventy-f ve years old. He wants to sell and has been contacted by American competitors. But Mister X. is from Thetford Mines. He was born there, founded his business in his garage, and grew up with his employees. Therefore, selling off to pocket millions of dollars is of no interest to him if that means employees will likely lose their jobs. This is where we come in, buying the whole company. We strike a deal with Mister X., which is probably inferior to what strategic investors could offer, but which has other advantages. At Industry X., the management team was very strong. So, we conduct the transaction with management, but we also involve employees: we either form a worker cooperative, or devise a share ownership plan that is advantageous for the employees. Our long-term objective, in ten to f fteen years or a little longer depending on the company's growth, is to transfer the ownership back to the management and employees. Once the company belongs to its employees, it is rooted in the region. No one will be able to relocate it any longer. (My translation)

9 Now referred to as the Scottish National Investment Bank: https://beta
   .gov.scot/publications/national-investment-bank-implementation-plan
   -terms-of-reference/

10 From 15% in 2014 to 0% in 2017 (Canada 2013, 207–9). The federal tax
   credit was re-established at 15% in 2016 and for subsequent years by the
   Liberal government, elected in October 2015.

11 The disappointment for the entire industry, including for the FSTQ and
   FACSN obviously, was the federal government's lack of understanding of
   our ecosystem. That this system failed elsewhere in Canada doesn't mean
   that it didn't work in Quebec. It works in Quebec. Is everything perfect? No,
   there are adjustments to make. But scrapping the tax breaks altogether …?
   The great disappointment within the industry really was the indifference of
   the federal government to the numerous interventions of our members, who
   showed that it was killing something that works. (My translation)

12 Unless otherwise indicated, all dollar f gures in the book refer to Canadian
   dollars.

13 Brian McVey, Director of Strategy at Scottish Enterprise. Personal
   interview, Edinburgh, 5 September 2014.

14 See Bélanger et al. (2018); Henderson (2007); Lachapelle and Gagné (2003);
   Lachapelle (2000); Curtice (1999); Surridge and McCrone (1999).

15 See Abdelal (2001); Baughn and Yaprak (1996); Boulanger (2002, 2006);
   Campbell and Hall (2009); Crane (1998, 1999); D'Costa (2012); Fougner
   (2006a); Greenfeld (1995, 2001, 2006); Herrera (2005); Kangas (2013); Levi-
   Faur (1997a, 1997b); Nagy (2014); Nakano (2004); Nayar (1997); Pickel
   (2006); Rioux (2012a); Shulman (2000).

16 See also Mazzucato and Penna (2016) and Mazzucato and Semieniuk
   (2017, 2018).

17 For Quebec, see: https://qe.cirano.qc.ca/theme/marche-travail/main
-doeuvre/tableau-taux-syndicalisation-secteur-dactivite-2017. For Scotland,
see: https://www.gov.uk/government/uploads/system/uploads/
attachment_data/f le/711651/Trade_Union_Statistics.xlsx.

18 United Kingdom (2018) and Statistics Canada (n.d.c).

19 This includes a geographical share of offshore oil and gas production.

20 SMBs = 499 employees or less. For Scotland, see: http://www.gov.scot/
Resource/0050/00509984.pdf. For Quebec, see: https://www.ic.gc.ca/
eic/site/061.nsf/vwapj/PSRPE-KSBS_Juin-June_2016_fra-V3.pdf/$f le/
PSRPE-KSBS_Juin-June_2016_fra-V3.pdf.

2. Explaining Public Involvement in Venture Capital

1 BVCA (2001); Don and Harrison (2006).

2 This refers to Scotland's percentage share of the UK's total number of VC
investments, divided by Scotland's percentage share of the UK's registered
private businesses (Mason and Harrison 2002a, 436).

3 Macdonalds & Associates Limited (2001).

4 Macdonalds & Associates Limited (2001).

5 See also Eisinger (1991); Harrison and Mason (2000a); Karsai (2004);
Klonowski (2012).

6 See Martinez Sanchez (1992); Florida and Smith (1993); Murray (1998);
Harrison and Mason 2000a; Sorensen and Stuart (2001); Chen et al. (2010);
Cumming and Dai (2010, 2012); Li (2012); Samila (2012).

7 See Murray (1998); Aernoudt (1999); McGlue (2002); Powell et al. (2002);
Gilson (2003); Leleux and Surlemont (2003); Carpentier and Suret (2005b);
Duruf é (2010); Samila and Sorensen (2011); Bonini (2012).

8 We are living at a time when, in our country as elsewhere, regional
jurisdictions have a specif c role to play in economic policy ... We are
willing to accept this diff cult role, but we should then be allowed to play
it; more precisely, I should say, we should ourselves acquire the means to
play it. (My translation)

9 The previous government allowed private interests, Canadian or foreign,
as well as the federal government to freely seize our available savings and
use them for purposes that often did not benef t us. (My translation)

10 As the "Desjardins movement" and its involvement in many public or
government-backed initiatives will often be referred to throughout this
book, and for the benef t of readers unfamiliar with the story, it will
be useful at this point to mention that Desjardins, with a f rst credit
union founded in 1900, is one of the oldest Francophone-led f nancial
institutions in Quebec and was almost always associated with the
nationalist movement in the province (Bélanger 2012). During Quebec's

Quiet Revolution, from the 1960s onward, Desjardins was deeply involved in many of the state-sponsored initiatives which led to the development of the Francophone business community, the so-called "Québec Inc." (Lévesque et al. 1997). Today, Desjardins remains one of the largest f nancial institutions in the world, by far the most important depository institution in Quebec, and as demonstrated on many occasions in this book a frequent collaborator of the Quebec government and other institutional investors in the realm of entrepreneurial f nance.

11 The interests of the Québécois, after all, are not limited to the safety of their retirement savings. Funds as considerable as these must be channeled to achieve accelerated development of the public and private sectors, so that Quebec's economic and social objectives can be met as rapidly and as eff ciently as possible. In sum, the Caisse should not be considered as a mere investment fund like all the others but as a tool for growth, a lever more powerful than all the others we have had in this province up to now. (My translation.)

12 Notably, after 1975, through very active participation in the Sociétés d'investissement dans l'entreprise québécoise (SODEQ) and the PQ government's new Régime d'épargne-actions du Québec (RÉAQ), offering tax incentives for the channelling of Québécois' savings into local SMBs' equity. On the SODEQ, RÉAQ, and RÉAQ-D (specif cally focused on development-stage SMBs), see Suret (1990, 1993); Suret and Cormier (1997); Carpentier and Suret (2005a, 2005b); Godbout et al. (2005).

13 The role played here by the SDI is a daily reminder, with each project we bring forward, of how much our industrial development stems from our own initiative. (My translation.)

14 By then head of Quebec's Ministère de l'industrie, du commerce et de la technologie (MICT), where he served from 1989 to 1994.

15 The MIC became the MICT in 1988.

16 All of our Liberal friends across the aisle, all the big f nanciers of the world of St. James Street cannot f nd risk capital to help the workers of the Exeltor company and their employers, who are searching for investors … This company risks bankruptcy if it does not f nd venture capital, because it is undercapitalized like many other businesses in Quebec. (My translation)

17 A very large number of LSIFs were introduced in Ontario during the 1990s. By 2001, twenty-nine were incorporated (Cumming and MacIntosh 2006, 580) and by 2005, a whopping sixty-nine (Cumming 2007, 3). By 2015 however, almost all of Ontario's LSIFs had been either closed or acquired by pan-Canadian investment funds, after the provincial tax credits were phased out in 2011. See also Ayayi (2004).

18 For contrasting assessments of the benef ts and downsides of the FSTQ model, see Suret (1990, 1993); Osborne and Sandler (1998); Ayayi (2004); Cumming and MacIntosh (2006, 2007); Bourque (2012); Zorn et al. (2018).

19 For a detailed account of the Scottish Off ce's history since 1885, see Torrance (2006).
20 Hansard (1965, cc.1175).
21 See also Clay and Cowling (1996); Bailey and De Propris (2001); Lee (2005); Deakins, Whittam, and Wiper (2010); Mason (2010); North, Baldock, and Ekanem (2010).

3. Quebec, 1990–2003

1 Web: http://www.pum.umontreal.ca/apqc/89_90/blais/blais.htm.
2 I maintain that interest rates are needlessly high, threaten economic growth and contribute to keep the Canadian dollar's exchange rate at a level which undermines the competitiveness of our businesses. (My translation.)
3 In numerous sectors, Quebec's businesses are characterized by their small size and by the multiplicity of production units. As the market becomes increasingly continental in nature, it is imperative to promote business and production consolidation, to allow for the advent of more competitive f rms. (My translation.)
4 This initiative was taken in the wake of the ratif cation of the Montreal Protocol on Substances that Deplete the Ozone Layer, on January 1st, 1989.
5 Quebec's industrial structure essentially rests on SMBs and still comprises too few businesses in high-technology sectors … In order to broaden the base of Quebec companies active in the technology-intensive sector, it is therefore important to increase government support for the research activities of SMBs operating in the f eld of advanced technologies. (My translation.)
6 One of the benef ts from the establishment of boards of decision-makers in the wake of the industrial clusters strategy is that our contractors found numerous Quebec-based suppliers capable of producing quality goods and services at competitive prices … In Quebec, we have the skills and capacity to innovate and develop original, high-quality products that would otherwise be imported. (My translation.)
7 The objective is not only to intervene in times of hardship or to maintain the local ownership of our companies with a core of shareholders forming control blocks; it is also to plan joint operations with structuring effects on Quebec's economy. (My translation.)
8 A seventeenth was added in 1998.
9 My translation.
10 "La déportation québécoise: les fonds mutuels", *L'Action Nationale*, vol. 86, no. 8.
11 "La déportation québécoise: deuxième partie", *L'Action Nationale*, vol. 87, no. 11–12.

12 This led to the setting up of the "Commission on Fiscal Imbalance" by the PQ in 2001 (Québec 2002a; Rioux 2014).

13 According to Gérald St-Aubin, VP for Strategic Investments and Partnerships at CRCD, the provision of "patient capital" with lower expectations of return really was, as had been the case with the FSTQ and FACSN, a central objective of the government in creating CRCD (personal interview).

14 Among the active funds sponsored by Fil*action* are, notably, the Fonds Tourisme PME and Femmessor.

15 The FDQ will act in complementarity or in partnership with f nancial institutions, respecting their usual f elds of intervention but also covering the sectors neglected by those institutions ... Thus, we could call it the merchant bank of Quebec's SMBs. (My translation.)

4. Scotland, 1990–2003

1 Personal interview, Edinburgh, September 5th 2014.

2 When the reform took effect, in April 1991, twenty-three LECs had been formed: thirteen in SE's network and ten under HIE's network.

3 For details about the methodology behind this indicator, see Dow and Kirk (2000, 29).

4 Personal interview, Glasgow, 17 August 2015.

5 According to Hood and Paterson (2002, 239), the BBRS largely failed to engender such large-scale mobilization and collaboration across Scotland. The BBRS initiatives mentioned in this section qualify this conclusion somewhat.

6 *Business Gateway* for instance, a public business support organization collaborating closely with SE and HIE, was born out of the *Business Shop Network* (O'Hare 2004).

7 Geoffrey Whittam, personal interview, Glasgow, 17 August 2015.

8 Personal interview, Glasgow, August 17 August 2015.

9 Web: https://www.rse.org.uk/cms/f les/advice-papers/inquiry/comm/c01.pdf (11/30/2016).

10 The members of the SCC, a coalition of devolutionists formed in 1989, included the SLP, the SLD, the Scottish Trades Union Congress, the SCDI, and the FSB Scotland. Although the SNP decided not to become an off cial member and to continue promoting Scotland's secession from the UK rather than devolution, it still supported both devolution and most of the SCC's positions.

11 For a list of economic and f scal powers devolved to Scotland by the *Scotland Act 1998*, see Keating (2010, 233); CSD (2008, 3–5). See also Rioux (2016).

12 These agencies and their VC funds were relatively short-lived however, and were all dissolved by 2012 in the wake of the establishment of the

British Business Bank. On these agencies and funds, see UK (1999); Harding (2000); Allen (2002); Mason and Harrison (2003); Sunley et al. (2005); NESTA (2009); Webster (2009).

5. Quebec, 2003–2019

1 In 1998–9, the provincial government was contributing 60% of the CLD budgets; by 2007–8, this contribution reached 70% (Québec 2009a, 6).

2 David Brulotte, Personal interview, Paris, 18 May 2015; Hugo T. Lacroix, Personal interview, Paris, 18 May 2015.

3 To this f gure should be added the important contribution of the CDPQ: by 2007, the CDPQ was investing over $50 million per year in business succession, through its *Accès Relève* program.

4 Jack Chadirdjian, CEO, Réseau Capital. Personal interview, Montréal, 1 March 2015.

5 Alain Denis, Vice-Président principal Nouvelle économie, FSTQ. Personal interview, Montréal, 9 April 2015.

6 The Brunet report was a starting point. Brunet said that there was a lack of cohesion and size. Without this concertation, without this alignment of interests between institutional players and people ready to invest in private funds, we would probably never have achieved anything tangible. (My translation.)

7 FIER-Partenaires really was a "creation of Quebec's government," in that tax-advantaged funds were presented with a fait accompli: *"honnêtement, ce n'est pas nécessairement ce qu'on aurait priorisé. On ne l'aurait pas fait. Mais on a été poussés à le faire."* [Honestly, this wasn't necessarily what we would have prioritized. We wouldn't have done it. But we were pushed to.] Gérald St-Aubin, CRCD, Personal interview, Montreal, 1 March 2015.

8 Personal interviews: André Petitclerc (IQ), phone interview, 13 April 2015; Alain Denis (FSTQ); Gérald St-Aubin (CRCD).

9 Personal phone interview, 10 February 2015.

10 Quebec should become the Canadian leader in the environmental and green-tech industry, which would contribute to the Quebec brand on the international scene. (My translation)

11 Beyond immediate problems, the current crisis risks annihilating the framework put in place by the government and the efforts made by all players to create a local seed-funding industry for technological businesses … The current f nancial stranglehold threatens i) the survival of technological f rms and of the technological VCs which fund them, ii) the anchoring in Quebec of the expertise and technological wealth generated by successive generations of technological enterprises supported over the last f fteen years, iii) our capacity to valorize in Quebec the sums invested in R&D for years … If the chain is broken talents will relocate, eventually outside of Quebec. (My translation.)

12 Personal interviews, André Petitclerc (IQ) and Alain Denis (FSTQ). Quote from Alain Denis.

13 Before Teralys, everyone was doing pretty much anything. There was no concertation, no complementarity. It was every man for himself, and from time to time we would form alliances for personal reasons. It was not concerted. It was precisely this lack of concertation that led to the creation of Teralys. We realized that if we wanted Quebec to stand out, we could create a group with the expertise to make the right choices and implement a sustainable strategy. (My translation.)

14 Gérald St-Aubin, personal interview.

15 Gérald St-Aubin, personal interview.

16 The intervention of IQ in venture capital will be concerted and will take the orientations of economic ministries into account … in order to target and intervene in priority sectors as def ned by the government. The concerted action of the ministries and IQ will constitute an exceptional striking force and benef t Quebec's economy. (My translation.)

17 André Petitclerc, personal interview.

18 With the establishment of the Fund, the government asserts its leadership in economic development, business support, and the coordination of foreign investment prospectors … Interventions made through f nancial assistance programs and other mandates managed by the Fund will be structuring and will have to generate important economic benef ts for Quebec. However, the risk associated with such interventions, generally higher than that incurred through IQ's regular activities, will be endorsed by the government. The government assumes this risk considering the impacts associated with those projects in terms of job creation, local development, the creation of economic niches of excellence, business restructuring, and the development of new export markets. (My translation.)

19 François Gilbert, Personal interview.

20 Reorganized by then as the Ministère des Finances et de l'Économie (MFE).

21 The BDÉQ might play a leading role to allow successful businesses to develop, thereby supporting their transition from SMBs to MBs, facilitating business transfers, and maintaining headquarters in Quebec. (My translation.)

22 This pledge was reiterated in the 2014–15 budget (Québec 2014a, B46).

23 Web: http://www.lapresse.ca/affaires/economie/grande-entrevue/ 201409/23/01-4802691-jacques-daoust-moins-de-subventions -plus-de-participations.php.

24 André Petitclerc, personal interview.

25 To the angel who has less capacity we will say: "invest as much as you are willing to risk in this f rm, and we can double or triple that amount." We are obviously going to act in collaboration. We have to motivate angels

to help the company grow. Later, when an American investor comes in and wants to inject $15 million in this company in exchange for a specif c valuation and the elimination of other shareholders' benef ts, dilution can be strong ... What we are telling the angels is that when they reach this phase, we will protect them. We have the capital to do so, and we will substitute for the offer from abroad. (My translation.)

26 Web: http://www.f l-information.gouv.qc.ca/Pages/Article.aspx?aiguillage=ajd&idArticle=2211104045.

27 Capitalized by IQ ($20 million), the FSTQ ($15 million), and Merck ($15 million): https://betakit.com/amorchem-closes-44-2-million-biotech-fund/.

28 Web: http://www.ocgc.gov.on.ca/index_en.php?page=northleaf-venture-catalyst-fund.

29 Quebec is a Canadian leader in venture and development capital. With this announcement, we are taking the necessary steps to maintain this position. (My translation). Web: https://www.newswire.ca/fr/news-releases/lancement-de-teralys-capital-fonds-dinnovation-516360211.html.

30 We have an amazing pulse on the economy, so governments will often consult with us and say: "we thought of doing this or that, how would that work out for you?" There is a lot of consultation and, conversely, the government can often bring us opportunities by telling us: "We want to develop this or that industry." Once we know the government focuses on this or that sector of Quebec's economy, we can also orient our strategies to aim at mutual reinforcement. (My translation.)

31 The government regularly informs us of its priorities. Now, for example, it is implementing a maritime strategy, so collaboration and corresponding initiatives from funds such as the FSTQ are certainly expected. The government itself does not tell us to act, but we are smart enough to align ourselves with government priorities. (My translation.)

32 Web: http://www.ledevoir.com/economie/actualites-economiques/468945/le-fonds-ftq-veut-investir-dans-les-infrastructures-socio-economiques.

33 My emphasis. Bold italics point to words and formulations which were not present in the previous Act on IQ.

6. Scotland, 2003–2019

1 The ERDF also committed funds soon after the off cial launch, in March 2003 (Kemp et al. 2017).

2 Personal interview, Glasgow, 15 August 2015.

3 On the particular issue of "entrepreneurial recycling," its impacts on regional economic development, and its implications for VC policy, see Mason and Harrison (2006).

4 Investment Director, Scottish Investment Bank. Personal interview, Glasgow, 11 August 2015.

5 Web: http://news.bbc.co.uk/2/shared/bsp/hi/pdfs/11_05_07 _agreement.pdf.

6 The ITI programme was later terminated, in March 2013, after having spent only £231 million of the £450 million originally earmarked for it. In terms of R&D commercialization and business spin-offs, the program was described as a policy failure, because of a design poorly matched with Scotland's existing entrepreneurial and innovation ecosystems. See Brown, Gregson, and Mason (2016).

7 Web: https://www.mygov.scot/national-renewables-infrastructure-fund -n-rif/.

8 For a balanced critical perspective on Scotland's recent policy approaches to high-growth f rms, see Brown and Mawson (2016).

9 To which the public sector contributed £55 million (including £22 million from the ERDF).

10 Web: http://www.offshorewind.biz/2012/10/10/scotlands-renewable -energy-investment-fund-opens-for-business/.

11 Web: http://www.offshorewind.biz/2012/10/10/scotlands-renewable -energy-investment-fund-opens-for-business/.

12 Rock Spring Ventures became Epidarex Capital in 2014. Epidarex still manages the SLSF.

13 Web: http://news.gov.scot/news/500m-new-support-for-businesses.

14 Web: https://www.gov.scot/publications/national-investment-bank -implementation-plan-terms-of-reference/.

15 In the 2018–19 Draft Budget, moreover (Scotland 2018a), a new £60 million Low Carbon Innovation Fund and a whole new economic development agency, the South of Scotland Enterprise agency, were notably announced.

7. Discussion and Conclusions

1 In late 2016 and early 2017, the CDPQ launched three new VC funds capitalized with over $550 million: the Fonds Espace CDPQ, Fonds Croissance CDPQ, and Fonds Relève-CDPQ (see f gure 1.2). Along with CRCD, moreover, the CDPQ invested in a new funding round of CCPME, bringing its overall capitalization to $540 million. In the spring of 2018, the CDPQ also partnered with Desjardins, the FSTQ and others to launch a new $75 million VC fund, Luge Capital, specialized in artif cial intelligence and f nancial technologies.

2 Now rebranded as the Energy Investment Fund (EIF).

3 Web: http://www.gov.scot/Topics/Statistics/Browse/Business/Publications/ GrowthSectors/Database.

4 As measured by the number of business deaths as a proportion of the existing stock of businesses. For sources, see graph 7.4.
5 Institut d'Estadistica de Catalunya: http://www.idescat.cat/economia/inec?tc=3&id=6004&lang=en.

Bibliography

Abdelal, Rawi. 2001. *National Purpose in the World Economy: Post-Soviet States in Comparative Perspective*. Ithaca: Cornell University Press.

ACLDQ. 2003. "Mémoire sur les orientations d'Investissement Québec." Québec.

Adamek, Petr. 2007. "Intermediary Technology Institutes, Scotland, United Kingdom." OECD Discussion Paper.

Aernoudt, Rudy. 1999. "European Policy towards Venture Capital: Myth of Reality?" *Venture Capital* 1, no. 1: 47–57.

Aldecoa, Francisco, and Michael Keating. 2013. *Paradiplomacy in Action: The Foreign Relations of Subnational Governments*. New York: Routledge.

Alesina, Alberto and Enrico Spolaore. 1997. "On the Number and Size of Nations." *The Quarterly Journal of Economics* 112, no. 4: 1027–56.

Alexander, Wendy. 2003. *Chasing the Tartan Tiger: Lessons From a Celtic Cousin?* London: The Smith Institute.

Allen, Grahame. 2002. "Regional Development Agencies (RDAs)." Research Paper 02/50, Economic Policy and Statistics Section, House of Commons Library.

Altenberg, Per. 2016. "Protectionism in the 21st Century." *Kommerskollegium* 1, no. 2.

Amin, Ash, and John Tomaney. 1995. "The Regional Dilemma in a Neo-Liberal Europe." *European Urban and Regional Studies* 2, no. 2: 171–88.

Arnott, Margaret, and Jenny Ozga. 2010. "Nationalism, Governance and Policy-making in Scotland: The Scottish National Party (SNP) in Power." *Public Money and Management* 30, no. 2: 91–6.

Ashcroft, Brian. 1988. "Scottish Economic Performance and Government Policy: A North-South Divide?" In *Scottish Government Yearbook 1988*, 238–58.

Ashcroft, Brian, James H. Love, and Eleanor Malloy. 1991. "New Firm Formation in the British Counties with Special Reference to Scotland." *Regional Studies* 25, no. 5: 395–409.

Audit Scotland. 2013. "Renewable Energy." Prepared for the Auditor General for Scotland, Edinburgh.

Ayayi, Ayi. 2002. "Good News, Bad News: Ten Years' Lessons From the Canadian Labour-Sponsored Venture Capital Corporations." Conference Paper, CESifo Conference Center, Munich.

– 2004. "Public Policy and Venture Capital: The Canadian Labor-Sponsored Venture Capital Funds." *Journal of Small Business Management* 42, no. 3: 335–45.

Bailey, David, and Lisa De Propris. 2001. "The Role for a Scottish Development Bank in a Devolved Scotland." *Scottish Affairs*, no. 35: 104–25.

Baldock, Robert, and David North. 2012. "The Role of the UK Government Equity Funds in Addressing the Finance Gap Facing SMEs with Growth Potential." Conference Paper, Institute for Small Business and Entrepreneurship Conference, Dublin.

Balke, Florence. 2005. "L'Écosse dans l'Union Européenne depuis l'Acte de Dévolution de 1998." Unpublished Masters' Thesis, Institut d'études politiques de Lyon, Université Lyon 2.

Barber, Lionel. 1982. "The Scottish Economy at Mid-Term – More Than an Invisible Hand at Work." *Scottish Government Yearbook 1982*, 168–80.

Baughn, C. Christopher, and Attila Yaprak. 1996. "Economic Nationalism: Conceptual and Empirical Development." *Political Psychology* 17, no. 4: 759–8.

BDC. 2012. "Rapport annuel." Montréal.

Beaulieu, Léopold. 1996. "Fondaction-CSN: Un démarrage réussi au-delà des espérances." *L'Action Nationale*. Accessed March 8, 2016. http://goo.gl/dowfaY.

Beiner, Ronald, ed. 1999. *Theorizing Nationalism.* Albany: State University of New York Press.

Béland, Daniel, and Robert Henry Cox, eds. 2011a. *Ideas and Politics in Social Science Research.* New York: Oxford University Press.

– 2011b. "Introduction: Ideas and Politics." In *Ideas and Politics in Social Science Research*, edited by Daniel Béland and Robert H. Cox, 3–20. New York: Oxford University Press.

Béland, Daniel, and André Lecours. 2004. "Nationalisme et protection sociale: une approche comparative." *Canadian Public Policy* 30, no. 3: 319–31.

– 2005a. "The Politics of Territorial Solidarity: Nationalism and Social Policy Reform in Canada, the United Kingdom and Belgium." *Comparative Political Studies* 38, no. 6: 676–703.

– 2005b. "Nationalism, Public Policy and Institutional Development: Social Security in Belgium." *Journal of Public Policy* 25, no. 2: 265–85.

– 2006a. "Décentralisation, mouvements nationalistes et politiques sociales: les cas du Québec et de l'Écosse." *Lien social et Politiques*, no. 56: 137–48.

– 2006b. "Sub-state Nationalism and the Welfare State: Quebec and Canadian Federalism." *Nations and Nationalism* 12, no. 1: 77–96.
– 2007. "Federalism, Nationalism and Social Policy Decentralization in Canada and Belgium." *Regional and Federal Studies* 17, no. 4: 405–19.
– 2008. *Nationalism and Social Policy: The Politics of Territorial Solidarity.* New York: Oxford University Press.
Bélanger, Éric, Richard Nadeau, Ailsa Henderson, and Eve Hepburn. 2018. *The National Question and Electoral Politics in Quebec and Scotland.* Montreal and Kingston: McGill-Queen's University Press.
Bélanger, Guy. 2012. *Alphonse Desjardins 1854–1920.* Québec: Septentrion.
Bélanger, Paul R., and Benoît Lévesque. 1994. "La modernité par les particularismes. Le modèle québécois de développement économique." In *Entre tradition et universalisme,* edited by Françoise-Romaine Ouellette and Claude Bariteau, 79–96. Québec: L'Institut québécois de recherche sur la culture.
Bennett, Mike, and John Fairley. 2003. "Policy Conf ict in Intergovernmental Relations: The Changing Role of Local Authorities in the Governance of Local Economic Development in Post-Devolution Scotland." *International Journal of Economic Development* 5, no. 1: 1–23.
Berger, Suzanne, and Ronald Dore, eds. 1996. *National Diversity and Global Capitalism.* Ithaca: Cornell University Press.
Bernier, Luc, Marie Bouchard, and Benoît Lévesque. 2003. "Attending to the General Interest: New Mechanisms for Mediating between the Individual, Collective and General Interest in Quebec." *Annals of Public and Cooperative Economics* 74, no. 3: 321–47.
Bernier, Luc, and Eoin Reeves. 2018. "The Continuing Importance of State -Owned Enterprises in the Twenty-First Century: Challenges for Public Policy." *Annals of Public and Cooperative Economics* 89, no. 3: 453–8.
Bertrand, Catherine. 2003. "Les nouvelles formes de gouvernance et les investissements régionaux: le cas de Capital régional et coopératif Desjardins." Unpublished Master's Thesis, Université du Québec à Montréal.
Bérubé, Gérard. 2003. "Perspectives – La dérive de la Caisse." *Le Devoir,* March 13, 2003. http://www.ledevoir.com/economie/actualites-economiques/22324/perspectives-la-derive-de-la-caisse.
– 2004a. "Perspectives – La mort de Gaspésia." *Le Devoir,* February 26, 2004. http://www.ledevoir.com/economie/actualites-economiques/48368/perspectives-la-mort-de-gaspesia.
– 2004b. "Perspectives – Dommage." *Le Devoir,* April 1, 2004. http://w22.ledevoir.com/economie/actualites-economiques/51222/perspectives-dommage.

Birch, David L. 1979. "The Job Generation Process." Unpublished Report, MIT Program on Neighbourhood and Regional Change for the Economic Development Administration, Washington, DC.

Block, Fred. 2008. "Swimming Against the Current: The Rise of a Hidden Developmental State in the United States." *Politics & Society* 36, no. 2: 169–206.

Block, Joern, Geertjan De Vries, and Philipp Sandner. 2012. "Venture Capital and the Financial Crisis: An Empirical Study across Industries and Countries." In *The Oxford Handbook of Venture Capital*, edited by Douglas J. Cumming, 37–60. New York: Oxford University Press.

Blyth, Mark. 1997. "Any More Bright Ideas? The Ideational Turn of Comparative Political Economy." *Comparative Politics* 29, no. 2: 229–50.

– 2002. *Great Transformations: Economic Ideas and Institutional Change in the Twentieth Century.* New York: Cambridge University Press.

Bonini, Stefano. 2012. "The Development of Venture Capital: Macroeconomic, Political, and Legal Determinants." In *The Oxford Handbook of Venture Capital*, edited by Douglas J. Cumming, 824–63. New York: Oxford University Press.

Botham, Ron, and David Clelland. 2005. "Corporate Headquarters in Scotland: Their Nature and Contributions to Scotland's Economic Development." A Report to Scottish Enterprise, Training and Employment Research Unit, University of Glasgow.

Botham, Ron, and Bob Downes. 1999. "Industrial Clusters: Scotland's Route to Economic Success." *Scottish Affairs*, no. 29: 43–58.

Boucher, Jacques L., and Joseph-Yvon Thériault, eds. 2005. *Petites sociétés et Minorités nationales. Enjeux politiques et perspectives comparées.* Sainte-Foy: Presses de l'Université du Québec.

Boulanger, Éric. 2002. "Le nationalisme économique dans la pensée et les politiques publiques du Japon: particularisme, pragmatisme et puissance." Cahiers de recherche 02-02, Centre Études internationales et mondialisation. February, 2002. http://www.ieim.uqam.ca/IMG/pdf/LE_20NATIONALISME.pdf.

– 2006. "Théories du nationalisme économique." *L'Économie politique* 3, no. 31: 82–95.

Bourdeau, Gilles, Alain Noël, and Jean-Marie Toulouse. 1994. "Un prof l de l'industrie du capital de risque au Québec." Cahier de recherche 94-03-01, École des Hautes Études Commerciales.

Bourque, Gilles L. 1995. "Le néo-corporatisme comme angle d'analyse de la nouvelle politique industrielle du Québec." Cahiers du CRISES, Collection acteurs sociaux, no. ET9506.

– 2000. *Le modèle québécois de développement: De l'émergence au renouvellement.* Québec: Presses de l'Université du Québec.

– 2012. "Fonds de travailleuses et de travailleurs et avantages f scaux: Une comparaison avantageuse." *Note d'intervention de l'IRÉC*, no. 13, February.

Boyer, Robert, and Daniel Drache, eds. 1996. *States against Markets: The Limits of Globalization*. New York: Routledge.

Boylan, Brandon M. 2015. "In Pursuit of Independence: The Political Economy of Catalonia's Secessionist Movement." *Nations & Nationalism* 21, no. 4: 761–85.

Breuilly, John. 1994. *Nationalism and the State*. 2nd ed. Chicago: University of Chicago Press.

British Labour Party. 1964. "The New Britain." Election Manifesto. http:// politicsresources.net/area/uk/man/lab64.htm

– 1974. "Britain Will Win With Labour." Election Manifesto. http://www .politicsresources.net/area/uk/man/lab74oct.htm

British Liberal Party. 1964. "Think for Yourself." Election Manifesto. http:// politicsresources.net/area/uk/man/lib64.htm

Brooks, Stephen, and A. Brian Tanguay. 1985. "Quebec's Caisse de Dépôt et Placement: Tool of Nationalism?" *Canadian Public Administration* 28, no. 1: 99–119.

Brown, Ross. 2002. "The Future of ICT Industries in Scotland: Towards a Post-Branch Plant Economy?" In *Scotland in the Global Economy: The 2020 Vision*, edited by Neil Hood, Jeremy Peat, Ewen Peters, and Stephen Young, 130–48. New York: Palgrave Macmillan.

Brown, Ross, Geoff Gregson, and Colin Mason. 2016. "A Post-Mortem of Regional Innovation Policy Failure: Scotland's Intermediate Technology Initiative (ITI)." *Regional Studies* 50, no. 7: 1260–72.

Brown, Ross, and Colin Mason. 2012. "The Evolution of Enterprise Policy in Scotland." In *Government, SMEs and Entrepreneurship Development: Policy, Practices and Challenges*, edited by Robert A. Blackburn and Michael T. Shaper, 17–30. New York: Routledge.

Brown, Ross, and Suzanne Mawson. 2016. "Targeted Support for High-Growth Firms: Theoretical Constraints, Unintended Consequences and Future Policy Challenges." *Environment and Planning C: Government and Policy* 34: 816–36.

BVCA. 1999. *Report on Investment Activity 1998*. London: Essex House.

– 2001. *Report on Investment Activity 2000*. London: Essex House.

– 2005. *Report on Investment Activity 2004*. London: Essex House.

– 2007. *Report on Investment Activity 2006*. London: Essex House.

– 2014. *Report on Investment Activity 2012*. London: Essex House.

Calhoun, Craig 1998. *Nationalism*. Minneapolis: University of Minnesota Press.

Campbell, John L. 1998. "Institutional Analysis and the Role of Ideas in Political Economy." *Theory and Society* 27, no. 3: 377–409.

Campbell, John L., and John A. Hall. 2009. "National Identity and the Political Economy of Small States." *Review of International Political Economy* 16, no. 4: 547–72.

Canada. Government of Canada. 2013. "Jobs Growth and Long-Term Prosperity: Economic Action Plan 2013." https://www.budget.gc.ca/2013/doc/plan/budget2013-eng.pdf.

– Canadian Labour-Market and Productivity Center. 1995. "The Role and Performance of Labour-Sponsored Investment Funds in the Canadian Economy: An Institutional Prof le." Ottawa.

Carbasse, Mathieu. 2018. "Les 100 engagements de la CAQ au pouvoir." *L'Actualité*, 2 octobre.

Cardinal, Linda, and Martin Papillon. 2011. "Le Québec et l'analyse comparée des petites nations." *Politique et Sociétés* 30, no. 1: 75–93.

Carney, Richard W. 2018. *Authoritarian Capitalism: Sovereign Wealth Funds and State-Owned Enterprises in East Asia and Beyond*. Cambridge: Cambridge University Press.

Carpentier, Cécile, and Jean-Marc Suret. 2005a. "The Indirect Costs of Venture Capital in Canada." *CIRANO Scientific Series*, June, 2005. http://www.cirano.qc.ca/pdf/publication/2005s-25.pdf.

– 2005b. "Initiatives gouvernementales en capital de risque: les leçons des expériences européennes." *Research Report, CIRANO*, March, 2005. http://www.cirano.qc.ca/pdf/publication/2005s-12.pdf.

CDPQ. 1989. "Rapport annuel 1988." Montréal.

– 1993. "Rapport annuel 1992." Montréal.

– 1998. "Rapport d'activités 1997." Montréal.

– 1999. "Rapport d'activités 1998." Montréal.

– 2007. "Rapport annuel 2006." Montréal.

– 2008. "Rapport annuel 2007." Montréal.

– 2010–19. "Rapport annuel." Montréal.

Cerny, Philip. 1997. "Paradoxes of the Competition State: The Dynamics of Political Globalization." *Government & Opposition* 32, no. 2: 251–74.

– 2010. "The Competition State Today: From *Raison d'État* to *Raison du Monde*." *Policy Studies* 31, no. 1: 5–21.

Chandan, Harish C., and Bryan Christiansen, eds. 2019. *International Firms' Economic Nationalism and Trade Policies in the Globalization Era*. Hershey, PA: IGI Global.

Chang, Ha-Joon. 2003. *Globalisation, Economic Development and the Role of the State*. New York: Zed Books.

Charest, Jean. 2000. "De Québec Inc. à Québec.com." In *La Révolution tranquille, 40 ans plus tard: un bilan*, edited by Yves Bélanger, Robert Comeau, and Céine Métivier, 187–95. Montréal: VLB.

Chen, Henry, Paul Gompers, Anna Kovner, and Josh Lerner. 2010. "Buy Local? The Geography of Venture Capital." *Journal of Urban Economics* 67: 90–102.

Chen, Kun. 2011. "Producing China's Innovative Entrepreneurship: Nationalism, Cultural Practices, and Subject-Making of Transnational Chinese Professionals." Unpublished PhD Thesis, University of California, Berkeley.

Clay, Nick, and Marc Cowling. 1996. "Small Firm and Bank Relationships: A Study of Cultural Differences between English and Scottish Banks." *Omega, International Journal of Management Science* 24, no. 1: 115–20.

Clift, Ben, and Cornelia Woll. 2015. *Economic Patriotism in Open Economies.* London: Routledge.

Conseil de la science et de la technologie. 2004. "Mémoire sur le rôle de l'État québécois dans le capital de risque." Québec: Éditeur off ciel.

Cowling, Marc. 1997. "Regional Determinants of Small Firms Loan under the UK Loan Guarantee Scheme." Working Paper No. 37, Warwick Business School.

Coyle, Diane, Wendy Alexander, and Brian Ashcroft, eds. 2005. *New Wealth for Old Nations: Scotland's Economic Prospects.* Princeton: Princeton University Press.

CPQ. 2010. "Commentaires du Conseil du patronat du Québec soumis à la commission des f nances publiques dans le cadre des consultations sur le projet de loi no 123." Montréal.

Crane, George T. 1998. "Economic Nationalism: Bringing the Nation Back In." *Millenium – Journal of International Studies* 27, no. 1: 55–75.

– 1999. "Imagining the Economic Nation: Globalisation in China." *New Political Economy* 4, no. 2: 215–32.

CRCD. 2002. "Rapport annuel 2001." Montréal.

– 2004. "Rapport annuel 2003." Montréal.

– 2006–8. "Rapport annuel." Montréal.

Crevoisier, Olivier. 1997. "Financing Regional Endogenous Development: The Role of Proximity Capital in the Age of Globalization." *European Planning Studies* 5, no. 3: 407–15.

CRISES. 2000. "Un cas exemplaire de nouvelle gouvernance." Montréal. http://www.25ansfondsftq.com/PDFs/CasExemplaireNouvelle Gouvernance.pdf.

Crouch, Colin, Martin Schröder, and Helmut Voelzkow. 2009. "Regional and Sectoral Varieties of Capitalism." *Economy and Society* 38, no. 4: 654–78.

Crouch, Colin, and Wolfgang Streeck, eds. 1997. *Political Economy of Modern Capitalism: Mapping Convergence & Diversity.* London: SAGE Publications.

CSD. 2008. "The Scotland Act 1998: Allocation of Parliamentary Powers and Ministerial Functions, and Their Exercise since the Creation of the Scottish Parliament." Edinburgh.

Cumming, Douglas J. 2007. "Government Policy towards Entrepreneurial Finance: Innovation Investment Funds." *Journal of Business Venturing* 22: 193–235.

– 2012. "Introduction." In *The Oxford Handbook of Venture Capital*, edited by Douglas J. Cumming, 1–12. New York: Oxford University Press.

Cumming, Douglas J., and Na Dai. 2012. "The Role of Geographic proximity in Venture Capital." In *The Oxford Handbook of Venture Capital*, edited by Douglas J. Cumming, 897–937. New York: Oxford University Press.

– 2010. "Local Bias in Venture Capital Investments." *Journal of Empirical Finance* 17: 362–80.

Cumming, Douglas J., and Sof a Johan. 2010. "Phasing Out an Ineff cient Venture Capital Tax Credit." *Journal of Industry, Competition and Trade* 10: 227–52.

Cumming, Douglas J., and Jeffrey G. MacIntosh. 2007. "Mutual Funds That Invest in Private Equity? An Analysis of Labour-Sponsored Investment Funds." *Cambridge Journal of Economics* 31: 445–87.

– 2006. "Crowding Out Private Equity: Canadian Evidence." *Journal of Business Venturing* 21, no. 5: 569–609.

Curtice, John. 1999. "Is Scotland a Nation and Wales Not?" In *Scotland and Wales: Nations Again?*, edited by Bridget Taylor and Katarina Thomson, 119–47. Cardiff: University of Wales Press.

CVCA. 2015a. "2014 Canadian Private Equity Market Overview." http://www .cvca.ca/wp-content/uploads/2014/07/CVCA-2014-PE-data-deck.pdf.

– 2015b. "Sommaire du marché canadien du capital de risque en 2014." http://www.cvca.ca/wp-content/uploads/2014/07/FR-2014-VC-data -deck.pdf.

– 2015c. "Sommaire du marché québécois du capital de risque en 2014." http:// www.cvca.ca/wp-content/uploads/2014/07/FR-2014-Quebec-VC-data-deck.pdf.

– 2016a. "Sommaire du marché canadien du capital de risque en 2016." http://www.reseaucapital.com/docs/statistiques_2015_venture_capital _2015_repor t_fr.pdf.

– 2016b. "Sommaire du marché du capital de risque. 2015 Québec." http:// www.reseaucapital.com/docs/statistiques_2015_quebec_vc____2015_fr.pdf.

– 2016c. "2015 Canadian Private Equity Market Overview." http://www .cvca.ca/wp-content/uploads/2016/03/CVCA-Private-Equity-2015-Report .pdf.

– 2017. "Aperçu du marché québécois du CR et du CD // 2016." https:// reseaucapital.com/wp-content/uploads/2017/06/CVCA-2016-Quebec -Overview-Fr_Final.pdf.

– 2018. "Aperçu du marché québécois du CR et du CD // 2017." https:// reseaucapital.com/documents/apercu-du-marche-quebecois-du-capital-de -risque-et-du-capital-de-developpement-s1-2018/.

– 2019. "Aperçu du marché canadien du CR et du CD // 2018." https:// central.cvca.ca/wp-content/uploads/2019/05/CVCA_FR_Canada_Q4 -2018_Final2.pdf.

Danson, Michael, John Fairley, M.G. Lloyd and D. Newlands. 1990. "Scottish
Enterprise: An Evolving Approach to Integrated Economic Development in
Scotland." *Scottish Government Yearbook 1990*, 168–94.

Danson, Michael, Ewa Helinska-Hughes, Stuart Paul, Geoff Whittam and
Michael Hughes. 2006. "An Analysis of Business Angels in Scotland and
Poland." *Zagreb International Review of Economics and Business*, Special
Conference Issue: 61–79. http://goo.gl/ky7nvQ.

Danson, Michael W., and M. Greg Lloyd. 1992. "The Enterprise Zone
Experiment in Scotland: Strategic Planning or Crisis Management." *Scottish
Government Yearbook 1992*, 206–23.

D'Costa, Anthony P., ed. 2012. *Globalization and Economic Nationalism in Asia*.
Oxford University Press Scholarship Online.

Deakins, David, Robert Sullivan, and Geoff Whittam. 2000. "Developing
Business Start-Up Support Programmes: Evidence From Scotland." *Local
Economy* 15, no. 2: 159–75.

Deakins, David, Geoff Whittam, and Janette Wyper. 2010. "SME's Access to
Bank Finance in Scotland: An Analysis of Bank Manager Decision Making."
Venture Capital 12, no. 3: 193–209.

De La Calle, Luis, and André Fazi. 2010. "Making Nationalists Out of
Frenchmen? Substate Nationalism in Corsica." *Nationalism and Ethnic
Politics* 16: 397–419.

Denver, David. 1997. "The 1997 General Election in Scotland: An Analysis of
the Results." *Scottish Affairs*, no. 20: 17–34.

Denver, David, and Iain MacAllister. 1999. "The Scottish Parliament Elections
1999: An Analysis of the Results." *Scottish Affairs*, no. 28: 10–32.

Denver, David, James Mitchell, Charles Pattie, and Hugh Bochel. 2000.
Scotland Decides: The Devolution Issue and the 1997 Referendum. New York:
Routledge.

Déry, Yves. 1994. "Le GATIQ et la société Innovatech. Deux piliers du
développement technologique." *Le Devoir*, October 22, p. F9.

Devine, Thomas M. 2008. "The Challenge of Nationalism." In *Scotland and
the Union 1707–2007*, edited by Thomas M. Devine, 143–56. Edinburgh:
Edinburgh University Press.

Devine, Tom M., Clive H. Lee, and George C. Peden, eds. 2005. *The
Transformation of Scotland: The Economy Since 1700*. Edinburgh: Edinburgh
University Press.

Dieckhoff, Alain, and Christophe Jaffrelot, eds. 2006. *Repenser le nationalisme:
Théories et pratiques*. Paris: Presses de la Fondation nationale des sciences
politiques.

Dmitrieva, Anna. 2008. "Scotland's Representation in Europe in the Post-
Devolution Era: Results and Expectations." Unpublished Masters' Thesis,
Humboldt-Universität zu Berlin.

Don, Gavin, and Richard T. Harrison. 2006. "The Equity Risk Capital Market for Young Companies in Scotland 2000–2004." Research Report, in collaboration with Scottish Enterprise, Glasgow.

Dow, Alexander, and Catherine Kirk. 2000. "The Numbers of Scottish Businesses and Economic Policy." *Quarterly Economic Commentary* 25, no. 4: 28–34.

Drover, Glenn, and K.K. Leung. 2001. "Nationalism and Trade Liberalization in Quebec and Taiwan." *Pacific Affairs* 74, no. 2: 205–24.

Dufour, Valérie. 2003. "La Caisse toujours hantée par Vidéotron." *Le Devoir*, March 11, 2003. http://www.ledevoir.com/non-classe/22203/la-caisse -toujours-hantee-par-videotron.

Duruf é, Gilles. 2010. "Government Involvement in the Venture Capital Industry: International Comparisons." *Canadian Venture Capital and Private Equity Association*. http://goo.gl/hSEIPg.

Dutrisac, Robert. 2003. "Place au privé dans le capital de risque." *Le Devoir*, December 18, 2003. http://web1.ledevoir.com/non-classe/43197/place-au -prive-dans-le-capital-de-risque.

– 2004. "Une industrie qui veut se développer – À qui le risque: au public ou au privé?" *Le Devoir*, February 28, 2004. http://www.ledevoir.com/ economie/actualites-economiques/48558/une-industrie-qui-veut-se -developper-a-qui-le-risque-au-public-ou-au-prive.

Eatwell, Roger, and Matthew Goodwin. 2018. *National Populism: The Revolt against Liberal Democracy*. London: Pelican Books.

Edinburgh Green Investment Bank Group. 2012. "Location of the Green Investment Bank: Self-Assessment for Edinburgh." Edinburgh.

Eisinger, Peter. 1991. "The State of State Venture Capitalism." *Economic Development Quarterly* 5, no. 1: 64–76.

Ekos Limited. 2008. "Review of Co-operative Development Scotland." Report for Scottish Enterprise, Glasgow and Inverness.

Evenett, Simon J., and Johannes Fritz. 2015. "The Tide Turns? Trade, Protectionism, and Slowing Global Growth." 18th Global Trade Alert Report, Center for Economic Policy Research.

FACSN. 2003. "La pertinence renouvelée d'Investissement Québec dans un contexte en transformation." Montréal.

– 2004. "Rapport annuel 2003–2004." Montréal.

– 2007. "Rapport annuel 2006–2007." Montréal.

Fairley, John, and M. Greg Lloyd. 1995. "Economic Development and Training: The Roles of Scottish Enterprise, Highlands and Islands Enterprise and the Local Enterprise Companies." *Scottish Affairs*, no. 12: 52–73.

FCCQ. 2010. "Mémoire présenté par la FCCQ à la commission parlementaire des f nances publiques." Projet de loi 123. Montréal.

FCEI. 2010. "Commentaires de la FCEI concernant le projet de loi no 123." Montréal.

– 2013. "Pour un développement économique misant sur les PME." Montréal.

Florida, Richard, and Martin Kenney. 1988. "Venture Capital and High Technology Entrepreneurship." *Journal of Business Venturing* 3, no. 4: 301–19.

Florida, Richard, and Donald F. Smith Jr. 1993. "Venture Capital Formation, Investment, and Regional Industrialization." *Annals of the Association of American Geographers* 83, no. 3: 434–51.

Fortin, Louise-E. 1985. "La politique technologique québécoise." *Politique*, no. 8: 23–44.

Fougner, Tore. 2006a. "Economic Nationalism and Maritime Policy in Norway." *Cooperation and Conflict: Journal of the Nordic International Studies Association* 41, no. 2: 177–201.

– 2006b. "The State, International Competitiveness and Neoliberal Globalisation: Is There a Future beyond 'the Competition State?'" *Review of International Studies* 32: 165–85.

Fournier, Louis. 1991. *Solidarité Inc. Un nouveau syndicalisme créateur d'emplois.* Montréal: Québec/Amérique.

Fournier, Pierre. 1979. *Les sociétés d'État et les objectifs économiques du Québec: une évaluation préliminaire.* Québec: L'Éditeur off ciel.

– 1987. "Les sociétés d'État au Québec." *Interventions économiques*, no. 18: 173–92.

Frangoul, Anmar. 2017. "Scotland Goes Big on Renewables and Low Carbon Innovation With a New $107 Million Fund." *CNBC*, December 21, 2017. https://www.cnbc.com/2017/12/21/scotland-goes-big-on-renewables -and-low-carbon-innovation-with-a-new-107-million-fund.html.

Fraser of Allander Institute. 2001. "Promoting Business Start-Ups: A New Strategic Formula." Report for Scottish Enterprise.

Fraser, Matthew. 1987. *Québec Inc. Les Quebecois prennent d'assaut le monde des affaires.* Montréal: Éditions de l'Homme.

FSTQ. 2003. "Promouvoir la complémentarité institutionnelle pour mieux appuyer le développement économique et social du Québec." Montréal.

– 2007. "Notre capital est d'abord humain." Rapport annuel 2007. Montréal.

– 2010–2019. "Rapport annuel." Montréal.

– 2010. *Mémoire de la FTQ et du FSTQ sur le projet de loi no 123.* Montréal.

Gagnon, Alain-G., ed. 2000. *L'Union sociale canadienne sans le Québec: Huit études sur l'entente-cadre.* Montréal: Éditions Saint-Martin.

Gagnon, Alain-G., and Mary Beth Montcalm. 1992. *Quebec beyond the Quiet Revolution.* Montreal: VLB.

Gagnon, Alain-G., and Ferran Requejo, eds. 2011. *Nations en quête de reconnaissance: Regards croisés Québec-Catalogne.* Brussels: P.I.E. Peter Lang.

Gagnon, Alain-G., and Marc Sanjaume-Calvet. 2016. "Trois grands scénarios pour la Catalogne au XXIe siècle: Autonomie, fédéralisme et sécession." In *Repenser l'autodétermination interne*, edited by Michel Seymour, 135–74. Montréal: Éditions Thémis.

Gagnon, Alain-G., and James Tully, eds. 2001. *Multinational Democracies*. Cambridge: Cambridge University Press.

Galenson, Walter, ed. 1985. *Foreign Trade and Investment: Economic Growth in the Newly Industrialising Asian Countries*. Madison: University of Wisconsin Press.

Gamble, Andrew. 1994. *The Free Economy and the Strong State: The Politics of Thatcherism*. London: MacMillan Press.

Garrett, Geoffrey. 1998a. *Partisan Politics in the Global Economy*. New York: Cambridge University Press.

– 1998b. "Global Markets and National Politics: Collision Course or Virtuous Circle?" *International Organization* 52, no. 4: 787–824.

Gellner, Ernest. 1983. *Nations and Nationalism*. Ithaca: Cornell University Press.

Genschel, Philipp, and Laura Seelkopf. 2015. "The Competition State: The Modern State in a Global Economy." In *The Oxford Handbook of Transformations of the State*, edited by Stephan Leibfried, Evelyne Huber, Matthew Lange, Jonah D. Levy, and John D. Stephens, 237–52. Oxford: Oxford University Press.

Gibb, Kenneth, Duncan Maclennan, Des McNulty, and Michael Comerford, eds. 2017. *The Scottish Economy: A Living Book*. New York: Routledge.

Giddens, Anthony, ed. 2000. *The Global Third Way Debate*. Malden: Blackwell Publishers.

Gilpin, Robert. 2001. *Global Political Economy: Understanding the International Economic Order*. Princeton: Princeton University Press.

Gilson, Ronald J. 2003. "Engineering a Venture Capital Market: Lessons from the American Experience." *Stanford Law Review* 55: 1067–103.

Global Entrepreneurship Monitor Scotland. 2002–8. "Hunter Center for Entrepreneurship." The University of Strathclyde in Glasgow.

Godbout, Luc, Suzie St-Cerny, Marc-André Lapointe, and Robert Laplante. 2005. "La f n du moratoire du regime d'épargne-actions." Research Paper, Chaire de recherche en f scalité et en f nances publiques & Institut de recherche en économie contemporaine.

Gompers, Paul, Anna Kovner, Josh Lerner, and David Scharfstein. 2008. "Venture Capital Investment Cycles: The Impact of Public Markets." *Journal of Financial Economics* 87: 1–23.

Gordon, Joan. 2013. *Tailored Approach to Implementation of Advanced Financial Instruments: Scotland*. Glasgow: Scottish Investment Bank.

Graefe, Peter. 2003. "Nationalisme et compétitivité: le Québec peut-il gagner si les Québécois perdent?" In *Québec: État et Société. Tome 2*, edited by Alain-G. Gagnon, 481–503. Montréal: Québec Amérique.

– 2000. "The High Value-Added, Low-Wage Model: Progressive Competitiveness in Québec from Bourassa to Bouchard." *Studies in Political Economy* 61: 5–30.

– 2005. "The Contradictory Political Economy of Minority Nationalism." *Theory and Society* 34, nos. 5–6: 519–49.

Graefe, Peter, and X. Hubert Rioux. 2017. "From the Bailiffs at Our Doors to the Greek Peril: Twenty Years of Fiscal Urgency and Quebec Politics." In *Canadian Provincial and Territorial Paradoxes: Public Finances, Services and Employment in an Era of Austerity*, edited by Bryan Evans and Carlo Fanelli. Montreal and Kingston: McGill-Queen's University Press.

Gray, Caroline 2015. "A Fiscal Pact to Sovereignty? The Basque Economic Agreement and Nationalist Politics." *Nationalism and Ethnic Politics* 21: 63–82.

Greene, Francis J., Kevin F. Mole, and David J. Storey. 2004. "Does More Mean Worse? Three Decades of Enterprise Policy in the Tees Valley." *Urban Studies* 41, no. 7: 1207–28.

Greenfeld, Liah. 1995. "The Worth of Nations: Some Economic Implications of Nationalism." *Critical Review* 9, no. 4: 555–84.

– 2001. *The Spirit of Capitalism: Nationalism and Economic Growth*. Cambridge, MA: Harvard University Press.

– 2006. *Nationalism and the Mind: Essays on Modern Culture*. Oxford: Oneworld Publications.

Gregson, Geoff, Sacha Mann, and Richard Harrison. 2013. "Business Angel Syndication and the Evolution of Risk Capital in a Small Market Economy: Evidence From Scotland." *Managerial and Decision Economics* 34: 95–107.

Guibernau, Montserrat. 1999. *Nations without States: Political Communities in a Global Age*. Malden: Polity Press.

Gulliver, Stuart. 1984. "The Area Projects of the Scottish Development Agency." *The Town Planning Review* 55, no. 3: 322–34.

Haddow, Rodney. 2015. *Comparing Quebec and Ontario: Political Economy and Public Policy at the Turn of the Millennium*. Toronto: University of Toronto Press.

Hall, Derek. 2005. "Japanese Spirit, Western Economics: The Continuing Salience of Economic Nationalism in Japan." In *Economic Nationalism in a Globalizing World*, edited by Eric Helleiner and Andreas Pickel, 118–38. Ithaca: Cornell University Press.

Hall, Douglas James. 1998. "An Evaluation of Ontario's Industrial Policy Efforts: 1985–1995." Unpublished PhD Thesis, Queen's University.

Hall, Peter A. 1993. "Policy Paradigms, Social Learning, and the State: The Case of Economic Policymaking in Britain." *Comparative Politics* 25, no. 3: 275–96.

Hall, Peter A., and Daniel W. Gingerich. 2009. "Varieties of Capitalism and Institutional Complementarities in the Political Economy: An Empirical Analysis." *British Journal of Political Science* 39, no. 3: 449–82.

Hall, Peter A., and David Soskice, eds. 2001. *Varieties of Capitalism: The Institutional Foundations of Comparative Advantage*. New York: Oxford University Press.

Hamilton, Paul. 2004. "Converging Nationalisms: Quebec, Scotland and Wales in Comparative Perspective." *Nationalism and Ethnic Politics* 10, no. 4: 657–85.

Hancké, Bob, ed. 2009. *Debating Varieties of Capitalism*. Oxford: Oxford University Press.

Hansard UK. 1965. "Highland Development (Scotland) Bill." vol. 708, cc. 1079–204. March 16, 1965. http://goo.gl/PVoFwe.

– 1975. "Scottish Development Agency Bill." vol. 894, cc. 462–592. June 25, 1975. http://goo.gl/wU95tP.

– 1990. "Enterprise and New Towns (Scotland) Bill." vol. 164, cc. 838–912. January 9, 1990. http://goo.gl/9FpNwL.

Harding, Rebecca. 2000. "Venture Capital and Regional Development: Towards a Venture Capital 'System.'" *Venture Capital* 2, no. 4: 287–311.

Harrison, Richard T., Tiago Botelho, and Colin M. Mason. 2016. "Patient Capital in Entrepreneurial Finance: A Reassessment of the Role of Business Angel Investors." *Socio-Economic Review* 14, no. 4: 669–89.

Harrison, Richard T., Gavin Don, Keith Glancey Johnston, and Malcolm Greig. 2010. "The Early-Stage Risk Capital Market in Scotland since 2000: Issues of Scale, Characteristics and Market Eff ciency." *Venture Capital* 12, no. 3: 211–39.

Harrison, Richard T., and Colin M. Mason. 1989. "The Role of the Business Expansion Scheme in the United Kingdom." *OMEGA International Journal of Management Science* 17, no. 2: 147–57.

– 1996. "Developing the Informal Venture Capital Market: A Review of the Department of Trade and Industry's Informal Investment Demonstration Projects." *Regional Studies* 30, no. 8: 765–71.

– 2000a. "Editorial: the Role of the Public Sector in the Development of a Regional Venture Capital Industry." *Venture Capital* 2, no. 4: 243–53.

– 2000b. "Venture Capital Market Complementarities: The Links between Business Angels and Venture Capital Funds in the United Kingdom." *Venture Capital* 2, no. 3: 223–42.

Hay, Colin. 2011. "Ideas and the Construction of Interests." In *Ideas and Politics in Social Science Research*, edited by Daniel Béland and Robert H. Cox, 65–82. New York: Oxford University Press.

Hayton Consulting. 2008. "Evaluation of the Scottish Co-Investment Fund." A Report to Scottish Enterprise, Glasgow.

Hayton, Keith, and Ewan Mearns. 1991. "Progressing Scottish Enterprise." *Local Economy* 5, no. 4, 305–16.

Hechter, Michael. 1999. *Internal Colonialism: The Celtic Fringe in British National Development*. London: Transaction Publishers.

– 2000. "Nationalism and Rationality." *Studies in Comparative International Development* 35, no. 1: 3–19.

Heilperin, Michael A. 1960. *Studies in Economic Nationalism.* Geneva and Paris: Publications de l'Institut Universitaire de Hautes Études Internationales, No. 35.

Helleiner, Eric. 1994. *States and the Reemergence of Global Finance: From Bretton Woods to the 1990s.* Ithaca: Cornell University Press.

– 2005. "Conclusion: The Meaning and Contemporary Signif cance of Economic Nationalism." In *Economic Nationalism in a Globalizing World*, edited by Eric Helleiner and Andreas Pickel, 220–34. Ithaca: Cornell University Press.

Helleiner, Eric, and Andreas Pickel, eds. 2005. *Economic Nationalism in a Globalizing World.* Ithaca: Cornell University Press.

Henderson, Ailsa. 2001. "Scottish International Initiatives: Internationalism, the Scottish Parliament and the SNP." Conference Paper, Forum of Federations, Ottawa.

– 2007. *Hierarchies of Belonging: National Identity and Political Culture in Scotland and Quebec.* Montreal and Kingston: McGill-Queen's University Press.

Hepburn, Eve. 2008. "The Neglected Nation: The CSU and the Territorial Cleavage in Bavarian Party Politics." *German Politics* 17, no. 2: 184–202.

Herman, Dan. 2016. "Responses to Change in the Global Political Economy of Innovation: The Role of Subnational States in Industrial Transition." Unpublished PhD Thesis, Wilfrid Laurier University.

Herrera, Yoshiko M. 2005. *Imagined Economies: The Sources of Russian Regionalism.* Cambridge: Cambridge University Press.

Highlands and Islands Development Board. 1967. "First Report: 1st November 1965 to 31st December 1966." Inverness.

– 1975. "Ninth Report: 1st January 1974 to 31st December 1974." Inverness.

– 1986. "20th Report: 1st January 1985 to 31st December 1985." Inverness.

– 1990. "24th Report: 1st January 1989 to 31st December 1989." Inverness.

Highlands and Islands Enterprise. 1993. "Second Report 1992–1993." Inverness.

– 1996. "Fifth Report 1995–1996." Inverness.

Hobson, John M., and M. Ramesh. 2002. "Globalization Makes of States What States Make of It: Between Agency and Structure in the State/Globalization Debate." *New Political Economy* 17, no. 1: 5–22.

Hobson, John M., and Leonard Seabrooke, eds. 2007. *Everyday Politics of the World Economy.* New York: Cambridge University Press.

Holder, Michael. 2018. "Scottish Government Launches £60 Million Low Carbon Infrastructure Fund." *Business Green*, January 22, 2018. https://www.businessgreen.com/bg/news/3024886/scottish-government-launches-gbp60m-low-carbon-infrastructure-fund.

Holitsher, Marc and Roy Suter. 1999. "The Paradox of Economic Globalization and Political Fragmentation: Secessionist Movements in Quebec and Scotland." *Global Society* 13, no. 3: 257–86.

Hopkins, Paul M. 2018. "Acquisitions in Scotland 2003–2017." A Report for
Scottish Enterprise.

Hood, Neil. 1990. "Scottish Enterprise: The Basis of a Scottish Solution to
Scottish Problems?" *Quartterly Economic Commentary* 16, no. 2: 65–75.

– 1991. "The Development and Implementation of a Strategic Role Within
Scottish Enterprise." *Quarterly Economic Commentary* 16, no. 3: 70–80.

– 2000. "Public Venture Capital and Economic Development: The Scottish
Experience." *Venture Capital* 2, no. 4: 313–41.

Hood, Neil and Calum Paterson. 2002. "The Growth and Development of
New Firms." In *Scotland in a Global Economy: The 2020 Vision*, edited by Neal
Hood, Jeremy Peat, Ewen Peters and Stephen Young, 237–57. New York:
Palgrave Macmillan.

Hood, Neil, Jeremy Peat, Ewen Peters and Stephen Young, eds. 2002. *Scotland
in a Global Economy: The 2020 Vision*. New York: Palgrave Macmillan.

Hughes, J. T. 1980. "An Outline of the Powers and Work of the Highlands
and Islands Development Board." *Highlands and Islands Development Board*,
August, 1980. http://goo.gl/TlBXmy.

– 1982. "Policy Analysis in the Highlands and Islands Development Board."
Journal of the Operational Research Society, no. 33: 1055–64.

Imbeau, Louis M., and Mélissa Leclerc. 2002. "L'élimination du déf cit
budgétaire au Québec: contexte et réalisation d'un engagement électoral."
In *Le Parti Québécois: Bilan des engagements électoraux 1994–2000*, edited by
François Pétry, 67–81. Québec: Presses de l'Université Laval.

Imrie, Colin. 2006. "Internationalising Scotland: Making Scotland Global and
International in Its Outlook." *Scottish Affairs*, no. 54: 68–90.

Industry Canada. 2008–2015. "Venture Capital Monitor." http://www.ic.gc
.ca/eic/site/061.nsf/eng/h_02055.html.

Institut Català de Finances. 2012–19. "Annual Report." Barcelona.

Institut de la statistique du Québec. 2017. "Investissements en capital de
risque en pourcentage du PIB, Québec, Canada et quelques pays de la
zone OCDE et hors-OCDE, 1996–2016." www.stat.gouv.qc.ca/statistiques/
science-technologie-innovation/capital-risque/tab9.xlsx.

Institut du Québec. 2017. "Le vieillissement de la population et l'économie du
Québec." Note de recherche.

IQ. 1999–2018. "Rapports annuels." Montréal.

– 2011. "Plan stratégique 2011–2013." Montréal.

Jaaskelainen, Mikko, Markku Maula, and Gordon Murray. 2007. "Prof t
Distribution and Compensation Structures in Publicly and Privately
Funded Hybrid Venture Capital Funds." *Research Policy* 36: 913–29.

Jeng, Leslie A., and Philippe C. Wells. 2000. "The Determinants of Venture
Capital Funding: Evidence Across Countries." *Journal of Corporate Finance* 6:
241–89.

Jenkins, J. Craig, and Kevin T. Leicht. 1996. "Direct Intervention by the
    Subnational State: The Development of Public Venture Capital Programs in
    the American States." *Social Problems* 43, no. 3: 306–26.
Jérôme-Forget, Monique. 2000. "S'ajuster au vent de la concurrence et de la
    modernité." In *La Révolution tranquille, 40 ans plus tard: un bilan*, edited by
    Yves Bélanger, Robert Comeau, and Céline Métivier, 199–205. Montréal:
    VLB.
Jessop, Bob. 2002. *The Future of the Capitalist State*. Cambridge: Polity Press.
Johan, Sof a, Denis Schweizer, and Feng Zhan. 2014. "The Changing Latitude:
    Labor-Sponsored Venture Capital Corporations in Canada." *Corporate
    Governance: An International Review* 22, no. 2: 145–61.
Kacowicz, Arie M. 1999. "Regionalization, Globalization and Nationalism:
    Convergent, Divergent or Overlapping?" *Alternatives: Global, Local, Political*
    24, no. 4: 527–55.
Kangas, Anni. 2013. "Market Civilisation Meets Economic Nationalism: The
    Discourse of Nation in Russia's Modernisation." *Nations and Nationalism* 19,
    no. 3: 572–91.
Karsai, Judit. 2004. "Can the State Replace Private Capital Investors? Public
    Financing of Venture Capital in Hungary." Working Paper, Hungarian
    Academy of Sciences, Institute of Economics. http://econ.core.hu/doc/dp/
    dp/mtdp0409.pdf.
Kavanagh, Dennis. 1990. *Thatcherism and British Politics: The End of Consensus?*
    2nd ed. New York: Oxford University Press.
Keating, Michael. 1997a. *Les défis du nationalisme moderne: Québec, Catalogne,
    Écosse*. Montréal: PUM.
– 1997b. "Stateless Nation-Building: Quebec, Catalonia and Scotland in the
    Changing State System." *Nations and Nationalism* 3, no. 4: 689–717.
– 1997c. "The Political Economy of Regionalism." In *The Political Economy
    of Regionalism*, edited by Michael Keating and John Loughlin, 17–40. New
    York: Routledge.
– 1998. *The New Regionalism in Western Europe: Territorial Restructuring and
    Political Change*. Cheltenham: Edward Elgar.
– 2001. "Nations Without States: The Accomodation of Nationalism in the
    New State Order." In *Minority Nationalism and the Changing International
    Order*, edited by Michael Keating and John McGarry, 19–43. New York:
    Oxford University Press.
– 2010. *The Government of Scotland: Public Policy Making After Devolution*.
    Edinburgh: Edinburgh University Press.
– 2013. *Rescaling the European State: The Making of Territory and the Rise of the
    Meso*. New York: Oxford University Press.
Keating, Michael, and Harald Baldersheim, eds. 2016. *Small States in the
    Modern World: Vulnerabilities and Opportunities*. Northampton: Edward Elgar.

Keating, Michael, and John Loughlin, eds. 1997. *The Political Economy of Regionalism*. New York: Routledge.

Keating, Michael, and John McGarry, eds. 2001. *Minority Nationalism and the Changing International Order*. New York: Oxford University Press.

Keller, Matthew R., and Fred Block. 2013. "Explaining the Transformation in the US Innovation System: The Impact of a Small Government Program." *Socio-Economic Review* 11, no. 4: 629–56.

Kemp, Kenny, Graham Lironi, and Peter Shakeshaft. 2017. *The Archangels' Share: The Story of the World's First Syndicate of Business Angels*. Salford, England: Saraband.

Klonowski, Darek. 2012. "The Role of Government, Venture Capital and Banks in Closing Liquidity Gaps in the SME Sector of an Emerging Market." In *The Oxford Handbook of Venture Capital*, edited by Douglas J. Cumming, 966–95. New York: Oxford University Press.

Krugman, Paul. 1995. *Development, Geography and Economic Theory*. London: MIT Press.

Lachapelle, Guy. 2000. "Identity, Integration and the Rise of Identity Economy: The Quebec Case in Comparison With Scotland, Wales and Catalonia." In *Globalization, Governance and Identity: The Emergence of New Partnerships*, edited by Guy Lachapelle and John Trent, 211–31. Montréal: Presses de l'Université de Montréal.

Lachapelle, Guy, and Gilbert Gagné. 2003. "Intégration économique, valeurs et identités: les attitudes matérialistes et postmatérialistes des Québécois." *Politique et Sociétés* 22, no. 1: 27–52.

Lachapelle, Guy, and Stéphane Paquin, eds. 2005. *Mastering Globalization: New Sub-States' Governance and Strategies*. New York: Routledge.

Lalonde, Denis. 2018. "Capital de risque: Luge Capital lance un fonds de 75M$." *Les Affaires*, June 12, 2018. https://www.lesaffaires.com/strategie-d-entreprise/pme/capital-de--luge-capital-lance-un-fonds-de-75m/603277.

Landström, Hans, and Colin Mason, eds. 2016. *Handbook of Research on Business Angels*. Cheltenham, England: Edward Elgar.

Laplante, Serge. 1993. "Innovatech-Québec: vivement la mise en oeuvre." *Le Devoir*, December 4, p. B3.

Law, Alex, and Gerry Mooney. 2012. "Devolution in a 'Stateless Nation': Nation-building and Social Policy in Scotland." *Social Policy & Administration* 46, no. 2: 161–77.

Learmonth, Davie, Alison Munro, and J. Kim Swales. 2003. "Multi-sectoral Cluster Modelling: The Evaluation of Scottish Enterprise Cluster Policy." *European Planning Studies* 11, no. 5: 567–84.

Le Devoir. 2004. "Le PQ craint le désengagement de l'État." *Le Devoir*, February 24, 2004. http://web1.ledevoir.com/economie/actualites-economiques/48184/le-pq-craint-le-desengagement-de-l-etat.

Lee, Clive H. 2005. "The Establishment of the Financial Network." In *The Transformation of Scotland: The Economy Since 1700*, edited by Tom M. Devine, Clive H. Lee and George C. Peden, 100–27. Edinburgh: Edinburgh University Press.

Leibfried, Stephan, Evelyn Huber, Matthew Lange, Jonah D. Levy, and John D. Stephens, eds. 2015. *The Oxford Handbook of Transformations of the State*. Oxford: Oxford University Press.

Leicht, Kevin T., and J. Craig Jenkins. 1994. "Three Strategies of State Economic Development: Entrepreneurial, Industrial Recruitment, and Deregulation Policies in the American States." *Economic Development Quarterly* 8, no. 3: 256–69.

– 1998. "Political Resources and Direct State Intervention: The Adoption of Public Venture Capital Programs in the American States, 1974–1990." *Social Forces* 76, no. 4: 1323–45.

Leleux, Benoît, and Bernard Surlemont. 2003. "Public versus Private Venture Capital: Seeding or Crowding Out? A Pan-European Analysis." *Journal of Business Venturing* 18, no. 1: 81–104.

Lerner, Josh. 1998. "Angel Financing and Public Policy: An Overview." *Journal of Banking and Finance* 22: 773–83.

– 1999. "The Government as Venture Capitalist: The Long-Run Impact of the SBIR Program." *Journal of Business* 72, no. 3: 285–318.

– 2002. "When Bureaucrats Meet Entrepreneurs: The Design of Effective Public Venture Capital Programmes." *The Economic Journal* 112, no. 477: F73–F84.

– 2009. *Boulevard of Broken Dreams: Why Public Efforts to Boost Entrepreneurship and Venture Capital Have Failed – and What to Do About It*. Princeton: Princeton University Press.

– 2010. "The Future of Public Efforts to Boost Entrepreneurship and Venture Capital." *Small Business Economics* 35: 255–64.

Lerner, Josh, and Brian Watson. 2008. "The Public Venture Capital Challenge: The Australian Case." *Venture Capital* 10, no. 1: 1–20.

Lévesque, Benoît. 2000. "Originalité et impact de l'action des SOLIDE sur le développement local et sur l'emploi au Québec." CRISES-CRDC co-publication, Série pratiques économiques et sociales, No. 18.

Lévesque, Benoît, Yvan Comeau, Denis Martel, Jean Desrochers, and Marguerite Mendell. 2003. "Les fonds régionaux et locaux de développement en 2002." Cahiers du CRISES, No. ET0309.

Lévesque, Benoît, Marie-Claire Malo, and Ralph Rouzier. 1997. "La Caisse de Dépôt et Placement du Québec et le Mouvement des Caisses Populaires et d'Économie Desjardins: deux institutions f nancières, une même convergence vers l'intérêt général?" Cahiers du CRISES, No. ET9703.

Lévesque, Benoît, Marguerite Mendell, and Solange Van Kemenade. 1996. "Les fonds régionaux et locaux de développement au Québec: des

institutions f nancières relevant principalement de l'économie sociale."
Cahiers du CRISES, No. ET9610.

Levi-Faur, David. 1997a. "Friedrich List and the Political Economy of the
Nation-State." *Review of International Political Economy* 4, no. 1: 154–78.

– 1997b. "Economic Nationalism: From Friedrich List to Robert Reich." *Review
of International Studies* 26: 359–70.

Li, Yong. 2012. "Venture Capital Staging: Domestic versus Foreign VC-Led
Investments." In *The Oxford Handbook of Venture Capital*, edited by Douglas J.
Cumming, 354–72. New York: Oxford University Press.

Life Sciences Scotland. 2011. *Scottish Life Sciences Strategy 2011: Creating Wealth,
Promoting Health*. Edinburgh: Life Sciences Scotland.

Lijphart, Arend. 1971. "Comparative Politics and the Comparative Method."
The American Political Science Review 65, no. 3: 682–93.

List, Friedrich. 1998 [1841]. *Système national d'économie politique*. Paris:
Gallimard.

L'Italien, François, Lyne Nantel, and Clément Bélanger Bishinga. 2014.
"L'endettement des fermes au Québec: Un portrait contrasté." Research
paper, Institut de recherche en économie contemporaine.

Liu, Yang and Fabio Massimo Parenti. 2019. "Economic Nationalism and
Globalization, Evidence From China (Belt and Road Initiative)." In
*International Firms' Economic Nationalism and Trade Policies in the Globalization
Era*, edited by Harish Chandan and Bryan Christiansen, 59–73. Hershey, PA:
IGI Global.

Lloyd, Greg, and Stuart Black. 1993. "Highlands and Islands Enterprise:
Strategies for Economic and Social Development." *Local Economy* 8, no. 1:
69–81.

Lockett, Andy, Gordon Murray, and Mike Wright. 2002. "Do UK Venture
Capitalists *Still* Have a Bias Against Investment in New Technology Firms?"
Research Policy 31: 1009–30.

Macdonalds & Associates Limited. 1990–2005a. "Statistiques." Prepared for
Réseau Capital. Accessed March 9, 2016. http://www.reseaucapital.com/
statistiques.php.

– 1990–2005b. "Tables." Prepared for Réseau Capital. Accessed March 9, 2016.
http://www.reseaucapital.com/statistiques.php.

MacLeod, Gordon. 2001. "New Regionalism Reconsidered: Globalization and
the Remaking of Political Economic Space." *International Journal of Urban
and Regional Research* 25, no. 4: 804–29.

Manigart, Sophie, and Christof Beuselinck. 2001. "Supply of Venture Capital
by European Governments." Working Paper, Faculty of Economics and
Business Administration, University of Ghent, August 2001. http://
citeseerx.ist.psu.edu/viewdoc/download?doi=10.1.1.199.5020&rep=rep1&
type=pdf.

Mann, Michael. 1997. "Has Globalization Ended the Rise and Rise of the Nation-State?" *Review of International Political Economy* 4, no. 3: 472–96.

Martin, Pierre. 1997. "When Nationalism Meets Continentalism: The Politics of Free Trade in Quebec." In *The Political Economy of Regionalism*, edited by Michael Keating and John Loughlin, 236–61. New York: Routledge.

Martinez Sanchez, Angel. 1992. "Regional Innovation and Small High-Technology Firms in Peripheral Regions." *Small Business Economics* 4: 153–68.

Mason, Colin M. 2010. "Editorial Introduction: Entrepreneurial Finance in a Regional Economy." *Venture Capital* 12, no. 3: 167–72.

Mason, Colin M., and Tiago Botelho. 2013. "The Transformation of the Business Angel Market: Evidence from Scotland." Working Paper, Adam Smith Business School, University of Glasgow.

– 2014. "The Role of the Exit in the Initial Screening of Investment Opportunities: The Case of Business Angel Syndicate Gatekeepers." Working Paper, Adam Smith Business School, University of Glasgow.

Mason, Colin M., Tiago Botelho, and Richard Harrison. 2016. "The Transformation of the Business Angel Market: Empirical Evidence and Research Implications." *Venture Capital* 18, no. 4: 321–44.

Mason, Colin M., and Ross Brown. 2010. "High Growth Firms in Scotland." Final Report to Scottish Enterprise.

Mason, Colin M., and Richard T. Harrison. 1989. "Small Firms Policy and the North-South Divide in the United Kingdom: The Case of the Business Expansion Scheme." *Transactions of the Institute of British Geographers* 14, no. 1: 37–58.

– 1995. "Closing the Regional Equity Gap: The Role of Informal Venture Capital." *Small Business Economics* 7: 153–72.

– 1997. "Business Angel Networks and the Development of the Informal Venture Capital Market in the UK: Is There Still a Role for the Public Sector?" *Small Business Economics* 9: 111–23.

– 2000. "Inf uences on the Supply of Informal Venture Capital in the UK: An Exploratory Study of Investor Attitudes." *International Small Business Journal* 18, no. 4: 11–28.

– 2001. "Investment Readiness: A Critique of Government Proposals to Increase the Demand for Venture Capital." *Regional Studies* 35, no. 7: 663–8.

– 2002a. "The Geography of Venture Capital Investments in the UK." *Transactions of the Institute of British Geographers* 27, no. 4: 427–51.

– 2002b. "Barriers to Investment in the Informal Venture Capital Sector." *Entrepreneurship and Regional Development* 14: 71–287.

– 2002c. "Addressing Demand Side Constraints in the Informal Venture Capital Market: the Example of LINC Scotland's 'Trial Marriage' Scheme." Conference Paper, European Academy of Management, Stockholm. http://

citeseerx.ist.psu.edu/viewdoc/download?doi=10.1.1.201.7841&rep=rep1&
type=pdf.

– 2003. "Closing the Regional Equity Gap? A Critique of the Department of
Trade and Industry's Regional Venture Capital Funds Initiative." *Regional
Studies* 37, no. 8: 855–68.

– 2004. "Improving Access to Early-Stage Venture Capital in Regional
Economies: A New Approach to Investment Readiness." *Local Economy* 19,
no. 2: 159–73.

– 2006. "After the Exit: Acquisitions, Entrepreneurial Recycling and Regional
Economic Development." *Regional Studies* 40, no. 1: 55–73.

– 2010. "Annual Report on the Business Angel Market in the United Kingdom:
2008/09." UK Department for Business, Innovation & Skills, URN 10/994.

Mason, Colin M., and Yannis Pierrakis. 2013. "Venture Capital, the Regions
and Public Policy: The United Kingdom since the Post-2000 Technology
Crash." *Regional Studies* 47, no. 7: 1156–71.

Mazzucato, Mariana. 2014. *The Entrepreneurial State: Debunking Public vs.
Private Sector Myths.* New York: Anthem Press.

– 2016. "From Market Fixing to Market-Creating: A New Framework for
Innovation Policy." *Industry and Innovation* 23, no. 2: 140–56.

Mazzucato, Mariana, and Caetano C. R. Penna. 2016. "Beyond Market
Failures: The Market Creating and Shaping Roles of State Investment
Banks." *Journal of Economic Policy Reform* 19, no. 4: 305–26.

Mazzucato, Mariana, and Gregor Semieniuk. 2017. "Public Financing of
Innovation: New Questions." *Oxford Review of Economic Policy* 33, no. 1: 24–48.

– 2018. "Financing Renewable Energy: Who Is Financing and Why It
Matters." *Technological Forecasting and Social Change* 127: 8–22.

Mazzucato, Mariana, and Laurie Macfarlane. 2019. "A Mission-Oriented
Framework for the Scottish National Investment Bank." *Institute for
Innovation and Public Purpose*, Policy Paper (IPP WP 2019-02). https://www
.ucl.ac.uk/bartlett/publicpurpose/wp2019-02.

McBride, Stephen, and Russell A. Williams. 2001. "Globalization, the
Restructuring of Labour Markets and Policy Convergence." *Global Social
Policy* 1, no. 3: 281–309.

McCann, Philip. 1997. "How Deeply Embedded Is Silicon Glen? A Cautionary
Note." *Regional Studies* 31, no. 7: 695–703.

McCrone, David. 1999. "Opinion Polls in Scotland July 1988–June 1999."
Scottish Affairs, no. 28: 32–43.

McCrone, Gavin. 1999. "Industrial Clusters: A New Idea or an Old One?"
Scottish Affairs, no. 29: 73–7.

McEwen, Nicola. 2002. "State Welfare Nationalism: The Territorial Impact of
Welfare State Development in Scotland." *Regional and Federal Studies* 12,
no. 1: 66–90.

– 2006. *Nationalism and the State: Welfare and Identity in Scotland and Quebec.* Brussels: P.I.E.-Peter Lang.

McGlue, David. 2002. "The Funding of Venture Capital in Europe: Issues for Public Policy." *Venture Capital* 4, no. 1: 45–58.

McGregor, Peter, J. Kim Swales, and Ya Ping Yin. 2001. "The Impact on the Scottish Economy of an Expansion in Developmental Foreign Direct Investment in the Electronics Sector." *Quarterly Economic Commentary* 26, no. 1: 39–49.

McVey, Brian. 2000. "Response to Paper by Alexander Dow and Catherine Kirk 'The Number of Scottish Businesses and Economic Policy.'" *Quarterly Economic Commentary* 25, no. 4: 35–7.

Meadwell, Hudson, and Pierre Martin. 1996. "Economic Integration and the Politics of Independence." *Nations and Nationalism* 2, no. 1: 67–87.

Mehta, Jal. 2011. "The Varied Roles of Ideas in Politics: From Whether to How." In *Ideas and Politics in Social Science Research*, edited by Daniel Béland and Robert H. Cox, 23–46. New York: Oxford University Press.

MEQ. 2010. "Projet de loi 123: le bon point de depart pour une politique économique pleine d'avenir." Montréal.

Michie, Rona, and Fiona Wishlade. 2014. "Business Development Banks and Funds in Europe: Selected Examples." In *Briefing to the Scottish Government in the Context of the Scottish Business Bank Proposal.* Glasgow: European Policies Research Center.

Mitchell, James. 1997. "Scotland, the Union State and the International Environment." In *The Political Economy of Regionalism*, edited by Michael Keating and John Loughlin, 406–21. New York: Routledge.

Moore, Barry, and John Rhodes. 1974. "Regional Policy and the Scottish Economy." *Scottish Journal of Political Economy* 11, no. 3: 215–35.

Moore, Chris, and Simon Booth. 1986. "The Scottish Development Agency: Market Consensus, Public Planning and Local Enterprise." *Local Economy* 1, no. 3: 7–19.

Morin, Philippe. 2012. "The Fonds de Solidarité: Historical and Political Foundations, What Lessons for Economic Democracy?" *Review of Radical Political Economics* 44, no. 1: 82–99.

Murray, Gordon C. 1994. "The *Second* 'Equity Gap': Exit Problems for Seed and Early Stage Venture Capitalists and Their Investee Companies." *International Small Business Journal* 12, no. 4: 59–76.

– 1995. "Evolution and Change: An Analysis of the First Decade of the UK Venture Capital Industry." *Journal of Business Finance and Accounting* 22, no. 8: 1077–106.

– 1998. "A Policy Response to Regional Disparities in the Supply of Risk Capital to New Technology-Based Firms in the European Union: The European Seed Capital Fund Scheme." *Regional Studies* 35, no. 5: 405–19.

– 2007. "Venture Capital and Government Policy." In *Handbook of Research on Venture Capital*, edited by Hans Landström, 113–54. Cheltenham, England: Edward Elgar.

Murray, Gordon C., and Jonathan Lott. 1995. "Have UK Venture Capitalists a Bias Against Investment in New Technology-Based Firms?" *Research Policy* 24: 283–99.

Nagy, Stephen Robert. 2014. "Nationalism, Domestic Politics, and the Japan Economic Rejuvenation." *East Asia* 31, no. 1: 5–21.

Nakano, Takeshi. 2004. "Theorizing Economic Nationalism." *Nations and Nationalism* 10, no. 3: 211–29.

Nayar, Baldev Raj. 1997. "Globalisation, Nationalism and Economic Policy Reform." *Economic and Political Weekly* 32, no. 30: PE93–PE104.

NESTA. 2009. "From Funding Gaps to Thin Markets: UK Government Support for Early-Stage Venture Capital." Research Report, September 2009. https://ore.exeter.ac.uk/repository/bitstream/handle/10036/106659/Thin-Markets-v9.pdf?sequence=2.

Neumark, David, Brandon Wall, and Junfu Zhang. 2011. "Do Small Businesses Create More Jobs? New Evidence for the United States From the National Establishment Time Series." *The Review of Economics and Statistics* 93, no. 1: 16–29.

Newlands, David. 2005. "The Regional Economies of Scotland." In *The Transformation of Scotland: The Economy Since 1700*, edited by Tom M. Devine, Clive H. Lee and George C. Peden, 159–83. Edinburgh: Edinburgh University Press.

Noland, Marcus. 1990. *Pacific Basin Developing Countries: Prospects for the Future*. Washington, DC: Institute for International Economics.

North, David, Robert Baldock, and Ignatius Ekanem. 2010. "Is There a Debt Finance Gap Relating to Scottish SMEs? A Demand-side Perspective." *Venture Capital* 12, no. 3: 173–92.

OECD. 2016. *State-Owned Enterprises as Global Competitors: A Challenge or an Opportunity?* Paris: OECD Publishing.

– 2017. *The Size and Sectoral Distribution of State-Owned Enterprises*. Paris: OECD Publishing.

– 2018a. *OECD Economic Outlook 2018*. Paris: OECD Publishing.

– 2018b. *Financing SMEs and Entrepreneurs 2018: An OECD Scoreboard*. Paris: OECD Publishing.

O'Hare, Chris. 2004. "Business Gateway: Business Support in Lowland Scotland." *Business Information Review* 21, no. 4: 245–51.

Ontario, Legislative Assembly of Ontario. 1987. "Hansard Transcripts." Off cial Record for April 30, 1987. http://goo.gl/FcSLPH.

Osborne, Duncan, and Daniel Sandler. 1998. "A Tax-Expenditure Analysis of Labour-Sponsored Venture Capital Corporations." *Canadian Tax Journal* 46, no. 3: 499–574.

Ozaki, Toshiya. 2012. "Open Trade, Closed Industry: The Japanese Aerospace Industry in the Evolution of Economic Nationalism and Implications for Globalization." In *Globalization and Economic Nationalism in Asia*, edited by Anthony P. D'Costa. Oxford: Oxford University Press Scholarship Online.

PACEC. 2012. *Scottish Enterprise: Economic Impact of the Scottish Venture Fund. Final Report.* Cambridge and London: PACEC.

– 2013. *Economic Impact of the Scottish Enterprise Seed Fund. Final Report.* Cambridge and London: PACEC.

Paillé, Daniel. 1994. "Conférence de presse." November 15. Québec.

Painchaud, Paul. 1977. "Territorialization and Internationalism: The Case of Quebec." *Publius* 7, no. 4: 161–75.

Palley, Thomas I. 2011. "The Rise and Fall of Export-led Growth." Working Paper No. 675, Levy Economics Institute of Bard College.

Paquin, Stéphane. 2001. *La revanche des petites nations. Le Québec, l'Écosse et la Catalogne face à la mondialisation.* Montréal: VLB Éditeur.

– 2002. "Globalization, European Integration and the Rise of Neo-nationalism in Scotland." *Nationalism and Ethnic Politics* 8, no. 1: 55–80.

– 2003. "Paradiplomatie identitaire et diplomatie en Belgique fédérale: Le cas de la Flandre." *Canadian Journal of Political Science* 36, no. 3: 621–42.

– 2004. *Paradiplomatie et relations internationales: Théorie des relations internationales des régions face à la mondialisation.* Bruxelles: P.I.E.-Peter Lang.

– 2004b. "La paradiplomatie identitaire: Le Quebec, la Catalogne et la Flandre en relations internationales." *Politique et Sociétés* 23, nos. 2–3: 203–37.

Parizeau, Jacques. 1994. "Conférence de presse." November 4. Québec.

Parry, Richard. 1983. "Public Expenditure in Scotland." In *Scottish Government Yearbook 1983*, 98–120.

Paul, Stuart, and Geoff Whittam. 2010. "Business Angel Syndicates: An Exploratory Study of Gatekeepers." *Venture Capital* 12, no. 3: 241–56.

Paul, Stuart, Geoff Whittam, and Jim B. Johnston. 2003. "The Operation of the Informal Venture Capital Market in Scotland." *Venture Capital* 5, no. 4: 313–35.

Peden, George C. 2005. "The Managed Economy: Scotland, 1919–2000." In *The Transformation of Scotland: The Economy Since 1700*, edited by Tom M. Devine, Clive H. Lee and George C. Peden, 233–65. Edinburgh: Edinburgh University Press.

Pelletier, Mario. 2009. *La Caisse dans tous ses États: L'histoire mouvementée de la Caisse de dépôt et placement du Québec.* Outremont: Carte Blanche.

Peters, Ewen, and Neil Hood. 2002. "Scotland's Biotechnology Cluster: Strategic Issues and Responses." In *Scotland in a Global Economy: The 2020 Vision*, edited by Neil Hood, Jeremy Peat, Ewen Peters and Stephen Young, 91–111. New York: Palgrave Macmillan.

Pickel, Andreas. 2005. "Introduction: False Oppositions. Recontextualizing Economic Nationalism in a Globalizing World." In *Economic Nationalism in a Globalizing World*, edited by Eric Helleiner and Andreas Pickel, 1–17. Ithaca: Cornell University Press.

– 2006. *The Problem of Order in the Global Age: Systems and Mechanisms*. New York: Palgrave Macmillan.

Pierrakis, Yannis. 2010. "Venture Capital: Now and After the Dotcom Crash." NESTA, Research Report. July, 2010. https://media.nesta.org.uk/documents/venture_capital.pdf.

Pierrakis, Yannis, and Colin Mason. 2008. "Shifting Sands. The Changing Nature of the Early Stage Venture Capital Market in the UK." NESTA, Research Report, September, 2008. https://media.nesta.org.uk/documents/shifting_sands.pdf.

PLQ. 1989. "Une richesse à renouveler: Programme politique." Montréal.

– 1991. "Un Québec libre de ses choix: Rapport du comité constitutionnel." Montréal.

– 1998. "Le plan pour un Québec plus fort: Le résumé." Montréal.

– 2003. "Un gouvernement au service des Québécois: Ensemble, réinventons le Québec. Le plan d'action du prochain gouvernement libéral." Montréal.

– 2007. "S'unir pour réussir. Le Québec de demain. Plan d'action 2007–2012." Montréal.

– 2014. "Our Commitments." Montréal.

Porter, Michael E. 1994. "The Role of Location in Competition." *Journal of the Economics of Business* 1, no. 1: 35–9.

– 1998. *The Competitive Advantage of Nations*. New York: Free Press.

Powell, Walter W., Kenneth W. Koput, James I. Bowie, and Laurel Smith-Doerr. 2002. "The Spatial Clustering of Science and Capital: Accounting for Biotech Firm-Venture Capital Relationships." *Regional Studies* 36, no. 3: 291–305.

PQ. 1994. "Programme électoral du Parti Québécois." Montréal.

– 1998. "Les orientations du programme electoral du Parti Québécois: Ensemble, nous savons construire." Montréal.

Québec. Ministère des Finances. 1962a. "Discours du Budget 1962–1963." Éditeur off ciel.

– Assemblée Législative. 1962b. "An Act to Incorporate the General Investment Corporation of Quebec." July 6, 1962. http://goo.gl/QCtDix.

– 1965. "Notes du discours de l'Honorable Jean Lesage prononcé en Chambre le 9 juin 1965 lors de la présentation, en deuxième lecture, de la Loi de la Caisse de dépôt et placement du Québec (Bill 51)." June 9, 1965. http://goo.gl/ugGvNM.

– Assemblée Nationale. 1971a. "An Act Respecting the Fédération de Québec des Unions régionales des Caisses Populaires Desjardins." December 23, 1971. http://goo.gl/tOJBcT.

– Assemblée Nationale. 1971b. "Journal des débats 11, no. 24." Éditeur off ciel.
– Assemblée Nationale. 1971c. "An Act Respecting the Société de développement industriel du Québec." Updated August 21, 1998. http://goo.gl/yUhHgx.
– Ministère d'État au Développement économique. 1982. "Le virage technologique – programme d'action économique." Éditeur off ciel.
– Assemblée Nationale. 1983a. "Journal des débats 27, no. 41." Éditeur off ciel.
– Commission permanente du travail. 1983b. "Journal des débats 27, no. 129." Éditeur off ciel.
– Assemblée Nationale. 1983c. "An Act to Establish the Fonds de Solidarité des Travailleurs du Québec (F.T.Q.)." Updated May 1, 2019. http://goo.gl/H37IGH.
– Ministère des Finances. 1989. "Discours sur le budget 1989–1990." Éditeur off ciel.
– Société de développement industriel. 1990a. "Plan de développement 1988–1991 et Plan de dévelopement stratégique 1990–1993." Éditeur off ciel.
– Ministère des Finances. 1990b. "Discours sur le budget 1990–1991." Éditeur off ciel.
– Ministère des Finances. 1991. "Discours sur le budget 1991–1992." Éditeur off ciel.
– Assemblée Nationale. 1992. "Loi sur la Société Innovatech du Grand Montréal." June 23, 1992. http://goo.gl/gwC0W4
– Ministère de l'Industrie, du Commerce et de la Technologie. 1993a. "Industrial Clusters." Éditeur off ciel.
– Commission permanente de l'économie et du travail. 1993b. "Journal des débats 32, no. 80." Éditeur off ciel.
– Ministère des Finances. 1995a. "Discours sur le budget 1995–1996." Éditeur off ciel.
– Commission permanente de l'économie et du travail. 1995b. "Journal des débats 34, no. 33." Éditeur off ciel.
– Commission permanente de l'économie et du travail. 1995c. "Journal des débats 34, no. 36." Éditeur off ciel.
– Commission permanente de l'économie et du travail. 1995d. "Journal des débats 34, no. 20." Éditeur off ciel.
– Commission permanente de l'économie et du travail. 1995e. "Journal des débats 34, no. 35." Éditeur off ciel.
– Assemblée Nationale. 1995g. "An Act to Establish Fondaction, le Fonds de Développement de la Confédération des Syndicats Nationaux pour la Coopération et l'Emploi." Éditeur off ciel.
– Vérif cateur général. 1995h. "Rapport à l'Assemblée nationale pour l'année 1994–1995. Chapitre 4. L'aide gouvernementale au démarrage d'entreprises." Éditeur off ciel.

– Vérif cateur général du Québec. 1997a. "Rapport à l'Assemblée Nationale pour l'année 1996–1997." Éditeur off ciel.
– Secrétariat au développement des régions. 1997b. "Politique de soutien au développement local et régional." *Livre blanc.* Accessed June 4, 2019. https://goo.gl/uwzzl2.
– Assemblée Nationale. 1997c. "An Act Respecting the Ministère des Régions." Éditeur off ciel. December 19, 1997. http://goo.gl/Qce7Ae.
– Ministère des Finances. 1998a. "1998–1999 Budget Speech." Éditeur off ciel.
– Commission des f nances publiques. 1998b. "Journal des débats 35, no. 50." Éditeur off ciel.
– Ministère des Finances. 1998c. "Québec Objectif emploi. Vers une économie d'avant-garde. Plan d'action pour favoriser le développement du secteur f nancier." Éditeur off ciel.
– Ministère des Finances. 1998d. "Québec Objectif emploi. Vers une économie d'avant-garde. Accroître les investissements privés." Éditeur off ciel.
– Assemblée Nationale. 1998e. "An Act Respecting Investissement-Québec and Garantie-Québec." Éditeur off ciel.
– Ministère de la Recherche, de la Science et de la Technologie. 1999a. "Québec Objectif emploi. Vers une économie d'avant-garde. Accélérer la recherche et l'innovation." Éditeur off ciel.
– Ministère des Finances. 1999b. "Discours sur le budget 1999–2000." Éditeur off ciel.
– Assemblée Nationale. 2000a. "Journal des débats 36, no. 132." Éditeur off ciel.
– Commission de l'agriculture, des pêcheries et de l'alimentation. 2000b. "Journal des débats 36, no. 27." Éditeur off ciel.
– Ministère des Régions. 2001a. "Rapport triennal des Centres locaux de développement (CLD) 1998–2000." Éditeur off ciel.
– Ministère des Finances. 2001b. "Stratégie de développement économique des régions-ressources. La force des régions. Un maillon essentiel de notre économie." Éditeur off ciel.
– Ministère des Finances. 2001c. "Discours sur le budget 2001–2002." Éditeur off ciel.
– Assemblée nationale. 2001d. "Loi constituant Capital régional et coopératif Desjardins." Éditeur off ciel.
– Assemblée Nationale. 2001e. "Journal des débats 37, no. 35." Éditeur off ciel.
– Commission des f nances publiques. 2001f. "Journal des débats 37, no. 25." Éditeur off ciel.
– Ministère des Finances. 2001g. "Discours sur le budget 2002–2003." Éditeur off ciel.
– Ministère des Finances. 2001h. "AGIR. Le Plan d'action et la politique économique du gouvernement." Éditeur off ciel.
– Assemblée Nationale. 2001i. "Journal des débats 37, no. 68." Éditeur off ciel.

- Commission sur le déséquilibre f scal. 2002a. "Pour un nouveau partage des moyens f nanciers au Canada. Rapport." Éditeur off ciel.
- Ministère des Finances. 2002b. "Vers le plein emploi. Horizon 2005." Éditeur off ciel.
- Ministère des Finances. 2003a. "Politique de développement des coopératives. Horizon 2005." Éditeur off ciel.
- Ministère du Développement Économique et Régional. 2003b. "Rapport du groupe de travail sur le rôle de l'État québécois dans le capital de risque." Éditeur off ciel.
- Ministère des Finances. 2003c. "Discours sur le budget 2003–2004." Éditeur off ciel.
- Ministère des Finances. 2003d. "Renseignement additionnels sur les mesures f scales – Budget 2003–2004." Éditeur off ciel.
- Assemblée Nationale. 2003e. "Loi sur le ministère du Développement économique et régional et de la recherche."
- Assemblée Nationale. 2003f. "Journal des débats 38, no. 31." Éditeur off ciel.
- Commission des f nances publiques. 2003g. "Journal des débats 38, no. 9." Éditeur off ciel.
- Commission des f nances publiques. 2003h. "Journal des débats 38, no. 12." Éditeur off ciel.
- Commission des f nances publiques. 2003i. "Journal des débats 38, no. 13." Éditeur off ciel.
- Ministère des Finances. 2004a. "The Managed Economy: Scotland, 1919–2000." Éditeur off ciel.
- Commission des f nances publiques. 2004b. "Journal des débats 38, no. 27." Éditeur off ciel.
- Commission des f nances publiques. 2004c. "Journal des débats 38, no. 28." Éditeur off ciel.
- Commission des f nances publiques. 2004d. "Journal des débats 38, no. 30." Éditeur off ciel.
- Commission des f nances publiques. 2004e. "Journal des débats 38, no. 32." Éditeur off ciel.
- Ministère du Développement économique, de l'Innovation et des Exportations. 2005a. "L'Avantage québécois. Stratégie gouvernementale de développement économique." Éditeur off ciel.
- Commission d'enquête sur la Société Papiers Gaspésia. 2005b. "Rapport d'enquête sur les dépassements de coûts et de délais du chantier de la Société Papiers Gaspésia de Chandler." Éditeur off ciel.
- Ministère des Finances. 2005c. "Plan budgétaire 2005–2006." Éditeur off ciel.
- Ministère du Développement économique, de l'Innovation et des Exportations. 2006a. "Un Québec innovant et prospère. Stratégie québécoise de la recherche et de l'innovation." Éditeur off ciel.
- Ministère des Finances. 2006b. "Plan budgétaire 2006–2007." Éditeur off ciel.

– Ministère du Développement économique, de l'Innovation et des Exportations. 2006c. "Stratégie de développement de l'industrie aéronautique québécoise." Éditeur off ciel.
– Ministère du Développement économique, de l'Innovation et de l'Exportation. 2007. "Pour un secteur manufacturier gagnant. Plan d'action en faveur du secteur manufacturier." Éditeur off ciel.
– Ministère du Développement économique, de l'Innovation et de l'Exportation. 2008. "Pour un Québec vert et prospère. Stratégie de développement de l'industrie québécoise de l'environnement et des technologies vertes." Éditeur off ciel.
– Ministère du Développement économique, de l'Innovation et des Exportations. 2009a. "The Managed Economy: Scotland, 1919–2000." Éditeur off ciel.
– Vérif cateur général du Québec. 2009b. "Rapport spécial portant sur le Fonds d'intervention économique régional, volet 'fonds régionaux d'investissement.'" Éditeur off ciel.
– Ministère des Finances. 2009c. "2009–2010 Budget Plan." Éditeur off ciel.
– Ministère des Finances. 2010a. "Des choix pour l'avenir. Plan d'action économique et budgétaire." Éditeur off ciel.
– Assemblée Nationale. 2010b. "An Act Respecting the Amalgamation of the Société Générale de Financement du Québec and Investissement Québec." Éditeur off ciel.
– Commission des f nances publiques. 2010c. "Journal des débats 41, no. 91 à 108." Éditeur off ciel.
– Ministère du Développement économique, de l'Innovation et des Exportation. 2010d. "Le renouvellement de l'entrepreneuriat au Québec: un regard sur 2013 et 2018." Éditeur off ciel.
– Ministère du Développement économique, de l'Innovation et des Exportations. 2011a. "Le Fonds du développement économique. Des interventions structurantes au bénéf ce du développement économique du Québec." Éditeur off ciel.
– Ministère du Développement économique, de l'Innovation et des Exportations. 2011b. "Vers une stratégie de l'entrepreneuriat. Rapport de consultation." Éditeur off ciel.
– Ministère du Développement économique, de l'Innovation et des Exportations. 2011c. "Foncez! Tout le Québec vous admire. Stratégie québécoise de l'entrepreneuriat." Éditeur off ciel.
– Ministère des Finances. 2011d. "Plan budgétaire 2011–2012." Éditeur off ciel.
– Ministère des Finances. 2012. "2012–2013 Budget Speech." Éditeur off ciel.
– Ministère des Finances et de l'Économie. 2013. "Investing for Our Prosperity: The Government's Economic Cision." Éditeur off ciel.
– Ministère des Finances et de l'Économie. 2013b. "Banque de développement économique du Québec." Sommaire. Éditeur off ciel.

- Assemblée Nationale. 2013c. "Bill 36. An Act Respecting the Banque de Développement Économique du Québec." Éditeur off ciel.
- Ministère des Finances et de l'Économie. 2013d. "Priorité emploi. Politique économique." Éditeur off ciel.
- Ministère des Finances et de l'Économie. 2013e. "Priorité emploi. Politique industrielle québécoise 2013–2017." Éditeur off ciel.
- Ministère des Finances. 2014a. "Plan budgétaire 2014–2015." Éditeur off ciel.
- Groupe de travail sur la protection des entreprises québécoises. 2014b. "Le maintien et le développement des sièges sociaux au Québec." Éditeur off ciel.
- Ministère des Finances et de l'Économie. 2014c. "Qualif cation de gazelles et d'entreprises prometteuses dans le cadre de la Politique industrielle 2013–2017." Éditeur off ciel.
- Ministère des Finances. 2015a. "Le plan économique du Québec." Éditeur off ciel.
- Commission d'examen sur la f scalité. 2015b. "Se tourner vers l'avenir du Québec. Volume 1. Une réforme de la f scalité québécoise." Éditeur off ciel.
- Ministère de l'Économie, de la Science et de l'Innovation. 2015c. "PerforME. Qualif cation d'entreprises. Guide d'appel de candidatures en continu." Éditeur off ciel.
- Ministère de l'Économie, de l'Innovation et des Exportations. 2015d. "L'avenir prend forme. Stratégie québécoise de développement de l'aluminium 2015–2025." Éditeur off ciel.
- Secrétariat aux Affaires maritimes. 2015e. "La stratégie maritime à l'horizon 2030. Plan d'action 2015–2020." Éditeur off ciel.
- Ministère de l'Économie, de la Science et de l'Innovation. 2016a. "Plan d'action en économie numérique. Pour l'excellence numérique des entreprises et des organisations québécoises." Éditeur off ciel.
- Ministère de l'Économie, de la Science et de l'Innovation. 2016b. "Québec Aerospace Strategy: Redef ning the Horizon." Éditeur off ciel.
- Ministère des Finances. 2016c. "Le plan économique du Québec 2016–2017." Éditeur off ciel.
- Assemblée Nationale. 2019. "Bill n° 27: An Act Tespecting Mainly Government Organization as Regards the Economy and Innovation." Éditeur off ciel.
Raf qui, Pernilla S. 2010. "Varieties of Capitalism and Local Outcomes: A Swedish Case Study." *European Urban and Regional Studies* 17, no. 3: 309–29.
Réseau Capital. 2004. "Pour une industrie du capital de risque plus performante." Montréal.
- 2009. "Permettre à l'écosystème du f nancement technologique québécois de traverser la crise actuelle." Montréal.
- 2013. "Consultations sur la Banque de développement économique du Québec." Montréal.

Rich, David C. 1983. "The Scottish Development Agency and the Industrial Regeneration of Scotland." *Geographical Review* 73, no. 3: 271–86.

Riddell, Peter. 1989. *The Thatcher Decade: How Britain Has Changed During the 1980s*. Oxford: Basil Blackwell.

Rioux, X Hubert. 2012a. "Entre réingénierie et continuité: réforme libérale des sociétés d'État québécoises et nationalisme économique (2003–2012)." *Papers in Political Economy* 44, published online November 1, 2011. http://interventionseconomiques.revues.org/1602.

– 2012b. "Le 'lion celtique': néolibéralisme, régionalisme et nationalisme économique en Écosse." Unpublished Master's Thesis, Université du Québec à Montréal. http://www.archipel.uqam.ca/5477/1/M12749.pdf.

– 2014. "Quebec and Canadian Fiscal Federalism: From Tremblay to Séguin and Beyond." *Canadian Journal of Political Science* 47, no. 1: 47–69.

– 2015. "From Sub-state Nationalism to Subnational Competition States: The Development and Institutionalization of Commercial Paradiplomacy in Scotland and Quebec." *Regional and Federal Studies* 25, no. 2: 109–28.

– 2016. "Peut-on faire l'économie de l'autodétermination? Le cas écossais." In *Repenser l'autodétermination interne*, edited by Michel Seymour, 175–96. Montréal: Éditions Thémis.

– 2019a. "Les noces de porcelaine: Investissement Québec et le modèle québécois de développement (1998–2018)." In *L'État québécois: où en sommes-nous?*, edited by Robert Bernier and Stéphane Paquin, Chapter 8. Québec: Presses de l'Université du Québec.

– 2019b. "Vingt ans plus tard: une rétrospective des contributions d'Investissement Québec au développement régional." In *La politique territoriale au Québec. 50 ans d'audace, d'hésitations et d'impuissance*, edited by Marc-Urbain Proulx and Marie-Claude Prémont, 203–20. Québec: Presses de l'Université du Québec.

Rioux, Hubert, and Stéphane Paquin. 2017. "Intelligence artif cielle: un succès du modèle québécois." *La Presse*. November 8, 2017. http://plus.lapresse.ca/screens/7bd3ffe9-d1d6-4274-99fd-de2d0b582ef2__7C___0.html.

Robbins, Keith. 1998. "Britain and Europe: Devolution and Foreign Policy." *International Affairs* 74, no. 1: 105–18.

Robertson, Lewis. 1978. "The Scottish Development Agency." *Scottish Government Yearbook 1978*, 21–31.

Rocher, François. 1994. "Le Québec en Amérique du Nord: la stratégie continentale." In *Québec: État et Société*, edited by Alain-G. Gagnon, 461–84. Montreal: Québec/Amérique.

– 2003. "Le Québec dans les Amériques: de l'ALÉ à la ZLÉA." In *Québec: État et Société. Tome 2*, edited by Alain-G. Gagnon, 455–80. Montréal: Québec/Amérique.

Rodrik, Dani. 1998. "Why Do More Open Economies Have Bigger Governments?" *Journal of Political Economy* 106, no. 5: 997–1032.

Roger, Antoine. 2001. *Les grandes théories du nationalisme*. Paris: Armand Colin.

Roper, Stephen, Jim Love, Phil Cooke, and Nick Clifton. 2006. *The Scottish Innovation System: Actors, Roles and Actions*. Cardiff: Aston Business School, Cardiff University.

Rosiello, Alessandro. 2004. "Evaluating Scottish Enterprise's Cluster Policy in Life Sciences: A Descriptive Analysis." Working Paper No. 16, Innogen – ESRC Center for Social and Economic Research on Innovation in Genomics.

Royal Society of Edinburgh, Scottish Financial Enterprise, and the Institute of Chartered Accountants of Scotland. 2014. "The Supply of Growth Capital for Emerging High-potential Companies in Scotland." Joint Working Group Report, Glasgow.

Samila, Sampsa. 2012. "Regional Impact of Venture Capital." In *The Oxford Handbook of Venture Capital*, edited by Douglas J. Cumming, 791–809. New York: Oxford University Press.

Samila, Sampsa and Olav Sorensen. 2010. "Venture Capital as a Catalyst to Commercialization." *Research Policy* 39: 1348–60.

Sansfaçon, Jean-Robert. 2003. "Une Caisse indépendante!" *Le Devoir*, March 11, 2003. http://www.ledevoir.com/non-classe/22154/une-caisse-independante.

Schmidt, Vivien A. 2002. *The Futures of European Capitalism*. Oxford: Oxford University Press.

– 2007. "Bringing the State Back Into the Varieties of Capitalism and Discourse Back Into the Explanation of Change." Working Paper, Center for European Studies. http://aei.pitt.edu/9006/1/CES_152.pdf.

– 2008. "Discursive Institutionalism: The Explanatory Power of Ideas and Discourse." *Annual Review of Political Science* 11, no. 1: 303–26.

– 2009. "Putting the Political Back Into Political Economy by Bringing the State Back in Yet Again." *World Politics* 61, no. 3: 516–46.

– 2010. "Taking Ideas and Discourse Seriously: Explaining Change Through Discursive Institutionalism as the Fourth 'New Institutionalism.'" *European Political Science Review* 2, no. 1: 1–25.

Schmit, Matias, Laurent Gheeraert, Thierry Denuit, and Cédric Warny. 2011. "Roles, Missions and Business Models of Public Financial Institutions in Europe." Vienna: SUERF – The European Money and Finance Forum.

Schwab, Klaus, and Xavier Sala-i-Martin. 2013. *The Global Competitiveness Report 2013–2014*. Geneva: World Economic Forum.

Scotland, Scottish Executive. Enterprise and Lifelong Learning Committee. 2000a. "First Report: Inquiry into the Delivery of Local Economic Development Services in Scotland." Edinburgh.

– Scottish Executive. 2000b. "Created in Scotland: The Way Forward for Scottish Manufacturing in the 21st Century." Edinburgh.

– Scottish Executive. 2000c. "The Way Forward: Framework for Economic Development in Scotland." Edinburgh.

– Scottish Executive. 2001. "A Science Strategy for Scotland." Edinburgh.
– Scottish Executive. 2003. "Management Statement between Enterprise and Lifelong Learning Department and Scottish Enterprise." Edinburgh.
– Scottish Government. 2003–18. "Gross Expenditures on Research and Development (GERD)." Edinburgh.
– Scottish Executive. 2004a. "The Framework for Economic Development in Scotland." Edinburgh.
– Scottish Executive. 2004b. "Background Analysis to The Framework for Economic Development in Scotland." Edinburgh.
– Scottish Executive. 2004c. "A Smart, Successful Scotland. Strategic Direction to the Enterprise Networks and an Enterprise Strategy for Scotland." Edinburgh.
– Scottish Executive. 2004d. "Co-Operative Development Agency Consultation." Edinburgh.
– Enterprise and Culture Committee. 2006. "Fifth Report, 2006: Business Growth – The Next 10 Years." Edinburgh.
– Scottish Government. 2007a. "The Government Economic Strategy." Edinburgh.
– Economy, Energy and Tourism Committee. 2007b. "Off cial Report November 7th." Edinburgh.
– Scottish Government. 2007c. "Scottish Budget Spending Review 2007." Edinburgh.
– Scottish Government. 2008a. "International Framework." Edinburgh.
– Scottish Government. 2008b. "Action Plan on European Engagement." Edinburgh.
– Scottish Government Social Research. 2008c. "Evaluation of Regional Selective Assistance (RSA) in Scotland 2000–2004." Edinburgh.
– Economy, Energy and Tourism Committee. 2008d. "Off cial Report May 21st." Edinburgh.
– Scottish Government. 2008e. "Enterprising Third Sector Action Plan 2008–2011." Edinburgh.
– Scottish Government. 2008f. "Draft Budget 2009–2010." Edinburgh.
– Scottish Government. 2009a. "Public Services Reform: Simplif cation and Improvement Update Document." Edinburgh.
– Scottish Government. 2009b. "The Scottish Government's Response to the First Annual Report of the Council of Economic Advisers." Edinburgh.
– Scottish Government. 2009c. "Economic Recovery Plan: Update." Edinburgh.
– Scottish Government. 2009d. "Renewables Action Plan." Edinburgh.
– Scottish Government Social Research. 2010a. "Evaluation of Third Sector Investment and Support." Edinburgh.
– Scottish Government. 2010b. "The Scottish Economic Recovery Plan: Accelerating Recovery." Edinburgh.

– Scottish Government. 2010c. "A Low Carbon Economic Strategy for Scotland." Edinburgh.
– Economy, Energy and Tourism Committee. 2011a. "Second Report: A Fundamental Review of the Purpose of an Enterprise Agency and the Success of the Recent Reforms." Edinburgh.
– Scottish Government. 2011b. "The Scottish Economic Recovery Plan: Update." Edinburgh.
– Scottish Government. 2011c. "The Government Economic Strategy." Edinburgh.
– Scottish Government. 2011d. "2020 Routemap for Renewable Energy in Scotland." Edinburgh.
– Scottish Government. 2011e. "Draft Budget 2012–2013." Edinburgh.
– Scottish Government. 2012. "Draft Budget 2013–2014." Edinburgh.
– Scottish Government. 2013a. "Scotland's Economy: The Case for Independence." Edinburgh.
– Scottish Government. 2013b. "Sustainable, Responsible Banking: A Strategy for Scotland." Edinburgh.
– Scottish Government. 2013c. "Building Security and Creating Opportunity: Economic Policy Choices in an Independent Scotland." Edinburgh.
– Scottish Government. 2014. "Reindustrialising Scotland for the 21st Century: A Sustainable Industrial Strategy for a Modern, Independent Nation." Edinburgh.
– Scottish Government. 2015a. "Scotland's Economic Strategy." Edinburgh.
– Scottish Government. 2015b. "Annual GDP Growth Rates (Rolling Q4 on Q4) for GDP Targets to 2014 Q4." Edinburgh.
– Scottish Government. 2015c. "The Market for SME Finance in Scotland." Edinburgh.
– Scottish Government. 2016. "Draft Budget 2017–2018." Edinburgh.
– Scottish Government. 2017. "A Nation with Ambition: The Government's Programme for Scotland 2017–18." Edinburgh.
– 2018a. "Draft Budget 2018–2019." Edinburgh.
– Scottish Government. 2018b. "Scottish National Investment Bank Implementation Plan." Edinburgh.
– Scottish Government. 2018c. "A Consultation on the Scottish National Investment Bank. Analysis of Responses." Edinburgh.
Scottish Constitutional Convention. 1995. "Scotland's Parliament, Scotland's Right." Edinburgh.
Scottish Council for Development and Industry. 1961. "Inquiry into the Scottish Economy 1960–1961." Edinburgh.
Scottish Enterprise. 1992. "Strategies for the Nineties." Glasgow.
– 1993. "Annual Report 1992–1993." Glasgow.
– 1995. "Annual Report 1994–1995." Glasgow.

– 1996. "Annual Report 1995–1996." Glasgow.

– 1998. "Annual Report 1996–1997." Glasgow.

– 2000. "Annual Report 1999–2000." Glasgow.

– 2001. "Annual Report 2000–2001." Glasgow.

– 2005. "Annual Report 2004–2005." Glasgow.

– 2006. "Operating Plan 2006–2009." Glasgow.

– 2011. "Business Plan 2011–2014." Glasgow.

– 2012a. "Business Plan 2012–2015." Glasgow.

– 2012b. "Renewable Energy Investment Fund." Glasgow.

– 2013. "Evaluation of Enterprise Fellowships: Final Report for Scottish
Enterprise, Frontline Consultants." Glasgow.

– 2015. "Business Plan 2015–2018." Glasgow.

Scottish Enterprise Investments. 2009. "Annual Report 2008–2009." Glasgow.

Scottish Investment Bank. 2012. "Operating Plan 2012–2015." Glasgow.

– 2013. "Annual Report 2012–2013." Glasgow.

Scottish National Party. 2005. "Let Scotland Flourish: A Growth Strategy for
Scotland." Edinburgh.

– 2007. "It's Time." Edinburgh.

– 2011. "Re-Elect a Scottish Government Working for Scotland." Edinburgh.

Scottish Parliament. 2019. "South of Scotland Enterprise Bill." SP Bill 41B,
Session 5 (2019). Edinburgh.

SDI. 1990. "Plan de développement stratégique 1990–1993." Sillery.

SECOR. 2003. "Pour une industrie québécoise du capital-risque en santé."
Accessed July 6, 2016. http://reseaucapital.com/docs/pres_2003___20.pdf.

SECOR-KPMG. 2013. "Les sièges sociaux au Québec: Leur évolution, leur
contribution et leur expansion." Montréal.

SGF. 2000. "Rapport annuel 1999." Montréal.

– 2006. "Building Up: Annual Report 2005." Montréal.

– 2008. "Teaming Up to Measure Up: Annual Report 2007." Montréal.

Shulman, Stephen. 2000. "Nationalist Sources of International Economic
Integration." *International Studies Quarterly* 44, no. 3: 365–90.

Simard, Jean-François, and Yvon Leclerc. 2008. "Les Centres locaux
de développement 1998–2008. Une gouvernance en mutation: Entre
participation citoyenne et imputabilité municipale." *Revue Canadienne des
sciences régionales* 31, no. 3: 615–34.

Simard, Louis, Alain Dupuis, and Luc Bernier. 2006. "Entreprises publiques et
intérêt général à l'heure de la gouvernance." *Canadian Public Administration /
Administration publique du Canada* 49, no. 3: 308–33.

SIQCA. 2015. "Rapport annuel 2014–2015." Québec.

SISQ. 2015. "Rapport annuel 2014–2015." Québec.

Skogstad, Grace. 2000. "Globalization and Public Policy: Situating Canadian
Analyses." *Canadian Journal of Political Science* 33, no. 4: 805–28.

Smith, Anthony D. 1995. *Nations and Nationalism in a Global Era*. Cambridge: Polity Press.

Smith, James. 2010. "Sub-National Mobilization and the Scottish Government's Action Plan on European Engagement." *Public Policy and Administration* 25, no. 2: 216–33.

Smith, Maurice. 1992. "The Peripheral Interest: Scotland, 1992 and All That." In *Scottish Government Yearbook 1991*, 44–58.

Smith, Michael R. 1994. "L'impact de Québec Inc., répartition des revenus et eff cacité économique." *Sociologie et sociétés* 26, no. 2: 91–110.

Social Investment Scotland. 2014. *Evaluation of the Scottish Investment Fund*. Edinburgh: Social Investment Scotland.

Sorensen, Olav, and Toby E. Stuart. 2001. "Syndication Networks and the Spatial Distribution of Venture Capital Investments." *American Journal of Sociology* 106, no. 6: 1546–88.

Stewart, David. 2009. *The Path to Devolution and Change: A Political History of Scotland Under Margaret Thatcher*. London: Tauris Publishers.

Statistics Canada. n.d.a. *Table 36-10-0222-01: Gross Domestic Product, Expenditure-Based, Provincial and Territorial, Annual*. Last updated June 10, 2019. https://www150.statcan.gc.ca/t1/tbl1/en/tv.action?pid=3610022201.

– n.d.b. *Table 27-10-0273-01: Gross Domestic Expenditures on Research and Development, by Science Type and by Funder and Performer Sector*. Last updated June 10, 2019. https://www150.statcan.gc.ca/t1/tbl1/en/tv.action?pid=2710027301.

– n.d.c. *Table 14-10-0288-01: Employment by Class of Worker, Monthly, Seasonally Adjusted and Unadjusted, Last 5 Months*. Last updated June 10, 2019. https://www150.statcan.gc.ca/t1/tbl1/en/tv.action?pid=1410028801.

St-Jean, Étienne, and Marc Duhamel. 2016. "Situation de l'activité entrepreneuriale québécoise: rapport 2015 du Global Entrepreneurship Monitor." Institut de recherche sur les PME, Université du Québec à Trois-Rivières.

– 2017. "Situation de l'activité entrepreneuriale québécoise: rapport 2016 du Global Entrepreneurship Monitor." Institut de recherche sur les PME, Université du Québec à Trois-Rivières.

Sunley, Peter, Britta Klagge, Christian Berndt, and Ron Martin. 2005. "Venture Capital Programmes in the UK and Germany: In What Sense Regional Policies?" *Regional Studies* 39, no. 2: 255–73.

Surel, Yves. 2000. "The Role of Cognitive and Normative Frames in Policy-Making." *Journal of European Public Policy* 7, no. 4: 495–512.

Suret, Jean-Marc. 1990. "Les initiatives québécoises dans le domaine de la capitalisation des entreprises: Le point de vue des investisseurs." *Canadian Public Policy – Analyse de politiques* 16, no. 3: 239–51.

– 1993. "Une évaluation des dépenses f scales et subventions dans le domaine de la capitalisation des entreprises." *L'Actualité économique – Revue d'analyse économique* 69, no. 2: 17–40.

– 2004. "Le rôle du gouvernement québécois dans le capital de risque." Research Report 2004RB-01, CIRANO. March 2004. http://www.cirano .qc.ca/pdf/publication/2004RB-01.pdf.

Suret, Jean-Marc, and Élise Cormier. 1997. "Le régime d'épargne-actions du Québec: vue d'ensemble et évaluation." *CIRANO Scientific Series*, no. 97s–16.

Surridge, Paula, and David McCrone. 1999. "The 1997 Scottish Referendum Vote." In *Scotland and Wales: Nations Again?*, edited by Bridget Taylor and Katarina Thomson, 41–64. Cardiff: University of Wales Press.

Suzuki, Takaaki. 2012. "Globalization, Finance, and Economic Nationalism: The Changing Role of the State in Japan." In *Globalization and Economic Nationalism in Asia*, edited by Anthony P. D'Costa. Oxford: Oxford University Press Scholarship Online.

Swank, Duane. 1998. "Funding the Welfare State: Globalization and the Taxation of Business in Advanced Market Economies." *Political Studies* 46, no. 4: 671–92.

Talbot, Steve, and Alan Reeves. 1997. "Boosting the Business Birth Rate in Scotland: Evidence From the Lanarckshire Development Agency's Entrepreneurship Programme." *Quarterly Economic Commentary* 22, no. 2: 26–35.

Tanguay, A. Brian. 1980. "The Parti Québécois and the Politics of Concerted Action: A New Corporatism?" Unpublished Masters' Thesis, Carleton University. https://curve.carleton.ca/2aeeaf21-2eea-4c16-bff9-f9858f81cf94.

– 1990. "Rediscovering Politics: Organized Labour, Business, and the Provincial State in Quebec, 1960–1985." Unpublished PhD Thesis, Carleton University. https://curve.carleton.ca/system/f les/theses/22987.pdf.

Tarditi, Valeria. 2010. "The Scottish National Party's Changing Attitude Towards the European Union." Working Paper No. 112, Sussex European Institute.

Taylor, Bridget, and Katarina Thomson, eds. 1999. *Scotland and Wales: Nations Again?* Cardiff: University of Wales Press.

Taylor, Sandra, and Philip Raines. 2001. "Learning to Let Go: The Role of the Public Sector in Cluster Building in the Basque Country and Scotland." Regional & Industrial Policy Research Paper, No. 48, European Policies Research Center, University of Strathclyde.

Thomsen, Stephen, and Fernando Mistura. 2017. "Is Investment Protectionism on the Rise? Evidence from the OECD FDI Regulatory Restrictiveness Index." *OECD Global Forum on International Investment*. Paris: OECD Publishing.

Thomson Financial. 2006–8. "Bilan de l'industrie québécois du capital-risque." Accessed March 9, 2016. http://www.reseaucapital.com/statistiques.php.

Thomson Reuters. 2009–15. "Le marché québécois du capital de risque." Accessed March 9, 2016. http://www.reseaucapital.com/statistiques.php.

– 2011. "Canada's Buyout and Private Equity Market." Accessed June 3, 2016. http://www.thecmlink.com/wordpress/wp-content/uploads/2013/10/2010-December-Canadas-Buyou-Private-Equity-Market-in-2010-Thomson-Reuters.pdf.

– 2013. "Canada's Buyout and Private Equity Market." Accessed June 3, 2016. http://www.cvca.ca/wp-content/uploads/2014/07/Canadas_Buyout___Private_Equity_Market_in_2012_English.pdf.

– 2014. "Canada's Buyout and Private Equity Market." Accessed June 3, 2016. http://www.cvca.ca/wp-content/uploads/2014/07/Canadas_Buyout___Private_Equity_Market_in_2013.pdf.

– 2015. "Canada's Venture Capital Market in 2014." Accessed June 2, 2016. http://dmi.thomsonreuters.com/Content/Files/Canada%20VC%20Overview%2020 14_Rename.pdf.

Tilly, Charles. 1995. "To Explain Political Processes." *American Journal of Sociology* 100, no. 6: 1594–610.

– 2001. "Mechanisms in Political Processes." *Annual Review of Political Science* 4, no. 1: 21–41.

– 2008. *Explaining Social Processes*. New York: Paradigm Publishers.

Torrance, David. 2006. *The Scottish Secretaries*. Edinburgh: Birlinn Ltd.

Tremblay, André. 2000. "Pouvoir fédéral de dépenser." In *L'Union sociale canadienne sans le Québec. Huit études sur l'entente-cadre*, edited by Alain-G. Gagnon, 185–221. Montréal: Éditions Saint-Martin.

Tremblay, Diane-Gabrielle, and Vincent Van Schendel. 2004. *Économie du Québec: régions, acteurs, enjeux*. Montréal: Éditions Saint-Martin.

Tremblay, Gérald. 1991. "Vers une société à valeur ajoutée." MICT, Québec.

– 1993a. "Qualité totale: une condition essentielle à la relance économique du Québec." MICT, Québec.

– 1993b. "Ensemble vers la réussite." MICT, Québec.

Tremblay, Rodrigue. 1979. "Présentation du rapport annuel 1978–1979 de la Société de développement industriel." Public Speech, Montreal.

Trench, Alan. 2004. "The More Things Change the More They Stay the Same: Intergovernmental Relations Four Years On." In *Has Devolution Made a Difference? The State of the Nations 2004*, edited by Alan Trench, 165–92. Charlottesville: Imprint Academic.

Trigilia, Carlo. 1991. "The Paradox of the Region: Economic Regulation and the Representation of Interests." *Economy and Society* 20, no. 3: 306–27.

Tupper, Allan. 1983. *Bill S-31 and the Federalism of State Capitalism*. Kingston, ON: Institute of Inter-governmental Relations.

Turok, Ivan. 1993. "Contrasts in Ownership and Development: Local versus Global in 'Silicon Glen.'" *Urban Studies* 30, no. 2: 365–86.

– 1997. "Linkages in the Scottish Electronics Industry: Further Evidence." *Regional Studies* 31, no. 7: 705–11.

Turok, Ivan, and Ranald Richardson. 1991. "External Takeovers of Scottish Companies in the 1980s." *Royal Geographical Society* 23, no. 1: 73–81.

United Kingdom. 1965. "Highlands and Islands Development (Scotland) Act 1965." http://www.legislation.gov.uk/ukpga/1965/46/pdfs/ukpga_19650046_en.pdf?view =extent.

– 1975. "Scottish Development Agency Act 1975." November 12, 1975. http://www.legislation.gov.uk/ukpga/1975/69/pdfs/ukpga_19750069_en.pdf.

– Department of Trade and Indutry, Small and Medium Enterprise Policy Directorate. 1999. "Addressing the SME Equity Gap. Support for Regional Venture Capital Funds." Consultation Document, URN99/876.

– Capital for Enterprise Ltd. 2012. "Overview of Publicly-Backed Venture Capital and Loan Funds in the UK." Research Report.

– British Business Bank. 2014. "Strategic Plan June 2014." London.

– Off ce for National Statistics. 2018. "Statistical Bulletin: Public Sector Employment UK, December 2017." London.

Van Stel, Adriann, and David J. Storey. 2004. "The Link between Firm Births and Job Creation: Is There a Upas Tree Effect?" *Regional Studies* 38, no. 8: 893–909.

Vogel, Steven K. 1996. *Freer Markets, More Rules: Regulatory Reform in Advanced Industrial Countries*. Ithaca: Cornell University Press.

Vukov, Visnja. 2016. "The Rise of the Competition State? Transnationalization and State Transformations in Europe." *Comparative European Politics* 14, no. 5: 523–46.

Wannop, Urlan. 1984. "The Evolution and Roles of the Scottish Development Agency." *The Town Planning Review* 55, no. 3: 313–21.

Webster, David C. 2009. "England's Regional Venture Capital Funds: A Review of Programme Outcomes and Stakeholder Perspectives." Working Paper, University of Oxford. December 1, 2009. http://papers.ssrn.com/sol3/papers.cfm?abstract_id=1754482.

Weiss, Linda. 1998. *The Myth of the Powerless State*. Ithaca: Cornell University Press.

–, ed. 2003. *States in the Global Economy: Bringing Domestic Institutions Back In*. New York: Cambridge University Press.

– 2005. "Global Governance, National Strategies: How Industrialized States Make Room to Move Under the WTO." *Review of International Political Economy* 12, no. 5: 723–49.

Wolfe, David A., and Meric S. Gertler. 1999. "Globalization and Economic Restructuring in Ontario: From Industrial Heartland to Learning Region?" Conference Paper, NECSTS/RICTES-99 Conference on Regional Innovation Systems in Europe, Donostia-San Sebastian, Spain, September 30–October 2.

Woo-Cumings, Meredith. 2005. "Back to Basics: Ideology, Nationalism, and Asian Values in East Asia." In *Economic Nationalism in a Globalizing*

World, edited by Eric Helleiner and Andreas Pickel, 91–117. Ithaca: Cornell University Press.

Woods, Charlie. 2006. "Scotland's Birth Strategy: Entrepreneurial Culture and Attitudes, Entrepreneurship Policy Delivery." Discussion Paper, Entrepreneurship in the Districts Uckermark (Brandenburg) and Parchim (Mecklenburg-Western Pomerania), OECD LEED Local Entrepreneurship Series.

Woods, Ngaire, ed. 2000. *The Political Economy of Globalization*. New York: St Martin's Press.

Young Company Finance. 2006–18. "The Risk Capital Market in Scotland." Glasgow.

Zheng, Yongnian, and Rongfang Pan. 2012. "From Defensive to Aggressive Strategies: The Evolution of Economic Nationalism in China." In *Globalization and Economic Nationalism in Asia*, edited by Anthony P. D'Costa. Oxford: Oxford University Press Scholarship Online.

Zorn, Nicolas, Rodolphe Parent, and Robert Laplante. 2018. "Les fonds d'investissement de travailleurs, instruments de croissance inclusive?" Rapport de recherché de l'IRÉC, June.

Index

Studies in Comparative Political Economy and Public Policy

Lightning Source UK Ltd.
Milton Keynes UK
UKHW011955160721
387285UK00002B/21/J